Additional praise for *Message Not Received:*
Why Business Communication Is Broken and How to Fix It

"The message comes through loud and clear in Phil Simon's smart new book: Today's workplace is drowning in information overload, bad communication, and missed opportunities. Simon shows us the path forward with his savvy and practical advice."

—Dorie Clark
Adjunct Professor,
Duke University Fuqua School of Business;
Author of *Reinventing You*

"In a world where disjointed and disorganized communication is the norm, *Message Not Received* arrives at the perfect time. Phil Simon provides tremendous insights and practical approaches to improve our communication both in and out of the office. If you want to make sure your words are actually heard (not just delivered), then you need to read this book."

—Mike Vardy
Productivity Strategist;
Founder of Productivityist

"In today's business world, communication is more important and easily accessible than ever before—so why are we making it so complicated? In *Message Not Received*, Phil Simon closely examines why keeping it simple amounts to clear and efficient communication. I highly recommend that everyone in business take Simon's direction."

—Larry Weber
Chairman & CEO of Racepoint Global;
Author of *The Digital Marketer*

"Look behind any business failure and you'll find the lack of communication as a root cause. Phil Simon's latest book, *Message Not Received*, examines how and why the latest technologies that are intended to radically improve business communication too often obstruct it instead. Simon's book provides thorough, effective strategies for enabling effective organizational collaboration and communication to ensure business messages are indeed received. If you want to improve your organization's communication skills, you owe it to yourself to read this book."

—**Robert Charette**
President, ITABHI Corporation

"An essential resource for business clarity. Read *Message Not Received* to learn how to strip out the jargon and quit confusing people with buzzwords."

—**Anita Campbell**
Founder and CEO of Small Business Trends

"A refreshingly relevant critique of modern business communication."

—**Michael Schrenk**
Online Intelligence Consultant;
Author of *Webbots, Spiders, and Screen Scrapers*

DATE DUE

Message Not Received

Message Not Received

WHY BUSINESS COMMUNICATION IS BROKEN AND HOW TO FIX IT

Phil Simon

Cover design: Luke Fletcher

For general information on our other products and services or for technical support, please contact our Customer Care Department within the United States at (800) 762–2974, outside the United States at (317) 572–3993 or fax (317) 572–4002.

Wiley publishes in a variety of print and electronic formats and by print-on-demand. Some material included with standard print versions of this book may not be included in e-books or in print-on-demand. If this book refers to media such as a CD or DVD that is not included in the version you purchased, you may download this material at http://booksupport.wiley.com. For more information about Wiley products, visit www.wiley.com.

Library of Congress Cataloging-in-Publication Data:
Simon, Phil.
  Message not received: why business communication is broken and how to fix it/Phil Simon.
    pages cm
  Includes bibliographical references and index.
  ISBN 978-1-119-01703-5 (hardback); ISBN: 978-1-119-04812-1 (ePDF);
  ISBN: 978-1-119-04821-3 (ePub)
  1. Business communication.   2. Business communication–Technological innovations.
  I. Title.
  HF5718.S565 2015
  651.7—dc23

                                                                    2014038167

Printed in the United States of America

OTHER BOOKS BY PHIL SIMON

To Marillion:
Thank you for showing me a better way of life.

The real problem is not whether machines think but whether men do.
　　　　　　　　　　　　　　　　　　　　　—B. F. Skinner

We become what we behold. We shape our tools and then our tools shape us.
　　　　　　　　　　　　　　　　　　　—Marshall McLuhan

Contents

Part III

Message
Received

List of Figures and Tables

(Continued)

(*Continued*)

Preface

What we got here is . . . failure to communicate.
— Captain, Road Prison 36, *Cool Hand Luke*

On February 4, 2014, Microsoft concluded its extensive search to replace its retiring Chief Executive Officer (CEO), the easily excitable Steve Ballmer. On that day, the company named Satya Nadella as only the third CEO in its storied history. Given Microsoft's stature and reach, one could argue that Nadella represented the most significant executive appointment since Tim Cook succeeded Steve Jobs as Apple's head honcho on August 24, 2011.

Running a 50,000-employee corporation as powerful and culturally significant as Apple cannot be considered easy. In the whole scheme of things, though, few, if any, CEOs have inherited a company in better shape than Tim Cook did. He took over an extremely healthy organization with a record-setting hoard of cash,* a reportedly strong pipeline, a vibrant developer community, a favorable public image, and largely positive coverage from Wall Street.

The 46-year-old Nadella was not nearly as lucky. He had then and—has now—no small chore ahead of him. Many industry types, critics, ex-Microsoft employees, and activist investors have argued for years that the iconic tech company needs a drastic makeover. Ballmer's exit was just the first of many notable moves that it would need to make to remain relevant.

Long a tech powerhouse, Microsoft now finds itself at a crossroads, a potential victim of *The Innovator's Dilemma*, Clayton Christensen's

---

* At one point, Apple had more cash on hand than the U.S. government. The company could have bought Greece. For other interesting and crazy potential uses of its piggy bank, see http://tinyurl.com/wow-apple.

classic business text about disruptive innovation. Christensen astutely observed that very successful organizations have historically become complacent. They have tended to ignore the emerging trends and technologies that ultimately annihilated their businesses.

You might be thinking that that could *never* happen to a company as large, successful, and ubiquitous as Microsoft. It is too big to fail.

Think again.

Polaroid, Kmart, Eastman Kodak, Blockbuster Video, Tower Records, and Research in Motion (recently rebranded as Blackberry) were once economic juggernauts. They are now punch lines to jokes, historical footnotes, and the subjects of MBA case studies of what *not* to do. Briefly stated, each company failed to react to new consumer tastes, business realities, and technological changes until its song was over.

Now, Microsoft hasn't fallen as far as those companies did, and maybe it never will. Still, only a wild-eyed optimist can ignore the warning signs. Many of its recent high-profile product launches (e.g., Vista, Zune, Surface, and Soapbox) have performed much worse than anticipated, sometimes to embarrassing degrees.* Other than Xbox, the company hasn't had a true hit in a long time. The halcyon days of Windows and Office have long past, although each remains a multibillion-dollar franchise. Many questioned the wisdom of Microsoft's $7.2 billion Nokia purchase in September 2013. More than ever, there is cause to worry in Redmond, Washington.

A few chilling statistics will illustrate the point. In 2000, more than 90 percent of all devices connected to the Internet via some version of Windows. Thanks to the explosion of mobile devices and Microsoft's missteps, that number currently hovers around a shocking 20 percent—and continues to fall.[1] As of this writing, research firm International Data Corporation (IDC) reports that only 3 percent of mobile phones in the United States run a mobile version of Windows, putting Microsoft only marginally ahead of moribund Blackberry. Android dominates with a market share exceeding 80 percent, followed by iOS with roughly 12 percent.[2] It's not hard to find industry experts who believe that Microsoft has fallen and it won't be able to get up.

---

* To see a fairly comprehensive list of recently retired Microsoft products, check out this Pinterest board: http://tinyurl.com/ms-8208-pinterest3.

Nadella is quite familiar with Microsoft's culture and its challenges. He joined the software giant way back in 1992. As the new captain of a massive ship, he knows that steering it in a new direction will be much easier said than done. Forget any perceived or real hard technological challenges for a moment. Standing in Nadella's way are considerable "squishy" obstacles like Microsoft's legendary internal politics, bureaucracy, and organizational silos. Effecting his vision will require infusing a new way of thinking and working into Microsoft. Nadella will have to eliminate significant cultural and institutional impediments and, not surprisingly, make major personnel changes. To this end, the company will be parting ways with more than 18,000 employees. The reported 14 percent workforce reduction will represent Microsoft's biggest layoff to date.

On July 17, 2014, Nadella articulated his long-term vision for the company and broad steps on how to achieve it in the way that most CEOs do today: via a corporate memorandum. In a memo titled "Starting to Evolve Our Organization and Culture," Nadella begins inauspiciously:

> Last week in my e-mail to you I synthesized our strategic direction as a productivity and platform company.[*]

It only goes downhill from there. He continues:

> Microsoft has a unique ability to harmonize the world's devices, apps, docs, data and social networks in digital work and life experiences so that people are at the center and are empowered to do more and achieve more with what is becoming an increasingly scarce commodity—time!"[†]

Keep reading Nadella's memo and you'll find plenty of gems straight out of *Dilbert* and *Office Space*: regular *synergies, integration synergies* (evidently there's a difference between the two), *strategic alignment,* and others.

A few disclaimers are in order here. In my fourth book, *The Age of the Platform,* I was critical of Microsoft's tactics and decisions over

---

[*] Read that e-mail at www.microsoft.com/en-us/news/ceo/index.html.
[†] Read the whole memo at http://tinyurl.com/ptu99fh.

the past decade. Truth be told, though, I am certainly not anti-Microsoft.* In fact, I concur with much of Nadella's overall vision for the company—at least from the interviews he's given and the articles I've read. I also can't think of a painless way to announce that 18,000 people will soon be looking for work through no fault of their own. And, to be fair, Microsoft claims that it will grant generous severance packages.

I certainly don't know how Microsoft employees felt about their new CEO's memo. For all I know, the majority of "Softies" honestly found it to be positive, bold, clear, effective, and even necessary given the current state of the company. I strongly suspect, however, that that was the minority view. I'd also bet that many employees felt a sense of déjà vu (i.e., that they had seen this movie before). Nadella's vision hit employee screens nearly one year to the day that his predecessor sent his own terribly worded memo. In "One Microsoft" (sent on July 11, 2013), Steve Ballmer announced a major reorganization that included this 42-word dizzying sentence:

> Today's announcement will enable us to execute even better on our strategy to deliver a family of devices and services that best empower people for the activities they value most and the enterprise extensions and services that are most valuable to business.†

Just as Ballmer's message failed as an effective internal communications vehicle, so did Nadella's—a view shared by many. The media widely lampooned it as yet another example of the same old corporate blathering we've seen for decades. Shaun Nichols of *The Register* called it "coma-inducing." One could make the case that, because of the timing, Nadella's memo did more damage than his predecessor's did a year earlier. Sure, at that point, Ballmer was the face of Microsoft, serving as its CEO from January 2000 to February 2014. Still, most people knew that Ballmer would be departing soon; the only question during the last few years of his tenure surrounded his eventual replacement. In theory, Nadella may have had a clean(er)

---

*Yes, I wrote this book on my MacBook Pro, but for my money Microsoft Office is hands down the best productivity suite out there. And, more than five years after I "went Mac," I am still in search of a decent alternative to Microsoft Access.
† Read the whole memo at http://tinyurl.com/nlronl9.

slate with many Microsoft employees—or at least he did until he sent that eerily redolent and vacuous message.

The Wrong Way to Announce a New Product Launch

That's enough skewering of Microsoft's executive leadership. Let's move to another recent instance of truly awful corporate communications. The target this time: Computer Sciences Corporation (CSC). The company describes itself on its website as:

> a global leader of next-generation information technology (IT) services and solutions. The company's mission is to enable superior returns on clients' technology investments through best-in-class industry solutions, domain expertise, and global scale. CSC has approximately 79,000 employees and reported revenue of $13 billion for the 12 months ended March 28, 2014.*

A few days before I signed the contract to write the book you are now reading, the following press release came across the wire:

> **For Immediate Release: CSC Launches Next-Generation Big Data Platform as a Service**
> FALLS CHURCH, Va., June 26, 2014—CSC (NYSE: CSC), a global leader in next-generation IT services and solutions, has added new security, compliance, data infrastructure technologies, and cloud deployment options to its open source Big Data Platform as a Service (BDPaaS) offering, which enables enterprise and public sector clients to get up and running in 30 days or less across a variety of cloud and dedicated architectures.[3]

There's more to this press release, but let's stop right here.

Does that 61-word, one-sentence monstrosity make any sense at all to you? If your mind started wandering halfway through, don't fret. I'm in the same boat. After all, the jargon-laden monsoon contains *Big Data, platform, open source, infrastructure, cloud,* and *architectures.* Honorable mention goes to *next-generation, solutions,* and *deployment.* And let's not forget CSC's *pièce de résistance*: the horribly constructed acronym *BDPaaS.* Cramming all of these oft-bastardized technology

---

* See www.csc.com.

terms into a single sentence is quite the semantic achievement. The word *cacophony* comes to mind.

Before you continue reading, take a deep breath. It's about to get worse—much worse.

There. You've been warned.

CSC's press release continues with a tsunami of dense sentences and awkward jargon:

> The CSC BDPaaS has been engineered to support an "as-a-Service" on several cloud infrastructures including Amazon, CSC Cloud Solutions, RedHat OpenStack and VMware VSphere private clouds. This allows flexible deployment models within the customer's datacenter as well as trusted third party datacenters including CSC's. With the CSC BDPaaS, CSC customers are also able to leverage the ServiceMesh Agility Platform^{TM}, which provides cloud management, governance, and security across public, private and hybrid clouds.
>
> CSC BDPaaS offers batch analytics, fine-grained and interactive analytics, and real-time streaming analytics. Along with a suite of improved next-generation reference architectures for IBM, SAP, Oracle, and Teradata, it is the only "as a service" offering that seamlessly integrates with Hadoop, Ad-Hoc Query and Streaming analytics to support high volumes, high velocities and any type of data.
>
> "CSC is uniquely positioned to support predictive and prescriptive analytics for actionable insights from internal and external data to better manage customer intelligence, product innovation, risks and operational efficiencies," said Jim Kaskade, vice president and general manager, Big Data & Analytics, CSC. "Clients can minimize up-front costs and leverage existing technology investments without sacrificing time-to-market mandates. We're helping clients unlock the power and potential of Big Data with greater speed, efficiency, and confidence."

Full disclosure: I have no axe to grind here, but I cannot claim to be a completely uninterested party with respect to CSC. For nearly two years in the mid-2000s, I worked for the company. I implemented enterprise applications for its healthcare clients.

I have spent the duration of my professional career (nearly 20 years as of this point) at the nexus of business, technology, and data. As such, I am very familiar with most of the individual terms in the CSC press release, *and I still don't fully understand what this new product allegedly does.*

This begs the question, what was CSC thinking here? Admittedly, some of the terms in the press release are gaining in popularity. By no means, though, has every chief executive heard of cloud computing, Big Data, and Hadoop, never mind gems like *improved next-generation reference architectures.* Why toss them into one big tech bouillabaisse?

At the risk of piling on, it wouldn't be a proper technology press release if CSC didn't mention how it was "uniquely positioned" to do *exactly* what it purports to do. I challenge you to find a similar announcement these days that does *not* contain this two-word staple. (As an aside, I believe that word *unique* is a superlative. Something can't be *very* unique, *rather* unique, or *really* unique. A person or thing is either *unique* or it isn't. Period. Not every linguist shares this view, as Ammon Shea points out in *Bad English: A History of Linguistic Aggravation.*)

Lessons Learned

Comparing and contrasting the miscommunications of multibillion-dollar tech companies like Microsoft and CSC can teach us a great deal. The two messages exhibit both significant similarities and differences. Let's first address the latter.

The primary intended audience for each message is very different. Nadella wrote his memo mainly for Microsoft's current—and soon to be former—employees, although he's very mindful that it's impossible to keep messages like these private today. Chief executives carefully craft these communications with full knowledge that they will end up on the Web for all to read, often minutes afterward. Microsoft's primary goal surely wasn't publicity.

By contrast, CSC made its announcement chiefly to the outside world (hence the formal press release). BDPaaS is anything but a $1.99 iOS app or game; even the company's wealthiest executives aren't about to purchase its new product for their own personal use. Business is war, and companies are engaged in the same arms race for customers and profits. At a high level, CSC's marketing and PR strategies could have taken one of two forms: simplicity or complexity.

The company clearly doubled down on the latter. It is betting that its best chance for victory comes from creating and promulgating the most arcane, intricate-sounding terms possible. Ideally, from CSC's standpoint, current and prospective clients will do the following after reading its press release:

- Get really excited and/or intrigued.
- Click on a few links to learn more about BDPaaS.
- Call a sales rep.
- Schedule an in-person demo.
- Sit in amazement at what BDPaaS can do.
- Ask for pricing information.
- Eventually write a big check.

Was complexity the right bet? It's too early to say, but BDPaaS hasn't exactly taken the world by storm. Several times over the course of researching and writing this book (most recently on December 6, 2014), I searched Google for "CSC BDPaaS customers" and "CSC BDPaaS case studies." Beyond retreads of its press release, I retrieved zero meaningful results. What's more, the company's dedicated product Web page lacked a single BDPaaS success story.[*] I would wager that CSC would have seen far greater success in announcing its new service if it had chosen a simpler, more coherent path.

Let's now turn to the significant parallels between these two companies' messages. First, announcements like these are well-coordinated events. They represent the antitheses of an employee's ill-advised, alcohol-induced, and stream-of-consciousness tweets. (Chapter 1 begins by introducing Justine Sacco, the current queen of the dumb random tweet.) I assure you that Nadella didn't pen his memo late at night and hit the send button by his lonesome. Other high-ranking Microsoft employees developed it with or even for him. Ultimately, everyone involved signed off on its language.

By the same token, more than a handful of CSC's nearly 80,000 employees work in its public relations department. If CSC outsourced the BDPaaS release, it's highly unlikely that its PR firm operated with carte blanche. For such a critical corporate announcement, a team of people provides input. There are usually arguments over versions, terms, content, length, and even the specific words used. I have no

---

[*] See http://tinyurl.com/mfvxbfc.

doubt that some of CSC's most senior executives at the company ultimately signed off on its unfortunate press release. At best, the BDPaaS announcement is unclear; at worst, it's downright bewildering and counterproductive.

Second, consider the result of each message. Both fail despite the meticulous planning, editing, and consensus-building that happened behind the scenes. Because each message employed nearly impenetrable language, it's unlikely that either was fully received. A simpler, more straightforward approach would have been far more effective in each case. Less would have been more. Put differently, the problem isn't *what* Microsoft and CSC announced; it's *how* each company announced it.

Third, and most germane to this book, these messages are anything but isolated occurrences. Far from it. Lamentably, similar communications have become commonplace in many professional settings, and not only from some of the biggest technology vendors. Increasingly, confusing messages seem to be becoming the norm in the business world. Referring to Nadella's memo, Lee Hutchinson of Arts Technica echoes this sentiment: "This, sadly, is not a Microsoft-specific issue; it's standard all across not just the tech industry but essentially every large American company."[4]

The Good News about Bad Business Communication

I see Hutchinson and raise him. Pervasive technobabble is *not* confined to billion-dollar corporations and the people who work for them. Troll around the Web for a few minutes. You'll find no shortage of much smaller companies that describe their products and services in oblique manners. And this isn't just a sales or marketing problem. Ask many knowledge workers what they do, and you may very well need a site like AcronymFinder or AcronymSearch to translate. Myriad e-mails, internal corporate memos, press releases, and blog posts bastardize business and technology terms, not to mention seemingly a good deal of marketing copy on the Web. You might not even have to surf the Web. Think about your last few company meetings and the messages piling up in your inbox. I'll bet that you can find an example or two of poor communication.

What are the effects of this incessant noise? In a nutshell, they're not positive. For now, suffice it to say that intended audiences either completely tune out or don't (fully) receive the message, much less understand it.

As a general rule, the quality and clarity of business communication have deteriorated considerably over the past 10 years. Many people have lost the ability to communicate clearly (read: without business jargon). And, by relying far too much on one medium (e-mail), we muddy our messages even further.

Yes, we live in very busy and noisy times. Ours is an era marked by unprecedented technological change. Fortunately, there is good news on two levels. First, in this chaos lies enormous opportunity. The demand for simple and clear communication far exceeds its supply. Many us have forgotten that good things are more likely to happen when others actually understand our messages. (For example, imagine that you are a salesperson and your competitors speak technobabble. You are the one who speaks plain English.)

Second, we all can learn how to communicate better. Fret not; it is well within our grasp. It just requires a fundamental shift in what we say and how we say it.

Phil Simon
February 2015
Henderson, Nevada

Notes

1. Steven Vaughan-Nichols, "Windows Has Fallen Behind Apple iOS and Google Android," December 12, 2012, www.zdnet.com/article/windows-has-fallen-behind-apple-ios-and-google-android/.
2. Emil Protalinski, "IDC: Android Hit 81.0% Smartphone Share in Q3 2013, iOS Fell to 12.9%, Windows Phone Took 3.6%, BlackBerry at 1.7%," November 12, 2013, http://tinyurl.com/pge5kso.
3. "CSC Launches Next-Generation Big Data Platform as a Service," June 26, 2014, http://tinyurl.com/otcfxq8.
4. Lee Hutchinson, "Op-Ed: Microsoft Layoff E-mail Typifies Inhuman Corporate Insensitivity," July 17, 2014, http://arstechnica.com/staff/2014/07/op-ed-microsoft-layoff-e-mail-typifies-inhuman-corporate-insensitivity.

PART

I

WORLDS ARE COLLIDING

Part I begins by sketching out the roadmap for the book. It then turns to the tsunami of technology that is rapidly engulfing our lives. It examines the profound ways in which the business world is changing. Thanks to near-constant connectivity and ubiquitous technology, employees are becoming overwhelmed.

It includes the following chapters:

- **Introduction:** The Intersection of Business, Language, Communication, and Technology
- **Chapter 1:** Technology Is Eating the World: The Dizzying Nature of Today's Existence
- **Chapter 2:** The Increasingly Overwhelmed Employee: Is This Becoming the New Normal?

Introduction

The Intersection of Business, Language, Communication, and Technology

> *The single biggest problem in communication is the illusion that it has taken place.*
>
> —George Bernard Shaw

Although he died in 1950, Shaw's words live on, especially in the business world. Far too many executives, salespeople, consultants, and even rank-and-file employees just don't communicate very well.

No doubt, you know the type. Some think that they're speaking and writing effectively when they drop ostensibly sophisticated terms such as *paradigm shift, synergy, net-net, low-hanging fruit,* and *optics.*[*] These folks regularly rely on obscure acronyms, technobabble, jargon, and buzzwords when plain English would suffice. They constantly invent new tech-laden words, bastardize others, and turn nouns into verbs. They ignore their audiences, oblivious to the context of what they say and write. In other words, they "talk without speaking," to paraphrase a popular U2 song.

Forget for a moment a software vendor's poorly worded press release and an incoming CEO's cringe-worthy memo about "strategic synergies and alignments." There's an underlying question here: Is such jargon necessary? In other words, are today's business and technology environments so different and complicated that they require the use of an entirely new, usually confusing vocabulary?

For the most part the answer is *no.* At a high level, a good communicator should be able to explain confusing topics to teenagers without getting all technical. I have done so on several occasions. It's really not that hard. Just remember one thing:

---

[*] Weird Al Yankovic's "Mission Statement" hits the nail on the head: http://tinyurl.com/mvuvpwv.

At its most basic level, the word *communicate* means "to make common."[*]

Subject: The Other Scourge of Business Communication

Bad business communication is a disease with significant costs and far-reaching implications. The prevalence of hackneyed and utterly meaningless terms, however, is just one of its causes.

Let's say that I could wave my magic wand and single-handedly eliminate the use of jargon and confusing language in every organization in the world. No longer would you hear your manager say things like, "Let's take this offline, review our learnings, engage in some blue-sky thinking, and then circle back." *Poof!* *Value-adds* and *paradigm shifts* have been vanquished forever. Grammarians and English teachers around the world would rejoice in the streets.

Would this solve the business communication problem? Although we'd be off to a good start, the answer is *no*. Even the Orwellian abolishment of buzzwords would not guarantee that our colleagues, partners, bosses, underlings, clients, and prospects would effectively receive and understand our messages. A multitude of misses (miscommunications, misapprehensions, misunderstandings, and mistakes) would still result. How? From the way in which we overwhelmingly choose to send our messages.

Yes, I'm talking about the first killer app of the Internet, our widely preferred communications medium: e-mail. Many corporate folks depend almost exclusively on it as a ubiquitous communications tool. They pepper their staff, colleagues, prospects, and clients with torrents of messages. In the process, they actively resist new, user-friendly, affordable, powerful, and truly collaborative tools specifically designed to make people work, collaborate, and communicate better. (Chapter 8 introduces several exciting and progressive organizations that *have* adopted these new applications.)

Technology and the Cardinal Importance of Business Communication

In a way, nothing has changed. Business has always revolved around communication, and some people have always been better than

---

[*] The *Oxford English Dictionary* defines the word *communicate* as "to share or exchange information, news, or ideas." For instance, the prisoner was forbidden to communicate with his family.

others at writing and speaking. No one expects the squirrelly IT guy to be as debonair as the CEO or the head of sales or marketing. Not everyone can be Dale Carnegie. We expect different things from different people at work. We accept the fact that management consultants, techies, software salespeople, and chief execs may communicate in oblique manners. This holds true irrespective of the medium: writing a quick e-mail, penning a company-wide announcement, addressing thousands of people, or speaking individually to a colleague in person. For a long time now, the inability to communicate effectively has inhibited many organizations and derailed individual careers. We have always taken certain people with 50-pound bags of salt. Ignoring or tuning out blowhards may stop an oncoming migraine, but it's hardly a good solution to the problem, much less the ideal one.

In another way, *everything* has changed. Never before has the business world moved as fast as it does today—a trend that will only intensify for the foreseeable future. This is particularly true on technology-related matters. The need for clear and effective communication is more essential than ever. Not only will this problem persist if we ignore it, but it will exacerbate.

What's the Big Whoop?

You may think that relying on jargon and excessive e-mails is just par for the course. What's the big deal, anyway?

Several reasons readily come to mind. The first is that, as mentioned earlier, the need for clear, concise, and context-appropriate communication has never been more pronounced. As Chapter 2 demonstrates, employees are inundated with messages throughout the day, many of which arrive via confusing or inscrutable e-mails. Which of the following do you think is more likely to be effective?

- An endless chain of baffling, jargon-laden e-mails
- Simple, clear, and honest conversations either in person or via a truly collaborative tool

For a long time now, people have denounced the use of buzzwords when plain English would suffice. Yet jargon persists. The critics are helpless against "words" like *incent*. Beyond that, business folks turn nouns into verbs. In reality, they're only bloviating. (The now commonplace adoptions of *use case**** and *price point* are real pet peeves of mine.) They fail to consider the context of what they're saying, and they speak and write with zero regard for their audiences.

Second, you may believe that new times have always required new words and phrases. This is true, but not to the same extent currently exhibited. The verb "to Google" developed organically. Millions of people quickly understood what it meant. But what about horrible and contrived phrases such as *Next-Generation Big Data Platform as a Service?* Can we honestly make the same case here?

If technology were a fleeting trend, then perhaps we could excuse the growing use of jargon, the e-mail deluge, and bad business communication in general. Unfortunately, it isn't and we can't. Technology is permeating every instance of our lives—and not just in the workplace. The Internet of Things is arriving as we speak. *Every* company is becoming a tech company; some of them just haven't realized it yet. Few employees work in tech-free zones.

From Pencils to WhatsApp: A Little History Lesson

I'm no Renaissance man, but I fancy myself a student of history, particularly with respect to technology and language.† The creative use and misuse of language predates the modern-day corporation by centuries. It is anything but a new phenomenon, and neither is our complicated relationship between communication and technology.

Think about gadgets such as the computer, the smartphone, the Kindle, and the iPad. Compare them with the clay tablet, the printing press, the pencil, the telegraph, the typewriter, and other critical innovations from previous centuries. The former contain much more sophisticated technology than the latter, but the two groups have more in common than many people realize. Every one of these tools has faced highly influential detractors.

Dennis Baron makes this point in his impeccably researched 2009 book *A Better Pencil: Readers, Writers, and the Digital Revolution*. Baron examines the craft of writing via a fascinating historical lens. As he writes:

---

* Although many people currently use the two terms interchangeably, a *use case* is not a synonym for *use*. Rather, the former is a formal software and system engineering term describing how users use systems to accomplish particular goals. A use case defines the features to be implemented and the resolution of any errors that may be encountered. See http://tinyurl.com/kg38mu7.

† I used to speak Spanish fluently, and I still love the word *esposas*. It signifies both *wives* and *handcuffs*. It's a fascinating double meaning.

The World Wide Web wasn't the first innovation in communication to draw some initial skepticism. Writing itself was the target of one early critic. Plato warned that writing would weaken memory, but he was more concerned that written words—mere shadows of speech—couldn't adequately represent meaning. His objections paled as more and more people began to structure their lives around handwritten documents. Centuries later, the innovative output of Gutenberg's printing press was faulted for disrupting the natural, almost spiritual connection between the writer and the page. Eventually, we got used to printing, but Henry David Thoreau scorned the telegraph when it was invented in 1840s because this technology for quickly transporting words across vast distances was useless for people who had nothing to say to one another. The typewriter wasn't universally embraced as a writing tool when it appeared in the 1870s because its texts were impersonal, it weakened handwriting skills, and it made too much noise. And computers, now the writer's tool of choice, are still blamed by skeptics for a variety of ills, including destroying the English language, slowing down the writing process, speeding up writing to the point of recklessness, complicating it, trivializing it, and encouraging people to write who may, as Thoreau might put it, have nothing to say.

I hope to avoid the latter criticism in this book.

It turns out that, at least conceptually, writing with a pencil has a great deal in common with texting on a smartphone. Each has profound effects on how people process information and how they communicate with one another.

Book Overview and Outline

I like to think that business books, like their fictional counterparts, take their readers on a journey of sorts. If that's true, then it makes sense to provide a map. This section answers the following questions:

- Who should go?
- Do I need to bring anything?
- Where are we going?
- How will we get there?
- Who will benefit the most from this trip?
- What can I expect to learn along the way?

Central Premise of Book

The central premise of *Message Not Received* is quite simple and can be stated in six words:

> Most business communication simply doesn't work.

Because of raging technological change, the need to send clear, effective messages has never been more pronounced. All else being equal, the organizations and individuals that communicate well will do better than those that don't.

Fair enough, but how do we achieve this laudable goal? How do we maximize the chances that our professional messages are truly received and understood? At a high level, we must do two things. First, as a general rule, we need to use simpler language in our business communications as much as possible. Second, we need to wean ourselves from our e-mail *modus operandi* and related addiction. In its place, we need to adopt new, truly collaborative tools *where appropriate*.

This last part is just as crucial as the first. I am no anarchist. *Message Not Received* does *not* advocate an Edward Snowden–like approach to business communications. Some things ought to remain private, although the line between the two is shifting. Embracing transparency and communities—or ecosystems, if you like—may confer major potential benefits. Recent events demonstrate the outright trendiness of sharing and more open business practices. For example, consider Elon Musk, the CEO of Tesla, a manufacturer of high-performance electric sports cars. In June 2014, Musk announced a "patent pledge" on his company's blog making his company's intellectual property (IP) freely available.* Tesla will not initiate lawsuits against anyone who "in good faith" wants to use its technology to develop electric vehicles. In Musk's view, the benefits of such a risky gambit exceeded their costs.

The announcement was certainly newsworthy, but Musk is hardly the only chief executive singing that tune these days. Chris Anderson is the former *Wired* editor-in-chief, a best-selling author, and the current

---

* For more, see http://tinyurl.com/musk-x-pledge.

head of DIYDrones. Anderson believes that "community-driven companies will *always* win."* His company is pioneering tremendous innovation via open-source *hardware*. For his part, WordPress CEO Matt Mullenweg describes betting on the community as "the difference between long-term thinking and short-term thinking."

By espousing transparency and platform thinking, Musk, Anderson, Mullenweg, and hundreds of other CEOs are effectively betting that their companies will ultimately gain more than they surrender. Silly is the organization, however, that *arbitrarily* posts highly sensitive documents for all to see. Examples include IP, financial statements (if the company is privately held), proprietary software code, and employee performance reviews, salaries, and succession plans. Discretion, tact, privacy, and basic common sense still matter and always will. Some things have remained constant.

At the same time, many things have changed. In a nutshell, it's high time for many organizations and people to reevaluate their internal and external business communications. Aside from avoiding buzzwords and confusing language, *Message Not Received* argues that e-mail should not represent the default or sole means of sending messages and exchanging information. Better tools have been available for years, and this book introduces many of them, as well as a few of the companies that are reaping their considerable benefits.

Disclaimers

The central premise of *Message Not Received* is simple yet ambitious. Before continuing, several disclaimers are in order. Let me briefly explain what this book *does not* attempt to do.

Neither Necessary Nor Sufficient: No Guarantees   The prolific management author Tom Peters once wrote, "Communication is everyone's panacea for everything." I couldn't agree more. There's something inherently reassuring about getting everyone on the same page. Unfortunately, a bad idea is still a bad idea, even if everyone perfectly understands it. Coca-Cola's 1985 launch of New Coke was an unmitigated disaster. A better communications strategy would not have changed its fate.

---

*Watch the whole interview at http://tinyurl.com/anderson-comm-win.

Make no mistake: Clear, concise, timely, and context-appropriate communication is more important than ever. At the same time, though, it guarantees absolutely nothing in business. Communicating well at work is neither necessary nor sufficient for a successful outcome. Consider the following:

- An employee completely understands her manager's clearly defined expectations. Despite her best intentions, for whatever reason, she still does not meet his goals.
- An employee misinterprets his manager's vague or even undeclared directions and still somehow knocks his socks off.
- A developer knows her client well enough that, when he says one thing, she recognizes that he really means something else entirely.
- A middle manager has learned to ignore his VP's demands to immediately implement the latest shiny new thing. He knows that his VP will move on to another toy next week.
- A CEO totally grasps what a software vendor is trying to sell to his organization. Furthermore, he fully believes in the benefits and/or return on investment (ROI) of the product. Despite all of this, he still does not pull the trigger.
- A company president completely misconstrues what a software vendor has sold to her organization. Despite this inauspicious beginning, two years later, the new application is wildly successful.

Each of these scenarios is possible. There's a world of difference between *possible* and *probable*, though. These situations are the exceptions that prove the rule. All else being equal, a better message *is more likely* to yield better business results. This book stops short of making unrealistic promises. Effective messages in and of themselves won't ensure a successful project, partnership, merger, acquisition, product launch, new hire, marketing campaign, or sale. All sorts of internal and external variables can derail even the most promising prospects.

Intentional Omissions: Nonverbal Communication, Psychology, and Personality Types   Allow me to state the obvious: To a significant degree, our choice of words determines how—and whether—our audiences ultimately receive our messages. We shouldn't forget, however, that nonverbal factors are often just as important, if not more so. These include our facial expressions, gestures, body language, posture, and paralinguistics (e.g., tone of voice, loudness, inflection, and pitch). It would be irresponsible to dismiss the importance of nonverbal communication. This meaty topic is well beyond my realm of expertise. As such, it lies outside of the scope of this book. (If you're curious about the subject, *The Definitive Book of Body Language,* by Barbara Pease, is worth checking out.)

Next, *Message Not Received* is not a psychology book. It does not examine the most effective ways to communicate to disparate personality types. You won't find any overt references to psychometric questionnaires. No Myers-Briggs Type Indicators.[*] It also ignores the differences between introverts and extroverts. (If you're curious about this subject, check out *Quiet: The Power of Introverts in a World That Can't Stop Talking,* by Susan Cain.)

Tone   *Message Not Received* delves into our challenges with business communications (hence the subtitle). As I wrote in *Why New Systems Fail,* failure teaches us a great deal. Business books like *Good to Great* by Jim Collins suffer from relying exclusively on successful examples—or at least, companies that had been successful at certain points. That is never wise. As you know from reading the Preface, this book cites examples of how *not* to communicate but does not harp on negativity. *Message Not Received* is ultimately a positive book with a tone that is intended to be more instructive than paternalistic or snippy. You will not find any criticisms of honest grammatical errors and typos.

Who Should Read This Book?

It's the understandable, even necessary conceit of all nonfiction authors: *Everyone* should read our books! Who *wouldn't* benefit from our sage advice, insightful observations, profound theories, and predictions on the future? This is especially true with management gurus. Alas, *Message Not Received* is guilty of this as well. I'm

---

[*] In essence, the theory proposes that a great deal of ostensibly random variation in human behavior is actually quite orderly and consistent. It stems from basic differences in the ways individuals prefer to use our perception and judgment.

hard-pressed to think of any professionals who *wouldn't* benefit from improving their communications skills.

In any given week, I meet and talk to people who will soon be doing one or more of the following:

- Asking an angel investor or venture capitalist for money
- Interviewing for a new job
- Talking to their staff or subordinates about technology and change
- Trying to sell their companies' software or consulting services
- Explaining a complicated problem to their "tech-challenged" managers
- Addressing hundreds of people at a meeting or a conference

These people are all trying to achieve different things. Yet, paradoxically, they all have the same fundamental objective: to effectively communicate to their audiences. They need to ensure that their messages are received. What's more, the quality of their communications will dramatically impact whether they ultimately prosper in their professional endeavors.

Lamentably, far too many people think that successful business communication necessitates using buzzwords, jargon, and invented words. It doesn't. (In addition, they often choose the wrong medium for their communications [e-mail].) Think about talented colleagues and acquaintances with demonstrable skill and intelligence. Despite these assets, many people can't communicate well to a single layperson, let alone a group of them, and this is a big problem. As I learned a long time ago, skill and intelligence only get you so far.

Whether in public or behind closed doors, business communication has never been more essential. The tsunami of technology permeating our lives (a topic that Chapter 1 fully explores) has made simple, effective, and clear communication an extremely valuable currency for nearly everyone.

A Holistic Methodology

As of this writing, Amazon sells nearly 3,600 books under the general umbrella of "business communication."* I'm an avid reader,

---

* See http://tinyurl.com/bcbooks2.

but I can't claim to have read even 5 percent of them. Many of the more popular texts here seem to examine the topic in great depth but in relative vacuums. They appear to be very deep but not terribly wide. This isn't a criticism. In fact, many of my favorite nonfiction books don't stray too far from one relatively provincial subject.

On several levels, this book takes a decidedly different, more holistic approach. First, it fuses four highly intertwined fields: business, technology, language, and communication. At least for me, analyzing one of these subjects necessitates examining the other three. With each one, I have attempted to strike an appropriate balance between breadth and depth.

Second, as with my other books, *Message Not Received* combines theory and practice. When done right, the two serve as valuable complements. To the extent necessary, business texts generally benefit from sound scientific, academic, and sociological underpinnings.* By way of contrast, Seth Godin–type manifestos are occasionally inspirational, but they are typically devoid of sourcing, proper research, and outside opinions. As a result, they are usually less valuable and informative.

Next, to state the obvious, our choice of words definitely matters if we want our messages to be received. Still, *Message Not Received* does not focus exclusively on semantics; that would be grossly inadequate. What we say while we are on the clock is often as important as how we say it, if not more so. More than 50 years after he wrote them, Marshall McLuhan's iconic words continue to ring true: "The medium *is* the message."†

Fusing Data with Stories

Generally speaking, I believe in the power of data. Along these lines, this book cites large-scale studies conducted by McKinsey, the Project Management Institute (PMI), and many other respected institutions. Collectively, this research sheds much-needed light on the problem with business communications, gives it context, and manifests the enormity of the issue.

---

* Notable exceptions include company histories and biographies.
† I challenge you to find another five-word sentence that has spawned so much intense debate and analysis. See http://tinyurl.com/3ym58l.

This type of information by itself, though, often fails to expose the problem, much less drive the point home. Quantitative data does not always represent the best way to make an argument. Sometimes a more qualitative approach trumps a purely quantitative one. For a multitude of reasons, this is one of those circumstances.

First, it's often difficult to pinpoint—and find reliable data on—things like:

- The definitive moment at which poor communications tipped a project, organization, or group of employees for the worse
- The precise effect of poor communications on lost sales, employee morale, and the like
- How much time and money could be saved from better communications on any given task or project

Second, relying exclusively or even predominantly on statistics can be a bit lacking, impersonal, and even boring. They often fail to resonate with us as much as good yarns do. Next, stories actually *are* data. As Fred Shapiro, editor of *The Yale Dictionary of Quotations*, once wrote, "The plural of anecdote is data."

Finally, to quote Mark Twain, "There are lies, damned lies, and statistics." When it comes to business and technology, I tend to be a bit suspicious of most claims and promises. Throughout this book, I intentionally avoid making proclamations such as:

- Clear communication will decrease employee turnover by 12 percent.
- Adopting a new collaboration tool will double employee productivity.
- By sending fewer e-mails, your colleagues will be 23 percent less likely to tase you.

In any given circumstance, those predictions may turn out to be true. Still, an organization should never be mistaken for a chemistry lab. It's impossible to hold all other factors constant; we can't isolate cause and effect. Don't let anyone ever tell you any different. (See "Consultants, MBAs, and the Management 'Scientists'" in Chapter 4.)

No Man Is an Island: Looking Outward

At a high level, employees can be broken into two simple groups:

Group A: People who remain at one company for a long time (an increasingly rare feat these days)

Group B: People who regularly bounce around, usually by their choice. Examples include consultants, independent contractors, talk show host Keith Olbermann,[*] job-hoppers, freelancers, temps, and hired guns.

Those in Group A certainly garner a deep and valuable understanding of one company's processes, culture, politics, and inner workings. On the other hand, those who stay in the same place for ten years or more may become institutionalized. People in Group B benefit from their exposure to different corporate environments. They tend to see a wider array of situations than people in Group A do, even when they stay within a relatively narrow field or industry. If hired, they bring with them knowledge of other organizations' "best practices."[†] That is usually true, but there's a flip side to that coin. Those who move around too often and too quickly do so at their own potential peril. Recruiters and hiring managers may pass on them, questioning Group B's ability to hold a steady job. To be fair, this stigma has largely eroded over the past 15 years, especially in white-hot technology positions.

Like most current and former consultants, I put myself squarely in Group B. After several decades of working in probably more than 100 different environs, I have seen more than my fair share of effective and ineffective messages. The most interesting and instructive personal anecdotes have made their way into the following pages.

Still, I am no narcissist. No one can possibly know everything about any of the four subjects at the center of this book: technology, language, business, and communications. Moreover, *Message Not Received* is hardly the first text about business communications. On the contrary, an enormous amount of work has been done in this field long before I started writing this book.

---

[*] On his ESPN show *Olbermann* in 2014, the eponymous host mocked himself by holding a tournament of sorts. He presented a bracket of his 64 jobs similar to that of the NCAA Basketball Tournament. Yes, the 55-year-old Olbermann has held that many jobs over his career if you include college internships.

[†] I usually avoid this term at all costs. I'll feel better by putting it in quotes.

The opinions, theories, and professional experiences of people I respect inform much of my own thinking—and have for a long time. ("No man is an island," as the poet John Donne wrote nearly five centuries ago.) The same holds true with my writing. Whatever their form, the contributions of others—attributed, of course—enrich business books. To this end, *Message Not Received* includes a great deal of insightful advice, opinions, and examples from people with varied backgrounds. You'll read plenty of different viewpoints, relevant suggestions, and thought-provoking material from people not named Phil Simon, and this text is better for it.

Plan of Attack

Message Not Received consists of four parts. The first, "Worlds Are Colliding" starts with an overview of the book. It then explains where we are, recapping recent technological, societal, and business developments and trends. It concludes by examining one of the key effects of these trends as it relates to business communication.

Part II is titled "Didn't You Get That Memo? Why We Don't Communicate Good at Work." It delves into business communication and its two main problems.[*] It examines the increasing use of buzzwords, the evolution of e-mail, and our continued dependence on it. It concludes by describing some of the most inimical consequences of poor business communication.

Part III, "Message Received," focuses on solutions. It offers some general principles to increase the chances that our audiences will receive our messages. It then provides some specific communications tips around language and context before moving on to the case studies. You'll meet some fascinating companies that excel at communication and collaboration.

The book concludes with Part IV, "What Now?", in which I offer some final thoughts on business communication and how we can effect change in our jobs.

My Communication Bona Fides

It's a bit ironic that I've written a book about effective business communication. Before concluding this chapter, allow me a moment of personal reflection.

---

[*] This is an intentional error.

My Personal Communications Journey

By way of background, communication wasn't my strong suit early in my career. In fact, in my mid-twenties, my personal skills needed major work. I always tried to avoid using jargon, but my messages were often not effectively received. Sometimes I would inadvertently ignore the backgrounds of my audience. I sent far too much e-mail. In general, I'd even say that I was a bit "off."

I took constructive performance-review feedback to heart, changed my behavior, and read a few self-help and anger-management books. Dale Carnegie's classic *How to Win Friends and Influence People* really opened my eyes.

Beyond that, I thought long and hard about *how* I communicated. I reflected on my time at Cornell University from 1995 to 1997. I had taught myself Spanish after taking three years of it in high school. I realized that I could neither construct nor comprehend very involved and complicated sentences *en español*. Why not speak as simply as possible in *both* languages?

A light bulb went on.

This story has a happy ending. By 2002, my communication and people skills had begun to catch up with my technical skills. As I approached my five-year anniversary as a systems consultant, I had started coming into my own. I noticed that my clients were responding better to my suggestions. I found natural ways to infuse humor into tense situations. Arguments were less frequent and seemed less contentious, with a few notable exceptions. I remember realizing something that, in hindsight, now seems quite obvious:

When it comes to communication, one size does not fit all.

Alternatively stated, different people often need to hear the same message in very different ways. (I'll offer several personal stories that illustrate this point throughout this book.)

Even now I don't consider myself to be the world's best communicator, but I've made considerable strides. Heaven help me if I couldn't get my message across effectively most of the time. Today I make my living as a professional writer and speaker. When I meet people who have read my books, they often tell me that I write like I talk. More than a few times someone has said to me, "I can tell you didn't hire a ghostwriter." I explain myself clearly, especially when discussing technology trends. Evidently, this skill is in short supply these days.

These are, however, slightly mixed blessings. Having attended more conferences than I can count over my career—and spoken at many of them—I've noticed that most public speakers aren't terribly engaging. (Want proof? At your next event, just look at how many attendees are looking down at their smartphones, laptops, and tablets. Now count how many are looking up at the speaker.) And this goes double when the speaker is talking about business, technology, and/or data.

Next

Chapter 1 looks at the deluge of technology affecting seemingly every aspect of our lives. Yes, business communication has *always* been important. It is often the difference between success and failure. Sending effective messages is even more critical today, however, because our world has become noisier, busier, faster, and more chaotic than ever.

How hectic?

You're about to find out.

1

Technology Is Eating the World

The Dizzying Nature of Today's Existence

The future ain't what it used to be.

—Yogi Berra

Let's say that you're curious about Twitter, and one day you decide to take the plunge. You compose 140 characters or fewer and tweet.

You wait—and then wait some more.

Nothing happens. No retweets (RTs). No modified tweets (MTs). Just crickets.

You start to wonder if you have used Twitter correctly. Aren't tweets supposed to start conversations? Isn't that what social media experts[*] promise?

Don't worry. It's *not* your fault. The majority of tweets are ignored. Some estimates put that number at greater than 70 percent,[†] and I would suspect that that number is much higher for first-time users who are not named Tim Cook.[‡] On the other end of the spectrum, some are heard around the world. Let me tell you about one of them.

Whoops

Up until December 20, 2013, relatively few people had heard of a 30-something PR exec named Justine Sacco. That all changed at 10:19 a.m. on that now-infamous Friday morning. The senior director of corporate communications for Internet conglomerate Inter-Active Corp (IAC) boarded an 11-hour flight from London to Cape Town, South Africa. Right before takeoff, Sacco thought it either wise, funny, or both to tweet the following (see Figure 1.1):

---

[*] I don't like the term, but maybe I qualify as one. See http://tinyurl.com/ps-sm-exp.
[†] See http://tinyurl.com/q9zzq8y.
[‡] Cook, the CEO of Apple, signed up on September 20, 2013. Within days, he had amassed millions of followers.

Justine Sacco
@JustineSacco

Going to Africa. Hope I don't get
AIDS. Just kidding. I'm white!

12/20/13, 10:19 AM from Hillingdon, London

Figure 1.1   Justine Sacco's Infamous Tweet
Source: Twitter, December 20, 2013

Almost immediately after taking off on her Wi-Fi-free plane, Sacco's highly offensive tweet went viral. #HasJustineLandedYet soon started trending worldwide on Twitter. News reporters camped out at the Cape Town airport hoping to interview her.

Once Sacco landed, turned on her phone, and connected to the Internet, she realized the gravity of her joke gone bad. She deleted the offending tweet, along with her Twitter account. She issued a public apology. In her words, she was sorry "for being insensitive to this crisis—which does not discriminate by race, gender, or sexual orientation, but which terrifies us all uniformly—and to the millions of people living with the virus, I am ashamed."*

By that point, however, none of those actions mattered. No one could put that genie back in the bottle. The Twitter mob wanted blood. As the story developed, more disturbing details emerged. Twitter is public by default, and subsequent investigation of her activity on the social network revealed a pattern of insensitive and politically incorrect tweets. For instance, in February 2012, Sacco tweeted, "I had a sex dream about an autistic kid last night."†

Now, IAC is no mom-and-pop operation. Run by legendary media mogul Barry Diller, the corporation owns valuable online properties such as Match.com, OkCupid, The Daily Beast, Tinder, Dictionary.com, and Vimeo. No doubt that many of its millions of social-media-savvy customers quickly took to Twitter and other sites to express their outrage at the views of one of its most senior PR employees. IAC initially responded by condemning Sacco before doing the inevitable on December 22, 2013: terminating her employment amid the maelstrom.

---

* See www.cnn.com/2013/12/22/world/sacco-offensive-tweet.

† For some other doozies, see http://tinyurl.com/oh-justine.

Now, make no mistake: People who should know better have been making insensitive, racial, and misogynistic comments and jokes for a very long time—centuries before the advents of the Web and social media. Consider Donald Sterling, the octogenarian ex-owner of the Los Angeles Clippers of the National Basketball Association (NBA). Sterling wouldn't know Twitter if it bit him, yet he has a long history of controversial remarks and employment practices. In 2014, during the NBA playoffs, Sterling caused quite the stir after making what he thought were private remarks about African Americans to his mistress, V. Stiviano, a woman nearly 50 years his junior. (For whatever reason, Stiviano recorded Sterling. Maybe it was a sting operation.) Sterling's racist comments represented social dynamite, especially in a league comprising nearly 80 percent black players. New NBA commissioner Adam Silver promptly banned Sterling for life and forced him to sell the team. (Ironically, Steve Ballmer ponied up more than a record $2 billion for the franchise.)

So, what was different about Justine Sacco? Ten or 20 years ago, it was impossible to go from nearly anonymous to nearly ubiquitous in a few minutes. And Sacco didn't publish a lengthy, hate-filled screed. Her crime could be represented in fewer than 140 ill-advised characters. The kerfuffle illustrates not only the pervasive nature of technology today, but also how choosing the wrong communications medium can result in adverse consequences. (I certainly don't endorse Sacco's views, but she could have chosen a more private way to express them—one that wouldn't have resulted in her termination and permanently sullied her professional image.)

You may think that this was the only occurrence of an employee using technology and social media to cause major headaches for a prominent public company. Not even close. It happens almost every day. For instance, in January 2013, an employee from British electronics retailer HMV who had access to its social media channels "live tweeted" the company's layoffs.[*] A few months later, in August 2013, AOL CEO Tim Armstrong abruptly fired Patch creative director Abel Lenz on a call in front of 1,000 coworkers. Lenz's crime was taking a photo during a meeting, the details of which almost immediately went viral, including the actual recording of the call.[†] Armstrong issued an apology soon afterward.

---

[*] For more, see http://tinyurl.com/k6xjnx2.

[†] Listen to the call at http://tinyurl.com/patch-call-aol.

I could go on, but you get my point. Yogi Berra's quote at the beginning of this chapter has never been more apropos. We are living in a time of extraordinary technological and social change. Simply put, technology is everywhere now—or soon will be.

This chapter describes some of the key technological trends affecting not only every workplace on the globe, but just about every area of society. In so doing, it lays the groundwork for Part II of this book.

Accelerating Technological Change

Do you think that things happen faster these days than, say, 10 years ago? If so, you're not alone. More than ever, it seems like time flies. You may not be aware, though, that people have felt this way since the Industrial Revolution. *Speed dating* may be a relatively new term, but the notion that the pace of life is expediting is actually old hat. The dictionary company Merriam-Webster formally recognized the term *fast food* more than six decades ago.

The French cultural theorist and urbanist Paul Virilio has written extensively about emerging technology, speed, and power. Virilio contends that speed serves as the very foundation of technological society. Further, the velocity at which something happens often changes its very essence.* Moreover, Virilio states "that which moves with speed quickly comes to dominate that which is slower."[1] In two words, speed kills.

Virilio is no iconoclast. A gaggle of prominent academics and researchers has studied whether we are living in an era of accelerated technological change and concluded in the affirmative. Hermann Lübbe, Hartmut Rosa, Reinhart Koselleck, and many others have done extensive work to further our understanding of how rapid technological advances and our preoccupation with speed are collectively changing society. In his 2000 book *Faster: The Acceleration of Just About Everything,* James Gleick argues that this trend is only going to intensify in the coming years.

Research by the Federal Communications Commission (FCC) confirms that people are adopting technology more quickly than ever. Figure 1.2 shows the time that it has taken for inventions such as electricity, the VCR, and the telephone to reach one-quarter of the U.S. population.

---

* To this end, in 1997 Virilio posited the theory of *dromology* to explain the importance of speed in warfare and communication.

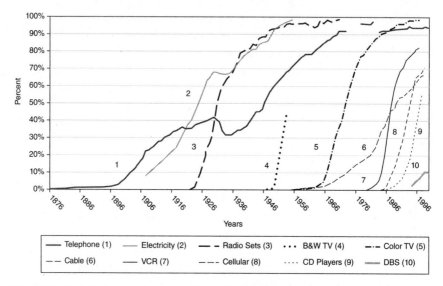

Figure 1.2   Penetration Rates of Consumer Technologies (1876–Present)
Source: FCC[2]

March 11, 2014, marked the 25th birthday of the World Wide Web. In honor of this historic event, several important technology media outlets released insightful research reflecting not only the development of the Internet, but also what's likely to happen in the coming years. Many media outlets, including *The Economist,* featured stories.[*] After all, it made for good fodder. Figure 1.3 presents the aforementioned FCC data.

On that same day, the Pew Research Center released a report called "The Future of the Internet."[†] The far-reaching analysis examined 15 theses about the digital future. At a high level, it surmised how trends like Big Data, mobility, and the Internet of Things will impact our lives by 2025. The Pew report peers into the future and offers some predictions that may or may not ultimately come true. Your guess is probably just as good as mine. Less uncertain, though, is the increasing rate at which we are adopting new technologies. As Pew's Drew Desilver wrote about the report:

> Using data from the website (of course) for futurist Ray Kurzweil's 2005 book *The Singularity Is Near, The Economist's* chart not only

---

[*] Read the whole article at http://tinyurl.com/kvbre4v.
[†] Access the entire report at http://tinyurl.com/pew5555.

depicts just how quickly the Web caught on, *but also shows a larger trend of ever-more-rapid adoption of new technologies over the past century and a half.* [Emphasis mine]

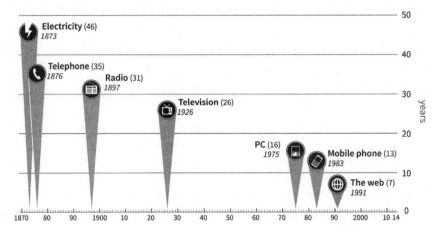

Figure 1.3   Technology Adoption: Years Until Used by One-Quarter of American Population
Source: FCC

Desilver cites the work of Ray Kurzweil, hands down the most prominent spokesperson on these types of subjects over the last several decades. The renowned inventor, author, and futurist has been banging the drums of technology, increasingly rapid change, and exponential growth for decades. In 2000 he wrote *The Age of Spiritual Machines: When Computers Exceed Human Intelligence.* Of note here is his Law of Accelerating Returns:

> As order exponentially increases, time exponentially speeds up (that is, the time interval between salient events grows shorter as time passes).
>
> The Law of Accelerating Returns (to distinguish it from a better-known law in which returns diminish) applies specifically to evolutionary processes. In an evolutionary process, it is order—the opposite of chaos—this is increasing. And, as we have seen, time speeds up.

Accelerating change goes hand in hand with automation, something that is also increasing faster than ever.

The Rise of the Machines

For a long time now, companies have been replacing humans with technology. Not that long ago, we needed to interact with another person at a bank to deposit checks and to withdraw cash. Not anymore. ATMs have us covered.

Automation is encroaching on our lives faster than ever, a point that Erik Brynjolfsson and Andrew McAfee of MIT make in their 2012 book *Race Against the Machine.* Research conducted at its Center for Digital Business proves that the digital revolution is accelerating. One of its principal effects is that computers are now capable of doing things that only humans used to be able to do.

Kurzweil has extrapolated current trends and arrived at an astonishing conclusion: Sometime around 2045, human and machine intelligence will merge. In his words, "the knowledge and skills embedded in our brains will be combined with the vastly greater capacity, speed, and knowledge-sharing ability of our own creations." Yes, man will be immortal.

Kurzweil has made many bold predictions such as these throughout the years. Unlike many experts, however, his prophecies have a remarkable knack of coming true—nearly five in six by his own estimation. For instance, in his 1990 book *The Age of Intelligent Machines,* he accurately prognosticated the fall of the Soviet Union as a result of "new technologies such as cellular phones and fax machines disempowering authoritarian governments by removing state control over the flow of information." In the same book, Kurzweil extrapolated the progress of chess software. Many laughed when he predicted that a computer would beat the world's best player by 2000. Kurzweil was actually too conservative. It happened even *earlier* than he predicted. In May 1997, the IBM supercomputer Deep Blue defeated world chess champion Garry Kasparov in a highly publicized tournament.

To be fair, Kurzweil is considered a controversial figure in many circles.* Many people find him and his views objectionable, although I am not one of them. I have enjoyed his writings and, based on my brief personal interaction with him, he is quite affable. In 2013, I had the pleasure of seeing him speak at the University of Nevada, Las Vegas. I was even able to ask him a question: Why did you decide to work at Google and do you like it? He answered that the com-

---

* Check out the 2009 documentary *Transcendent Man,* a fascinating look at the man.

pany's vast human and financial resources let him do things that he could not otherwise do. And, yes, he likes having a "real job."

The Deep Blue example is both instructive and endemic of a much more significant trend: Technology is capable of doing things that were once considered unthinkable or possible only on *Star Trek* episodes. Companies such as Tesla are changing the very nature of what automobiles can do. For its part, Google is wisely preparing for the inevitable twin declines in ad revenue and profits. The company's secret GoogleX division spends untold billions on "moonshot" projects. To this end, it hired Sebastian Thrun, at the time a professor of computer science and director of the Artificial Intelligence Laboratory at Stanford University. Thrun pioneered the company's foray into self-driving cars, making remarkable progress in just over three years. Note, however, that we are still a long ways away from seeing them on public highways and streets.

Things that we once thought unfathomable have started to become realities, as a few more examples will demonstrate. In 2011, IBM's Watson bested two of the greatest *Jeopardy!* champions in the show's history: Brad Rutter and Ken Jennings. After "reading" Wikipedia, the supercomputer soundly defeated its human competition. What's more, speech and voice recognition have made major strides. Apple's Siri might not be perfect, but it's getting better—and fast. Ditto for Microsoft's Cortana. Google Translate lets users effortlessly move between more than 80 languages from Afrikaans to Zulu—and usually very well.[*]

Forget robots on factory floors taking jobs from blue-collar workers. Technology is starting to eliminate the need for certain types of white-collar jobs, too. More than three years ago, Steve Lohr wrote in the *New York Times* about the ability of computers to mimic human reasoning. Companies like Narrative Science are using computers to generate passable news articles. As Lohr writes, its software:

> takes data, like that from sports statistics, company financial reports and housing starts and sales, and turns it into articles. For years, programmers have experimented with software that wrote such articles, typically for sports events, but these efforts had a formulaic, fill-in-the-blank style. They read as if a machine wrote them.[3]

---

[*] Try it yourself at https://translate.google.com.

Fewer jobs will remain immune from a greater level of automation and routinization.

Trailing the Goldfish: Our Declining Attention Spans

Perhaps you've heard of Herbert Simon (no relation to me, although he did teach at my *alma mater*). The man was a true polymath. Throughout his lengthy and legendary career, he did extensive research in a range of variegated fields, including cognitive psychology, computer science, public administration, economics, management, and sociology.

Simon is perhaps best known for coining the phrase *bounded rationality* in 1955.[*] This is the notion that, in decision making, the rationality of individuals is limited by:

- The information they have
- The cognitive limitations of their minds
- The finite amount of time they have to make decisions

Simon understood full well that *homo economicus* was a myth. Classic economic theory had it all wrong; most of the time, we cannot and do not make completely rational decisions. We do the best with what we have. Not only are we wholly inconsistent, but we are also easily manipulated in all sorts of ways. As a result, the field of *behavioral economics* has become downright chic, with authors like Dan Ariely extending Simon's work.

"In an information-rich world, the wealth of information means a dearth of something else," Simon wrote in 1970. If the world was replete with information more than 40 years ago, what would you call it *now*? And what are we lacking today?

For starters, how about the ability to pay attention for more than 15 seconds at a time? The number of distractions is orders of magnitude greater now than it was back then. The National Center for Biotechnology Information reported in 2014 that American "attention spans have been decreasing over the past decade with the increase in external stimulation."[†] How much? Look at the jarring data in Table 1.1.

---

[*] For more on this, see http://tinyurl.com/aclnans.
[†] See http://tinyurl.com/a7kmuce.

Table 1.1   Average Attention Spans

Attention Spans	Seconds
Average American in 2000	12
Average American in 2013	8
Goldfish in 2013	9

Source: National Center for Biotechnology Information (January 1, 2014)

You read that right: A garden-variety goldfish routinely pays attention for longer periods than the average American does these days. It's a good bet that the rise in the number of messages we regularly receive is at least partly responsible for our frighteningly short attention spans.

A Communications Revolution

On February 19, 2014, Facebook announced its acquisition of piping-hot mobile-messaging app WhatsApp for $19 billion, including $4 billion in cash. A few weeks earlier, Snapchat spurned a reported $3 billion offer from Mark Zuckerberg. Many pundits thought that Evan Spiegel and Bobby Murphy, the company's two 20-something founders, had lost their marbles.

The risky gambit seems to have paid off. In October 2014, *The Wall Street Journal* reported that Snapchat was in discussions with Yahoo. The latter would invest in the former at a $10-billion valuation.[4]

These numbers seem like Monopoly money and suggest that we have entered a new tech bubble. Whether these gargantuan rolls of the dice pay off for Facebook and Yahoo is anyone's guess. That aside, these loft valuations reflect the fact that we are in the middle of a veritable communications revolution.

Task-specific communications applications are immensely popular in the consumer world. Forget about social networks like Twitter, Facebook, and LinkedIn. Temporal message like Snapchat and WhatsApp, photo-sharing vehicles like Instagram and Pinterest, and video-sharing apps like Vine are fundamentally changing the way that consumers communicate with brands, not to mention with each other. Even the absurdly simple, oft-criticized Yo app served an indispensable communications function. In August 2014, Israeli citizens used it extensively to alert others of impending missile attacks.*

Those of us who want to stay in touch with each other are no longer restricted to the phone and e-mail. We've never had more communication options available to us—*at least outside of work.*

The Age of the Entrepreneur

During the dot-com bubble, overhyped companies like Pets.com, Webvan, eToys, and Kozmo quickly rocketed to unprecedented valuations—only to quickly and spectacularly crash. For every Amazon, eBay, Google, and other iconic company to emerge from that era, thousands more are historical footnotes. Back then, starting a tech company was a Herculean task. For instance, early Web magazine Salon.com reportedly needed to raise and spend an eye-popping $100 million to serve its first customer.

There's arguably even greater hype around the current batch of disruptive start-ups: Uber, Lyft, Pinterest, and Airbnb. On many levels, though, today's environment could not be more different from the late 1990s. Infrastructure costs have plummeted by orders of magnitude. Cloud computing has become an incredibly affordable and viable tool for myriad entrepreneurs who don't know if their ideas will thrive or fail. Why even buy software at all? The rise of software as a service (SaaS) has been meteoric, as the successes of Salesforce.com, Workday, and others have shown. Why buy when you can rent? And open-source software has continued to gain popularity, power, and mainstream acceptance. There has never been a greater variety of legally downloadable, free† applications available to anyone with an Internet connection. Sites like GitHub serve as central and robust code repositories.

As I write in *The Age of the Platform,* the prevalence of application programming interfaces (APIs) and software development kits (SDKs) has been a boon to developers and companies like Apple, Facebook, Google, LinkedIn, WordPress, and Twitter. Microsoft (via Nokia), Amazon, and BlackBerry may make quality smartphones, but each company has struggled with selling them. Developers are

---

* See http://time.com/2983226/yo-app-israel-missile.
† It's critical to remember that open-source software is much more like free speech than free beer.

choosing to concentrate their efforts on Android and iOS. Consumers have spoken loudly: They are loath to buy a phone that offers a relatively paltry selection of apps.

One of the most important effects of vastly more powerful and affordable technology is the ease of starting a company. It's no accident that Eric Ries's 2011 book *The Lean Startup* became a *New York Times* best-seller. Reis helped popularize the concept of a minimum viable product (MVP), a "version of a new product which allows a team to collect the maximum amount of validated learning about customers with the least effort."[5] Untold numbers of start-ups across the world are building their companies on top of Amazon Web services (AWS) and similar offerings from Microsoft, IBM, and Google. They are developing MVPs, collecting data via A/B testing, refining their products, and failing fast. (Beyond start-ups, some very prominent conglomerates have embraced lean methods. For instance, General Electric has trained more than 40,000 of its employees in the lean methodology.[6]) Reis has become a bona fide rock star.

Those lacking sufficient funds to bootstrap their own big ideas have plenty of alternatives. First, crowdfunding sites like Kickstarter are more popular than ever. Next, they can apply to popular start-up incubators like Y Combinator, TechStars, Seedcamp, and others. In return for relatively small ownership stakes, these accelerators provide their residents with seed money, advice, adult supervision, and connections. (Lest I overstate things, admission to A-list incubators is fiercely competitive; they reject the vast majority of applicants.) Failing that, ambitious founders and entrepreneurs can approach angel investors and venture capital (VC) firms.

No Shame: Entrepreneurialism, Failure, and American Risk Taking

Tech start-ups and mobile apps may be relatively recent advents, but they reflect the same American entrepreneurial ethos we've seen since the nineteenth century California Gold Rush. In the United States, there has never been shame in starting a company that eventually goes under. This is not true across the globe. For example, in many Asian countries such as Japan, failure is still widely stigmatized. In *Forbes*, Kevin Ready writes about the Japanese start-up gap. "Japan, as all modern societies, has benefited greatly from the innovation and value creation of entrepreneurship, yet has a culture that is highly resistant against, if not openly hostile to startups."[7]

(Continued)

(*Continued*)

It would be difficult to imagine Peter Theil of PayPal fame hatching his fellowship program in China. For the last four years, the billionaire entrepreneur and investor has paid 20 teenagers $100,000 each *not* to attend college. He believes that college debt is oppressive and that Theil Fellows will benefit more from the experience they gather even if their start-ups fail.

Theil is hardly the only American tech titan espousing the virtues of new, disruptive technologies like Bitcoin. Marc Andreessen is best known as coauthor of Mosaic, the first widely used Web browser. He cofounded Netscape Communications and currently serves as the general partner of the highly influential and successful venture capital firm Andreessen Horowitz, a firm that has perhaps the most impressive investment portfolio in the world.* As Andreessen famously remarked, "Software is eating the world." In his view, the American entrepreneurial ethos—and Silicon Valley in particular—drives a great deal of the world's innovation. Other countries cannot innovate as quickly as the United States does because they lack corresponding growth engines. This is very true, but deep cultural mores encourage Americans to start their own companies. In other cultures, the same societal forces strongly discourage their citizens from doing the same.

Disruption Is Cool

Because language is at the heart of this book, I would be remiss not to mention the metamorphosis of the word *disrupt* over the past decade. Consider its current *Oxford English Dictionary* definition:

- (v) Interrupt (an event, activity, or process) by causing a disturbance or problem;
- (v) Drastically alter or destroy the structure of (something)

Up until recently, the word's connotation was decidedly negative. As a kid, my parents sometimes told me that I was being *disruptive*. Why would anyone intentionally disrupt something or someone? The old notion of *disruption* has been, well, disrupted.

On a macroeconomic level, capitalism and disruption have always gone hand in hand. (The next chapter begins with one of my favorite related stories.) The Austrian economist Joseph Schumpeter popularized the notion of *creative destruction* in the early twentieth

---

* See it at http://a16z.com/portfolio.

century. Although it has long been an economic fact of life in capitalist societies, relatively few people have so outwardly *aspired* to actively disrupt entire industries.

My, how times have changed. Disruption is very much in vogue. TechCrunch runs trendy Disrupt conferences. Start-ups like Lyft, Uber, Airbnb, and countless others blatantly flout their goals of disrupting established industries. Behemoths like Google and Facebook are spending billions of dollars to effectively disrupt their own business models, the necessity of which Steve Jobs understood all too well. The mad genius once famously said, "If you don't cannibalize yourself, someone else will."

SEO and the *Really* Long Tail

If you're reading this book, it's safe to say that you sometimes search the Web for pictures, general information, videos, music (legal or otherwise), gifts to buy, and myriad other things. Whether you use Google, Yahoo, Bing, DuckDuckGo, or an alternative search engine, odds are that you rarely or never look at the second page of those search engines' results.[*]

Consider the following data from Chitika, an online ad network that delivers more than 4 billion strategically targeted ads each month to a network of more than 250,000 websites. In June 2013, the company released a study demonstrating what many marketers and technologists already knew: There's tremendous power in occupying the top spot in Google's organic search results.[†] Figure 1.4 displays some of the study's compelling data in a graphical format.

Other fascinating tidbits from the Chitika study include the following:

- Google's first page (read: the top 10 results) drives nearly 92 percent of all search traffic.
- The second page (read: results 11 through 20, inclusive) drives another 4.8 percent.
- Collectively, all of the remaining results drive less than 4 percent of Google search traffic.

---

[*] I'll further assume that, like most people, you have not adjusted your search settings from the default of 10. In case you didn't know, you can change that very easily. I set my default Google results to 100 per page.

[†] Read the entire study at http://tinyurl.com/rptChitika.

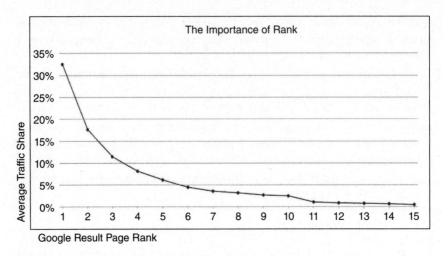

Figure 1.4   Traffic as a Function of Google Search Result Rank

Source: Data from Chitika

Figure 1.5 shows that people rarely go search beyond those first 10 to 15 results.

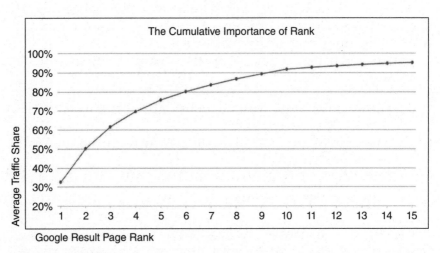

Figure 1.5   Cumulative Traffic as a Function of Google Search Result Rank

Source: Chitika

The Sliding Scale of Search

I am reminded here of the infamous quote by Alec Baldwin's character Blake in the movie *Glengarry Glen Ross*: "Second prize is a set of steak knives." Humor aside, statistics like these establish why search engine optimization (SEO) is essential today—and has been for more than 15 years. (SEO is "the process of getting traffic from the free, organic, editorial, or natural search results on search engines."*) Corporations often employ pricey SEO specialists whose sole jobs involve increasing their employers' organic ranking on search engines. These people study changes in the Google algorithm; the goal is to maintain and improve their organizations' existing site rankings. Companies without the budgets to hire SEO gurus often contract boutique SEO firms to accomplish the same goal.

A few more concrete examples are in order here. I've always loved French toast. Every month, roughly 8 million Google users type in "how to make French toast" or some similar variation.† Google handles so many searches that its software can almost always autocorrect user typos and even predict what they *really* want based on their initial keystrokes.

Now imagine that you run Instructables, a site that "lets you explore, document, and share your creations." When Google users search for "French toast recipes," a page from Instructables shows up at the top. Because of that key enviable placement, Instructables can expect to garner roughly one-third of all Google searches based on that query. (See Figure 1.4.) Note that that number is an aggregate one; it does not apply evenly across all searches. (The history of search is fascinating. John Battelle's *The Search: How Google and Its Rivals Rewrote the Rules of Business and Transformed Our Culture* is the best book I've read on the subject.)

Let's move to another example. You own Italianissimo, an upscale Italian restaurant in West Caldwell, New Jersey, not far from where I used to live. As the proprietor, you're curious about where Google organically ranks your establishment. You type in "best Italian restaurants in northern New Jersey" and find that Italianissimo shows up

---

*For more, see http://searchengineland.com/guide/what-is-seo.

† Through its AdWords product, Google lets anyone determine approximate search traffic. Just type in the word or phrase and hit "enter." For more, see http://tinyurl .com/google-toast.

on the fifth page of Google's results. As a result, it will receive only a tiny fraction of the traffic—and, more important, *the business*—than it would if Google had placed it at the top of page one. And, if your restaurant shows up on page 50 or 500, then it might as well be invisible to the average Googler.

A few disclaimers are in order here. First, you can buy your way to the top of the rankings via Google AdWords, but that can get very expensive very quickly. Second, although it is the dominant search engine in the United States, Google is hardly the only site by which people find restaurants. Bing, Yahoo, DuckDuckGo, and other search engines collectively account for the other one-third of U.S. searches. Beyond search engines, every day millions of people use sites like Facebook, OpenTable,* GrubHub, Yelp, Groupon, and others in deciding where to dine. And good old-fashioned word of mouth still matters. Third, users can opt to receive personalized results from Google, thus affecting the placement of any given website, business, and the like. Brass tacks: Your search results may not equate to mine, even if we enter precisely the same terms.

In the infamous words of the science-fiction writer William Gibson, "The future is already here–it's just not evenly distributed." The same applies with regard to Google's search results on any given topic. The highest-ranked result is orders of magnitude more valuable than the hundredth, never mind the thousandth, millionth, and so on. In this way, search is fairly pedestrian. It is just another example of a *power law*. (This is alternatively known as *the Pareto principle, the 80–20 rule, and the law of the vital few*.) For many events, roughly 80 percent of the effects stem from only 20 percent of its causes.

It's important to point out the sheer number of searches that take place every minute online. The site Internet Live Stats[†] reveals that Google alone handles more than a mind-blowing 2.4 million searches per minute per day—a number that has grown every year since the company's inception. As more and more people gain access to the Web, we can expect that number to keep rising. For the foreseeable future, the traditional index search business will not be disrupted.

---

* Acquired by Priceline for $2.6 billion on June 13, 2014.
† See http://tinyurl.com/lf8tjqk.

Let's go back to 1995, the nascent, pre-Google days of the Web. Assume for a moment that only 1 million or 10 million searches took place every day. Was there still value in being listed on the 6th or 26th page on Yahoo or Lycos? Sure, but not nearly as much as there is today. Now more than ever, even long-tail traffic can result in additional, business, revenue, and profits.

Search is certainly not an all-or-nothing game. For any given search query, Google's PageRank (named for Larry Page, the company's eponymous cofounder and current CEO) typically returns a very large set of results presented in descending order of importance—at least as its algorithm sees it.

In other words, "the head" (read: the top five or ten results) attracts most of the traffic and value in search. At the same time, though, there's still enormous *potential* value in the rest of the results (i.e., *the tail*). This is the thesis behind Chris Anderson's 2006 business text *The Long Tail.* Although few learned business folks dispute its existence, recent research suggests that the long tail is much thinner than Anderson had originally conceived.

Anita Elberse makes this case in her eye-opening 2013 book *Blockbusters: Hit-making, Risk-taking, and the Big Business of Entertainment.* She points to data on the music industry from Nielsen, a global information services firm. In her words:

> [O]f the eight million unique digital tracks sold in 2011 (the large majority for $0.99 or $1.29 through the iTunes Store), 94 percent—7.5 million tracks—sold fewer than one copy. Yes, that's right: of all of the tracks that sold at least one copy, about a third sold *exactly* one copy. (One has to wonder how many of those songs were purchased by the artists themselves, just to test the technology, or perhaps their moms out of a sense of loyalty.) And the trend is the opposite of what Anderson predicted: the recorded-music tail is getting thinner and thinner over time. Two years earlier, in 2009, 6.4 million unique tracks were sold; of those, 93 percent sold fewer than one hundred copies and 72 percent sold only one copy.

Elberse describes how the "head" of the tail is expanding—that is, fewer and fewer hits in the music, movie, book, and sports businesses are driving greater percentages of profits. She calls the levels of concentration in these markets "astonishing."

Google and the Never-Ending Jargon Train

Few learned folks doubt Google's immense power today. Consider this striking testament to its clout: As I write these words, European governments are working with the search giant to comply with new legislation on "the right to be forgotten." Its service is *too* good, *too* accurate.

The pressure to define and "own" a business and technology term has become more intense as our world has become noisier. For this very reason, software vendors and advisory firms such as CSC (mentioned in the Preface) coin and heavily promote their own terms.

Research firm Gartner defines *search-based data discovery tools* as "those that enable users to develop and refine views and analyses of structured and unstructured data using search terms."* IBM as of late has been marketing the concept of *cognitive computing*. As the company describes on its website,† cognitive computing represents systems that "learn and interact naturally with people to extend what either humans or machine could do on their own. They help human experts make better decisions by penetrating the complexity of Big Data." On an individual level, prominent thought leaders like Tom Davenport, a professor of management and information technology at Babson College, espouse newfangled terms like *Analytics 3.0*.‡

Now, businesses have been pushing their own wares for decades, and there's nothing unethical about this practice. Each company is understandably trying to market its own products and services. If Gartner promulgates a term like *search-based data discovery tools*, you can bet that competitors such as International Data Group (IDC), Forrester Research, and AMR Research will soon follow with their own facsimilies.

Let's look at a timely example of this type of term inflation. In my fifth book, *Too Big to Ignore*, I wrote the following about Big Data:

> Douglas Laney (then with the META group, now with Gartner) fired the first shot in late 2001. Laney wrote about the growth challenges and opportunities facing organizations with respect to increasing amounts of data. Years before the term Big Data was

---

* For more, see http://tinyurl.com/gartner-SBDT.
† See http://tinyurl.com/ibmccog.
‡ See http://hbr.org/2013/12/analytics-30/ar/1.

de rigueur, Laney defined three primary dimensions of the Data Deluge as the increasing amount of data (volume), the increasing range of data types and sources (variety), and the increasing speed of data (velocity).

Laney's three *v's* stuck, and today most people familiar with Big Data have heard of them. That's a far cry from saying, however, that everyone agrees on the proper definition of Big Data. Just about every major tech vendor and consulting firm has a vested interest in pushing its own agenda. To this end, many companies and thought leaders have developed their own definitions of Big Data. A few have even tried to introduce additional *v's* like veracity (from IBM) and variability (from Forrester Research). Among the technorati, arguments abound, and it often gets pretty catty.

Once Big Data became a *thing,* it didn't take long for other large software vendors and consulting firms to piggyback on Laney's oft-quoted work. Surely, there had to be more *v's!* It didn't take long for the herd to start zealously promoting variability, viability, veracity, validity, and value.

In reality, these extra *v's* don't alleviate the general sense of confusion about the topic, a point echoed by text analytics and data expert Seth Grimes. In a piece for *InformationWeek,* Grimes correctly notes that Laney's three terms more than adequately define *Big Data.* He further cautions readers and professionals to be wary of "wanna-*v's*" such as those previously mentioned.[8]

Marketing Madness

The precipitous drop in start-up costs discussed earlier has enabled anyone with an app or business idea to launch it. Of course, many concepts are terrible and destined for the morgue. When anyone can do something, just about everyone does. Thanks to rapid technological advances, creative endeavors such as starting a company or blog, writing and publishing a book, releasing an album, or shooting a movie have never been easier. Arguably, the principal downside of this trend is that it's never been tougher to get noticed. Beyond that, Andrew Keen contends in *The Cult of the Amateur* that the lack of proper gatekeepers has eliminated quality control. As a result, it is difficult to separate the wheat from the chaff. All of this noise means that relying only on organic traffic is unlikely to move the needle. (See "SEO, Google, and the *Really* Long Tail" earlier in this chapter.)

Google cofounder Sergey Brin once allegedly said, "Marketing is the cost you pay for lousy products." Brin is one of the smartest men on the planet, but he is dead wrong here. By way of background, search in 1998 was generally unreliable and ineffective. From the beginning, Google built a better mousetrap without the help of any formal marketing and advertising, relying instead on good old-fashioned word-of-mouth. Douglas Edwards makes this point in his excellent 2012 book *I'm Feeling Lucky: The Confessions of Google Employee Number 59.* The buzz around Google grew organically, as did its entrance into truly rarefied air, the marketing Holy Grail: the widespread adoption of "Google" as a verb.[*]

Although these stories are interesting and even inspirational, for the average company they are increasingly far-fetched. Google was the exception that proves the rule: More than ever, marketing matters. Sure, on rare occasions, YouTube videos, apps, songs, blog posts, photos, memes, and tweets go viral. (Justine Sacco, mentioned at the start of this chapter, is perhaps the best example of the latter.[†]) Foolish is the start-up founder, author, musician, or executive who dismisses the importance of marketing. In the words of Q Manning, CEO and founder of mobile-app firm Rocksauce Studios:

> All businesses require marketing. Digital products are no different. In our very first conversation with a prospective client, we emphasize the absolute necessity of marketing. We perform days of research to make sure we're building a beautiful product with the right features. We strongly advise them to make room in their budget for a solid marketing campaign.
>
> Of course we want our clients to be successful. That's not going to happen, however, if no one knows that the app exists.[9]

Manning is absolutely right. The vast majority of sales happen with the aid of some type of advertising and/or marketing. More broadly, marketing, disruption, and technology have always been inextricably linked. Think about it. Most industries and professions fall into one of two categories:

---

[*] *The Oxford English* Dictionary formally recognized it in 2006.
[†] Don't mistake good viral for bad viral.

1. *Those that have already been changed or obliterated by technology.* When was the last time you saw a Tower Records, Blockbuster, Fotomat,* or travel agency?
2. *Those that are being disrupted by technology—or soon will be.* Taxicabs and hotels are at the top of the list. Lyft, Uber, and Airbnb show no signs of backing down.

For a long time now, marketing and advertising budgets have been shifting from traditional print media, radio, and television to the online sources such as display ads, social media, content marketing, and search engines. Budgets tightened during the financial crisis, but they appear to have returned with a vengeance. Two statistics here are particularly instructive. Marketing expenditures on mobile paid search grew 98 percent globally in 2014 compared to 2013.[10] In June 2014, the Interactive Advertising Bureau (IAB) reported that:

> Internet advertising revenues in the U.S. reached $11.6 billion for the first quarter of 2014, marking a 19 percent increase over the same period in 2013, according to the latest [Internet] Advertising Revenue Report figures released today by the IAB and PwC US.[11]

Compared to its 1998 or even 2009 counterparts, marketing in a field in 2014 may be barely recognizable. Although the changes may be dramatic, the function is alive and well because it is a necessary evil. Companies that ignore marketing do so at their own peril; the alternative these days is virtual anonymity.

Marketing seems synonymous with noise today because it's 24/7. That is, people in industrialized societies are carrying more devices and almost constantly staring at screens. As a result, they are seeing more advertisements and marketing messages than ever. Jay Walker-Smith of Yankelovich Consumer Research estimates that American consumers have seen a ten-fold increase in marketing messages in the last 40 years. In his words, "We've gone from being exposed to about 500 ads a day back in the 1970s to as many as 5,000 a day today." This is a ten-fold increase over the past four decades.

---

* I'm dating myself here. Fotomat was an American-based retail chain of photo development drive-through kiosks located in shopping center parking lots.

Consider this amazing statistic: In their 2012 book, *The Human Face of Big Data,* Rick Smolan and Jennifer Erwitt write that today the average man is exposed to more data in a single day than his fifteenth century counterpart was *in his entire lifetime.*

Mobile Mania

Since the late 1990s, Mary Meeker of the VC firm Kleiner Perkins Caufield & Byers has published and presented her highly anticipated Internet Trends report. It scores oodles of press coverage. In May 2013, she was at it again.* Over the past few years, Meeker's research has emphasized both the increasing importance and usage of smartphones. She noted that people touch them an astonishing 150 times every day. Twenty-three of those times involved checking messages alone. All signs point to these numbers increasing.

That same year, IDC largely echoed Meeker's smartphone research. It found that 79 percent of people ages 18 to 44 keep their smartphones with them 22 hours per day.† (Yes, many people sleep next to them.) A full one-quarter of respondents couldn't remember a single time during the day in which they were not in the same room as their phones. Four out of five smartphone users check their phones within the first 15 minutes of waking up each morning. (I certainly do.) Nearly 80 percent of those people say that it's the first thing they do each morning after opening their eyes.

These statistics speak volumes about the adoption of smartphones. Most folks, though, don't need to see this type of data to grasp the profound influence that iPhones and Droids have had on our lives. Just watch people at your local supermarket, Target, and health club. Take a look at what just about everyone does once an air plane lands: Like trained rats, we immediately pick up our phones as soon as the wheels touch the ground, present company included.

BYOD

Back in the late 1990s, it was relatively easy for IT departments to block access to forbidden sites and other content that management deemed *NSFW.*‡ Services such as WebSense theoretically forbade

---

* Read her 2013 report at www.kpcb.com/insights/2013-internet-trends.
† To learn more about the report, see http://www.mediabistro.com/alltwitter/smartphones_b39001.
‡ Shorthand for "not suitable/safe for work."

employees from wasting time, at least while using a company computer. IT maintained site blacklists, easily blocking Hotmail, AOL, Gmail, porn sites, and other time-wasting online destinations.

IT is now almost completey ineffectual as this type of gatekeeper. Most employees take their own smartphones with them to work, a movement termed *bring your own device* (BYOD). This renders services like WebSense largely moot. Want to tweet or check Facebook at the office? Just whip out your smartphone. There's not much that IT can do to stop you or anyone else for that matter. If you connect via an AT&T, Verizon, or T-Mobile network (and not your organization's Wi-Fi), Big Brother will never know what you've been doing.

Security experts advise that the biggest threats lie *inside* of organizations' walls, not from outside hackers. Yes, recent high-profile data breaches have received plenty of publicity. Examples include LinkedIn, eBay, SONY, Michael's, Neiman Marcus, and JP Morgan Chase. Most CIOs know full well, however, that there's a much bigger risk: Employees, independent contractors, consultants, and freelancers could easily walk out with highly sensitive corporate information on a tablet, smartphone, or USB drive.[*]

The Rise of the Tech Celebrity

Many aspiring entrepreneurs fancy themselves the next Steve Jobs, the iconic leader who pioneered so many game-changing products. It's fair to call Jobs the first modern-day rock-star CEO, not to mention the inspiration for most of today's young, über-wealthy tech leaders. Facebook founder Mark Zuckerberg, Twitter cofounder and current Square CEO Jack Dorsey, and Tesla and SpaceX head honcho Elon Musk are bona fide celebrities. When they visit countries and appear at events, they evoke memories of the Beatles arriving in America for the first time in 1964. Outside of the United States, Jobs's influence is felt in places as far away as China. Lei Jun, the CEO of Beijing-based electronics behemoth Xiaomi, often dons the Jobsian uniform of a black shirt and jeans.

The sports and entertainment worlds have also caught technology fever. Cats and dogs are living together. High school jocks aren't afraid to hang out with geeks anymore. Luminaries such as LeBron James, Ashton Kutcher, and Leonardo DiCaprio are investing in tech

---

[*]For more of my thoughts on BYOD and security, see http://tinyurl.com/philbyod.

companies. In 2013, BlackBerry hired R&B singer, producer, and actress, Alicia Keys as its creative director. (Not long after, the company parted ways with her. The metadata from one of her tweets revealed that she had been using an iPhone.*) The company's new CEO John Chen is desperately trying to right the ship, but the trend is unmistakable: Marriages between celebrities and tech companies are on the uptick. As Julianne Pepitone writes on CNN, "Lately it's become popular for tech companies to sign on celebrities as 'creative directors,' which some see as glorified spokespeople. As of this writing, Lady Gaga holds the position at Polaroid, while rapper will.i.am does the same at Intel."[12] Apple paid $3 billion for headphone and streaming-music company Beats Music in May 2014. This was by far the most expensive acquisition in Apple's history. It's tough to see CEO Tim Cook making that unprecedented purchase had it not been for the star power of Beats's cofounders: rapper Dr. Dre and record and film producer Jimmy Iovine.

Want more proof that technology and pop culture have never been more intertwined? HBO's 2014 comedy *Silicon Valley* about a fictitious start-up has been hailed as a "hilarious critical and commercial darling."[13] The hit show tells the story of a bunch of geeks working on a file-compression algorithm, most certainly a sign of the times. Thomas Middleditch plays Richard Hendriks, the show's protagonist, a reclusive programmer who could easily be mistaken for an early Mark Zuckerberg in both appearance and disposition. Mike Judge's show perfectly captures the start-up zeitgeist, much like his cult classic *Office Space* did with Corporate America.

A New Body Politic

Beyond Hollywood, there's a growing sense that even governments are finally ending their sloth-like ways. The public sector is starting to recognize the importance of technology, especially as it pertains to future job growth. Soon after moving into the White House in 2009, President Obama issued a memorandum advocating a more open government. In his words, "Executive departments and agencies should harness new technologies to put information about their operations and decisions online and readily available to the public."

---

*For more on the hidden technology behind Twitter, see http://tinyurl.com/ke9a9sa.

More recently, Obama has asked Americans to learn computer science—and effected policies to that end.* Nonprofits such as Code for America are encouraging us to embrace our inner geek. At the city level, Thomas Menino of Boston, Edwin M. Lee of San Francisco, Rahm Emanuel of Chicago, Mike Bloomberg of New York, and other progressive mayors have been walking the walk. They have gone far beyond merely stating obvious yet vacuous platitudes about our technology-centered future. For instance, at the NY Tech Meetup in October 2011, Bloomberg said:

> Technology is going to define the twenty-first century economy, and I want to make sure those jobs are created in New York City. . . . The BigApps competition is just one of the ways we're making sure that's still true for today's entrepreneurs and for the visionaries of the future.†

Bloomberg entered office in 2002 resolute that technology could make New York City government more efficient, responsive, and transparent. Over the course of his three terms, he enacted many tech-friendly policies. (The Wikipedia entry for them runs a robust 500 words.) Although many politicians still struggle with turning on their smartphones, an increasing number understand the critical role that technology is playing in the world. Other prominent thought leaders include California Lt. Governor Gavin Newsom, author of *Citizenville: How to Take the Town Square Digital and Reinvent Government*, and Tim O'Reilly, founder of O'Reilly Media. Both have written and spoken extensively about promulgating a more open, more interactive government—one based on new technologies, greater citizen participation, and platform thinking. The popular and influential author Stephen B. Johnson echoes similar progressive sentiments in *Future Perfect: The Case for Progress in a Networked Age.*

Other Trends

I would be remiss if I didn't mention several other important technological trends that are changing our lives. Although the number of Facebook users seems to have plateaued at about 1.3 billion, social

---

* Watch him here on YouTube: www.youtube.com/watch?v=6XvmhE1J9PY.
† Watch him here on YouTube: www.youtube.com/watch?v=z6A6R7hI70o#t=93.

media has remained a major societal and business force. As I write these words, Facebook, Twitter, and LinkedIn have just reported strong or record earnings, and their stock prices have jumped considerably.

Wearable technology has arrived in earnest. The number of smartwatches continues to rise. Jawbone, the Apple Watch, and FitBit have arrived. Google has suspended development of its Glass product, but similar devices are coming soon. Scores of other potentially life-changing products will be released and improved in the next three to five years. Both Google and Apple announced plans at their annual 2014 development conferences to let users closely monitor their lives and health via future versions of their operating systems.

Long considered a pipe dream, virtual reality is very close to finally arriving. Led by a homeschooled 21-year-old named Palmer Luckey, Oculus Rift finally cracked the elusive VR code in 2013. The company's flagship headset was leaps and bounds better than competing products, so much so that in March 2014, Facebook plunked down more than $2 billion to acquire it.

Massive changes are coming in the form of personalized medicine, mobile payments, 3D printing, augmented reality, and the long-awaited arrival of the smart home via the Internet of Things. These advances—and many others—will affect just about every aspect of our lives. Pick an area or field. It's not a matter of *if* it will change, but *when*.

Next

This chapter has covered key technological trends affecting our personal and professional lives in profound ways. As it relates to business communication, the most important consequence of these trends is that they are collectively overwhelming us at work.

Let that serve as the starting point for Chapter 2.

Notes

1. John Armitage, "Beyond Postmodernism? Paul Virilio's Hypermodern Cultural Theory," November 15, 2000, www.ctheory.net/articles.aspx?id=133.
2. Sources of data: For "households" (1876–1900) and "homes with electricity" (1908–1911, 1913–1916, 1918–1920), staff estimates based on Census Bureau information; for CD players, Consumer Electronics Manufacturers Association data (June 1999); for Direct Broadcast Satellite, The Satellite Report 1999, by Global Satellite Research, C.E. Unterberg, Twobin (1999); for all other data, Statistical Abstracts of the United States, by U.S. Department of Commerce,

Bureau of the Census (1972, 1974, 1976, 1978, 1979, 1982-83, 1987, 1989, 1990, 1992, 1995, 1997, 1998) and Historical Abstract of the United States: From Colonial Times to 1970, by U.S. Department of Commerce, Bureau of the Census (1975).

3. Steve Lohr, "In Case You Wondered, a Real Human Wrote This Column," September 10, 2011, http://tinyurl.com/1722z.

4. http://online.wsj.com/articles/yahoo-nears-investment-in-snapchat-1412361684

5. Eric Reis, "Minimum Viable Product: A Guide," August 3, 2009, www .startuplessonslearned.com/2009/08/minimum-viable-product-guide.html.

6. Richard Clough, "General Electric Wants to Act Like a Startup," August 7, 2014, www.businessweek.com/articles/2014-08-07/ge-taps-lean-startup-ideas-for-faster-cheaper-product-rollout.

7. Kevin Ready, "In Search of Japan's Missing Startups," May 17, 2013, www.forbes .com/sites/kevinready/2013/05/17/in-search-of-japans-missing-startups.

8. Seth Grimes, "Big Data: Avoid 'Wanna V' Confusion," August 7, 2013, www.informationweek.com/big-data/big-data-analytics/big-data-avoid-wanna-v-confusion/d/d-id/1111077.

9. Personal conversation with Manning on August 7, 2014.

10. Jessica Lee, "Mobile Paid Search Spend Up 98% Globally vs. Last Year [Report]," July 15, 2014, http://searchenginewatch.com/article/2355483/Mobile-Paid-Search-Spend-Up-98-Globally-vs.-Last-Year-Report.

11. www.iab.net/about_the_iab/recent_press_releases/press_release_archive/ press_release/pr-061214.

12. Julianne Pepitone, "Alicia Keys Out as BlackBerry's 'Creative Director'," January 2, 2014, http://money.cnn.com/2014/01/02/technology/enterprise/ blackberry-alicia-keys.

13. Molly Mulshine, "'Silicon Valley' Cast: Peter Gregory Remains on Show Despite Actor's Untimely Death," May 21, 2014, http://betabeat.com/2014/05/silicon-valley-cast-peter-gregory-remains-on-show-despite-actors-untimely-death.

2

The Increasingly Overwhelmed Employee

Is This Becoming the New Normal?

It is not enough to be busy. The question is: What are we busy about?

—Henry David Thoreau

The *Oxford English Dictionary* defines the word *Luddite* as "a person opposed to increased industrialization or new technology." The fascinating genesis of the word dates back to the Industrial Revolution and reveals the complex interrelationship that has always existed among people, work, and technology.

In the early nineteenth century, a group of English textile artisans protested the deployment of labor-saving machinery in cotton and woolen mills. The tools included power looms and stocking and spinning frames. Collectively, these devices posed a threat to the artisans' livelihoods. Lesser-skilled laborers could now effectively do the same jobs for a fraction of the artisans' wages. In response, the group destroyed the new machinery. The term *Luddite* derives from the name of the artisans' alleged leader, Ned Ludlam.

We can debate the net effects, winners, and losers of the trends described in Chapter 1 ad nauseam. You may find them to be positive, negative, liberating, scary, or some combination of all of the above. Others may very well disagree with you. In a few decades, maybe scientists, anthropologists, psychologists, and neurologists will be able to fully appreciate how the Internet Age has affected us. Yes, you can access the vast quantities of information from your smartphone, but at what cost?

I don't know all of the answers to these heady questions, but less uncertain is the question of whether knowledge workers now find themselves overwhelmed. The answer here is a resounding *yes*.

Mad Men No More

Like millions of people, I watch AMC's *Mad Men,* historical fiction that takes place primarily in the 1960s. It will never supplant

Breaking Bad as my all-time favorite series and, in the last few seasons, *Mad Men* has become a bit too talky for my liking. Still, I feel compelled to tune in on Sunday nights. I watch it with a sense of amazement at how far technology has come in the last 40 to 50 years.

The show's protagonist, Don Draper (played by Jon Hamm), faces plenty of challenges at work and at home, most of which are of his own doing. He works at the Manhattan-based advertising firm Sterling Cooper Draper Pryce. Back then, it was far easier—and probably more common—for employees to leave work at the office. In those quaint days, people read newspapers to find out what happened yesterday.

Forget the 1960s. Consider just how much things have changed since the heydays of two other iconic TV shows: *Seinfeld and Friends*. Go ahead and watch an episode or two. You may still laugh, but you're sure to find them dated, even though they only went off of the air in 1999 and 2004, respectively. Those shows seem to have taken place in the distant past. No one uses a smartphone.* For example, consider "The Stock Tip," the fifth episode of the first season of *Seinfeld*. Jerry obsessively checks the newspaper every morning to find out how his investment performed yesterday. Not too many people do that anymore. Major newspapers are dying as we speak.†

In the *Mad Men* era, people wrote proper business memos on typewriters. Interoffice envelopes abounded. Each of these has gone the way of the dodo. (On April 25, 2011, Godrej and Boyce, the last typewriter manufacturer in the world finally closed its doors.)

Now, *consumers* are communicating via social networks, text messages, e-mail, Skype, more e-mail, and new means of communication on an almost-daily basis. Those who doubt the value of *messaging* (a relatively new word itself) only need to look at Facebook's aforementioned jaw-dropping $19 billion acquisition of WhatsApp in February 2014.

---

* Almost every episode of *Seinfeld* features an Apple Macintosh computer on Jerry's desk in the corner of his apartment.
† For a fascinating documentary on the health of one iconic newspaper, check out *Page One: Inside The New York Times.*

Information Overload: From Bad to Worse

LexisNexis is a leading global provider of legal, government, business, and high-tech research. In 2010, the company conducted its second International Workplace Productivity Survey* extending similar work performed in 2008. That seminal study "established information overload as a phenomenon driving American white-collar and legal professionals towards an 'information breaking point.'" What's more, the problem is exacerbating.

In the two years since the study was fielded in the United States, the problem among white-collar workers has gone from bad to worse. American professionals say they spend half their workday receiving and managing information, an increase of almost 10 percent since 2008.

"Workers across the globe are just about managing to keep their heads above water in a rising tide of information," said Michael Walsh, CEO of U.S. Legal Markets, LexisNexis. "The results of this survey reveal not just how widespread the problem is, but also the very real impact that information overload has on professionals' productivity and the bottom line. Employers need to do more than simply toss their workers a life preserver and hope for the best. They need to invest in practical solutions."

"The bad news is that wherever you find knowledge workers around the world, you'll also find information overload," Walsh continued. "The good news is that employers who take the initiative and invest in customized technology, tools and training can avoid significant costs in lost productivity. In fact, businesses that really come to grips with this problem could gain a competitive advantage over companies that do not."

Among the study's troubling findings:

- 51 percent of all those surveyed in each country say that if the amount of information they receive continues to increase, they will soon reach a "breaking point" at which they will be unable to handle any more. The avalanche of information is also taking a psychological toll on white-collar workers.
- 52 percent of professionals surveyed report feeling demoralized when they can't manage all the information that comes their way at work.
- A majority of professionals in all markets surveyed say the combination of constant accessibility and the incessant flow of e-mail makes it harder to focus on their work. More than eight in ten (85 percent) white-collar workers in Australia and more than two-thirds (69 percent) of South Africa's professionals say the constant flow of e-mail and other information is distracting, making it more difficult to focus on the task

---

*Read the study at http://tinyurl.com/ln-overload.

at hand. Six in ten workers in the U.S. (60 percent), U.K. (62 percent), and China (57 percent) echo this sentiment.

- To cope, a large majority of workers in every market admit deleting or discarding work information without fully reading it. Nine out of ten (91 percent) U.S. professionals say they have done this, as have eight in ten workers in China (84 percent) and Australia (82 percent), and almost three-quarters of professionals in the U.K. (73 percent) and South Africa (71 percent).
- Overall, almost nine in ten U.S. professionals and more than 94 percent of workers in the other four markets say their companies could do more to help them better handle information in their job.

One could only imagine the results if LexisNexis conducted this study today. Does anyone seriously doubt that these numbers would be even more disturbing across the board? Is it any wonder that Americans take only half of their allotted vacation time? More than 60 percent of employees frequently check in while they are out of the office, according to a 2014 survey by employment site Glassdoor. "American workers only used half of their eligible vacation time during the past 12 months," writes Aimee Picchi on CBS MoneyWatch. "The top reason for not taking vacation time was the concern that no other employee could do the job, followed by a fear of getting behind. Seventeen percent of respondents said they were afraid of losing their job."[1] In the words of Glassdoor's Rusty Rueff, "Every time a worker posts a beach photo to Facebook from her iPhone, she's just 'one button away' from work."

Additional research confirms this general problem. In March 2014, consulting firm Deloitte & Touche (D&T) released a study about current trends in global human capital titled "The Overwhelmed Employee."[2] From the report:

An explosion of information is overwhelming workers, while smartphones, tablets, and other devices keep employees tethered to their jobs 24/7/365.

Studies show that people check their mobile devices up to 150 times every day. Yet despite employees being always on and constantly connected, most companies have not figured out how to make information easy to find. In fact, nearly three-quarters (72 percent) of employees have told us they still cannot find the information they need within their company's information systems. D&T concludes that "nearly every company sees this phenomenon as a challenge to productivity and overall performance, but struggles to handle it."

Abundant Leisure: Keynes Was Wrong

In his 1930 paper, "The Economic Possibilities for Our Grandchildren," the British economist John Maynard Keynes famously predicted a relatively sanguine future in which employees would enjoy plenty of leisure time. In his words:

> We shall do more things for ourselves than is usual with the rich to-day. We shall endeavour to spread the bread thin on the butter—to make what work there is still to be done to be as widely shared as possible. Three-hour shifts or a fifteen-hour week may put off the problem for a great while. For three hours a day is quite enough to satisfy the old Adam in most of us!

Like many expert prognosticators, Keynes could not have been more wrong.* For a much more accurate prediction, consider the work of the German philosopher Josef Pieper. In his 1947 text *Leisure, The Basis of Culture,* Pieper wrote:

> The world of work is becoming our entire world; it threatens to engulf us completely, and the demands of the world of work become greater and greater, till at last they make a "total" claim upon the whole of human nature.
>
> Will it ever be possible to keep, or reclaim, some room for leisure from the forces of total work? And this would mean not merely a little portion of rest on Sunday, but rather a whole "preserve" of true, unconfirmed humanity: a space of freedom, of true learning, of attunement to the world-as-a-whole? In other words, will it be possible to keep the human being from becoming a complete functionary, or "worker"?

---

* This is just another example of the folly of trusting expert predictions, the topic of a talk I've given several times. See http://tinyurl.com/zzexperts.

More recently, Juliet Schor's 1993 book *The Overworked American: The Unexpected Decline of Leisure* examines the reasons that Americans work so much more than their counterparts in Germany, France, Scandinavia, and other European countries. Americans seem to be tethered to their devices and their jobs. Tim Ferris might have popularized the four-hour workweek with his bestselling book, but the data indicate otherwise. At least in many industrialized societies, employees are far more likely to be overwhelmed than bored—or even in balance.

We've been heading down this path for quite some time now. In "Hyperemployment, or the Exhausting Work of the Technology User," Ian Bogost in *The Atlantic* argues that we feel overwhelmed because we're actually working *dozens* of jobs. These include managing our different social media profiles, contributing to our friends' Kickstarter projects, coordinating that side gig on Etsy, and the like. In his words:

> For those of us lucky enough to be employed, we're really hyper-employed—committed to our usual jobs and many other jobs as well. It goes without saying that we're not being paid for all these jobs, but pay is almost beside the point, because the real cost of hyperemployment is time.[3]

Think about it. Are you ever truly bored at work? Do you ever feel like you have really accomplished everything that you should? Or do you think that you could be a little more active on social media, do some more research, or listen to another podcast?

Drowning in Data

There's a sense that there's *always* more to do, read, learn, consume, and produce. Freelance writer and artist Sarah Gooding perfectly captures this all-too-common feeling in a piece for Medium:

> It's never been easier to be productive, but it's also never been harder. With technology and a flood of information at my fingertips every time I turn on an Internet-connected device, my resolve crumbles. I reflexively click on headlines and tab upon tab opens with tantalizing news. This is why Woody Allen never bought a computer (sticking instead with his trusty typewriter) and still churns out a feature-length film every year.

Figure 2.1   Drowning, Not Browsing
Source: Sarah Gooding (@sarahgooding)

But not all of us are fortunate to have assistants to digitize our scripts. Given the patience and time required, I'm sure we could all transcribe ourselves. But it makes sense to take what is supposed to be the easy route. However, it's not digital devices that cause problems—it's what they enable you to do once you log on. And herein lies my dilemma.

The rush of speed-reading in an attempt to get through it all gives way to fatigue. Did I conquer that newsfeed, or did it conquer me? Explaining pieces I've skim-read to others can be difficult. How much can one retain when reading so urgently?[4]

Gooding also drew the accompanying picture in Figure 2.1. It perfectly sums up the sentiment felt by millions of people.

In my previous two books, I discussed how many organizations and their employees are inundated with data. I argued that a new mind-set and new tools can at least partially mitigate this problem. They can help us understand what's going on and make better business decisions. Still, one can't ignore the sheer enormity of content out there. It's become cliché, but accessing information today is like drinking from a fire hose.

Demonizing the Tech Companies

Far too many of us blame technology for feeling overwhelmed and for the decline in personal communication. After all, "technology" can't very well blame us back, It's tempting to criticize companies for making their products and services so damn irresistible and inexpensive, but it's also completely misplaced.

Consider Facebook for a moment. People forget that it is very much a business with a fiduciary responsibility to its shareholders to make money. It is neither a nonprofit nor a government utility. Sites like Facebook are designed to be extremely addictive or, as Mark Zuckerberg would prefer to call it, *sticky*. Is it any surprise that it conducts experiments on its users?

And let's not demonize Facebook. Tech behemoths such as Apple, Microsoft, Google, Amazon, and others do everything possible to prevent their customers and users from switching to competing products and services—aka, *vendor lock-in*. They attempt to do this via one of the following methods:

- **Carrots:** Free services, discounted rates, and interoperability
- **Sticks:** Loss of connections, loss of history, loss of data, and the like

Companies are sometimes far too zealous in their efforts to keep their customers. Technology journalist and critic Ryan Block discovered as much in July 2014. Block attempted to cancel his Comcast Internet service by calling the company's toll-free number. Simple enough, right? Not at all. For 20 minutes, an overzealous rep prevented him from doing so. Fortunately, Block recorded the excruciating call for the whole world to hear,* and the recording quickly went viral. Comcast justifiably took a great deal of flak for the incident and had to issue several public apologies.

---

* Listen to it at http://tinyurl.com/qfkcbrr. You'll be amazed at what you hear.

Tactics such as these are hardly the sole purview of technology companies. Why do casinos skimp on clocks and windows? Why are milk and eggs in the far back corners of grocery stores? These are not coincidences. Each tactic is designed to maximize that business's revenue and profits, just as basic economic theory prescribes.

Does this give companies a blank check to do whatever they want, legal or otherwise? Absolutely not. Certain ethical lines should not be crossed. Just remember, though, that *we* are responsible for how we use technology and how we communicate. We are not conscripted to update our Facebook statuses, tweet, and +1 something— although relatively few people actually do the latter.* We often forget that we control how we use the tools, not the other way around.

The Limits of Technology's Tentacles

Technology has always made many objectively positive and beneficial things possible. Forget advances in medicine, science, and transportation. Just think about what we can do now compared to 20 years ago. It's difficult not to be flabbergasted at how we can now easily:

- Keep in touch with our friends around the globe.
- Communicate with each other at a fraction of the pre-Internet cost.
- Access much greater amounts of information effectively for free.
- Choose from a far greater array of products.

Melvin Kranzberg taught history at Case Western Reserve University and Georgia Tech in the second half of the twentieth century. He is most famous for his six laws of technology. The most relevant one here is "Technology is neither good nor bad nor is it neutral." Translation: No technology is an unalloyed good. There's always a downside, and that holds as true with telephones as it does with Google Glass.

There's no dearth of texts suggesting that we may be ignoring or minimizing the detrimental effects of today's ubiquitous technology, social networks, and the like. *The Shallows: What the Internet Is Doing to Our Brains* by Nicholas Carr; *Distracted: The Erosion of Attention and the*

---

* Questionable statistics on monthly active users aside, Google+ is widely viewed as a digital ghost town.

Coming Dark Age by Maggie Jackson; and *You Are Not a Gadget* by Jaron Lanier are three important cultural critiques. These books suggest that we are losing at least some of our capacity for concentration, contemplation, reflection, and maybe even our humanity.

Is technology *solely* responsible for the overwhelmed employee? Let's not overstate things. Some much broader, more nuanced economic, political, and social factors are at play here, one of which I'll discuss next. Maybe Nate Silver is smart enough to determine the precise extent to which technology is culpable for employees feeling overwhelmed. For our purposes, however, exactitude is not necessary.

A Different Kind of Workplace

I began this book by discussing Satya Nadella's announcement that Microsoft would be cutting roughly 18,000 jobs. I chastised the CEO's unfortunate choice of words, not the necessity of the action or his right to take it. I don't know enough about the company's long-term plans to condemn its forthcoming personnel reductions. Even if the layoffs are ultimately shortsighted, an act of corporate greed, or just plain bad management, in a way it doesn't matter. Microsoft is well within its rights to downsize its workforce as its current management sees fit.

The Erosion of the Social Compact

A little history is in order here. Before the 1970s, corporate layoffs were exceedingly rare. Since the early 1980s, however, we've seen a significant uptick. Boards of directors hired turnaround specialists such as "Chainsaw Al" Dunlap specifically to right a sinking ship, even if that meant carnage (re: thousands of layoffs).* For a long time now, relatively healthy and profitable U.S.-based corporations have used cutbacks as a way to trim the fat and placate Wall Street. Even many Japanese companies are finally starting to reexamine the concept of *lifetime employment.* The costs of the practice might be too much for the country's economy to bear.†

Beyond exhibiting the willingness to cut jobs whenever necessary (discussed in the previous section), most large organizations have

---

* Dunlap even penned a self-aggrandizing manifesto in 1996: *Mean Business: How I Save Bad Companies and Make Good Companies Great.*
† For more on this, see http://tinyurl.com/pa2ylt.

enacted other cost-cutting measures. Just about all companies have retired the relatively generous defined-benefit pension plans that were so prevalent in the mid- to late twentieth century. Most now only offer employee-driven defined-contribution plans for the rank-and-file. The message: It's the individual employee's responsibility to plan for retirement, not the company's.

Not everyone is pleased with these trends. On the contrary, prominent critics abound. First and foremost is former U.S. Labor Secretary and prolific author Robert Reich. He has long decried the erosion of the employer–employee compact. Not only has this relationship changed, but so has the very nature of work.

From Organizations to Projects: The Evolution of Work

Who do you see yourself working for: the company or the project you are part of? If you had asked that question in the 1970s and into the mid-1980s, the answer would have been simple: I work for the company. However, the answer you would more than likely get today is that I work for the project first and the company second. Individual employee loyalty is no longer corporate-centric, but instead is project-centric.

Before the mid-1980s, when a company hired someone, there was an implicit social compact that in essence stated the following: Employees who worked hard and desired it had jobs for life with that company. Large companies like American Airlines, AT&T, Eastman Kodak, IBM, Motorola, Procter & Gamble, RJ Reynolds, and Texas Instruments had no-layoff policies even during recessions. Others that did lay off employees tended to try to hire them back as soon as possible. Employees were loyal to their company and vice versa.

However, in the mid-1980s, the investments made by organizations in automation over the course of the previous decade were now able to reduce significant employee headcount. In addition, deregulation of the airlines and telecommunications industries, among others, meant that companies in those markets could no longer count on the steady stream of revenue as they once had. Furthermore, corporate raiders had managed hostile takeovers of several major conglomerates, usually breaking them up through sales of different businesses in order to "unlock" the conglomerate's value. Finally, foreign competition was placing U.S. firms under increasing economic pressure. This forced many to downsize significantly their workforces to try to remain competitive.

In order to cope with this increasingly competitive business environment, companies started to look at how they could better organize themselves and become more cost-efficient. Management consultancies like McKinsey and

Andersen Consulting (now Accenture) urged companies to view their work in terms of projects with discrete beginnings and ends. Computer Sciences Corporation (CSC), Electronic Data Systems (EDS), and other system integrators reinforced this view. These companies had prospered by working on large-scale defense and IT projects. With more than a little self-interest, they claimed that companies could save significant money by outsourcing many of their support functions like IT to third parties (like them) who were more efficient and less costly than using in-house personnel.

To many companies under pressure to reduce costs, the idea of moving to projects made sense, but was still viewed as risky. In 1989, Eastman Kodak—which had recently ended its no-layoff policy—began outsourcing its information systems. Soon afterwards, dozens of other companies followed suit. Over the 1990s, more corporate functions were outsourced and/or downsized as ever more capable automation reduced headcount. Further downsized in the 1990s were the promises of no layoffs. By 2000, few major U.S. corporations still had such a policy in place.

The move to project-based work in conjunction with corporate outsourcing of work, not to mention the strong corporate bias to lay off workers quickly in times of trouble, has radically shifted worker loyalty from the organization to the projects they work for. And when those projects get into trouble or approach the natural ends of their lives, workers understand that the company will likely have little future employment for them if or when the project ends. This may help explain why, when a project gets into trouble, that information is often actively suppressed from reaching senior management.

Any attempt to improve corporate communications without recognizing this employee project-loyalty reality is bound to fail.

Robert Charette is President of ITABHI Corporation and a long-time enterprise risk management expert.

Layoffs and the Employee Psyche

Long gone are the days of indefinite job security. A declining percentage of American jobs entails ongoing or permanent responsibilities. As Charette points out, work has increasingly evolved—or *devolved*, depending on your point of view—to a more project-oriented basis. Coupled with the threat of layoffs, the current state of affairs has profound implications for both employees' workplace behavior and their willingness to share information with colleagues and management.

I have seen this firsthand. I have worked in several very tense environments in which employees would share only the bare minimum of information with others—and grudgingly at that. In other situations, the fear of being laid off represented the elephant in the room. People were afraid to leave the office. A friend of mine at General Electric once mentioned to me that his colleagues would regularly sneak *in* to the office during their vacations. They would tell others, "You didn't see me." Start-ups offer free food, Ping-Pong tables, and potentially lucrative equity, but those perks often come at significant personal cost. Work-life balance is often lacking or nonexistent. For example, conditions at mobile-payments start-up Square have been described as "brutal."[5] Even at companies that offer unlimited vacation time, employees often subordinate their personal lives to work.

Over the last three decades, the layoff threat has gone from virtually nonexistent to constant and very real. Still, for two reasons, it would be wildly inaccurate to claim that it has affected everyone equally. First, as the previous chapter explained, technology is eating the world. Salary-wise, app developers, software engineers, and other techies are the prime beneficiaries of this trend. Should the need arise, they can find gainful employment very quickly, sometimes within days of becoming free agents. Second, many recruiters will tell you that the war for talent has never been fiercer. Rock stars always have their pick of the job litter. Those who face the greatest risk of receiving pink slips are competent, average, entry-level and mid-management types. This is especially true for those who live in relatively remote areas of the country and who lack the skills currently demanded by the market (read: technology).

Is Being Overwhelmed Even a Choice Anymore?

So far, this chapter has explored the causes of what many believe to be a disturbing trend: Most knowledge workers today feel increasingly overwhelmed on the job. This chapter concludes by asking an even more disturbing question: What if being overwhelmed is becoming the new normal? Put differently, what if we continue to blindly accept this frenetic status quo? What if we never truly unplug from work?

While we're at it, consider some other profound questions:

- Have we acquiesced to the rat race?
- Is it healthy for us to principally define ourselves by our careers and our busyness?

- Should we always be as productive and connected as humanly possible?
- What are the long-term consequences of always being available?
- When and where should we draw the boundaries between work and leisure?
- In the end, are all of these sacrifices worth it?

These are lofty philosophical and psychological questions, and I can't answer all of them here. I'm not Friedrich Nietzsche; I'm just broaching some important issues.

All of us—on occasion—complain about work, present company included. From time to time, our jobs, managers, underlings, colleagues, professions, employers, partners, and clients annoy us. Most germane to this discussion, we might dislike our jobs' constantly increasing demands and incessant messages, but by and large we tolerate these irritants. The reasons run the gamut: We have bills to pay. We don't want to be fired. We want to get ahead. We want to achieve, to be successful. We fear change and the unknown. We think that there's a pot of gold at the end of the rainbow.

These reasons are all valid, but maybe they are secondary or even irrelevant. Perhaps it all comes down to two simple questions: What else are we going to do?* Would things be appreciably different if we chose another path?

We might loathe feeling like we're always on call, taking 9 p.m. conference calls, and responding to pointless e-mails for fear of political repercussions. When push comes to shove, though, how many of us are unhappy enough to actually do something about our situations?

What's Holding Us Back?

What's stopping us? What specifically is preventing us from switching jobs, companies, and/or fields? Why don't more of us draw lines—and actually enforce them? If we are tired of being tired, then why do we stay on the treadmill?

It's easier to name the reasons that we *don't* change our equations. For instance, relatively few of us face legal restrictions in democratic

---

* I am reminded here of the *Seinfeld* episode "The Revenge." George quits his job without really thinking it through. He sits down with Jerry to discuss his options, including ludicrous notions such as becoming the general manager of a baseball team.

societies. To wit, few of us are legally tied to our jobs. Only with rare exceptions do employees sign noncompetes, nondisclosure agreements, and other contracts limiting their future employment. Put differently, the vast majority of people in the United States are at-will employees. This means that they can be fired for a good reason, a bad reason, or any reason at all.* (Note that the at-will doctrine is not absolute. In the United States, different laws prohibit discrimination based on race, gender, age, whistleblower status, disability, pregnancy, and, increasingly, sexual orientation.) This sword cuts both ways. We can also quit our jobs without having to justify our motivations to our employers.

We can't blame the high costs of technology for our inertia, at least anymore. Maybe 15 years ago that argument held water. Today, however, it's never been easier and less expensive to build a professional website, take an online course, and learn a new skill if you're so inclined.

What is it, then? Maybe deep down we know that there's a good chance that very little would really change if we switched companies, changed careers, or even took the ultimate step of working for ourselves. Perhaps we would feel even *more* overwhelmed if we joined the ranks of the self-employed or started from scratch in a new vocation.

Humblebrags, Vanity, and the Cult of Busy

Let me offer a theory here: As much as we complain about always being busy and having too much work to do, we secretly crave this feeling. Many professionals think that being busy is tantamount to being important. It's a questionable contention. On his popular blog, Scott Berkun describes *the cult of busy*:

> [S]imply by always seeming to have something to do, we all assume you must be important or successful.
>
> It explains the behavior of many people at work. By appearing busy, people bother them less, and simultaneously believe they're doing well at their job. It's quite a trick.
>
> How busy a person seems is not necessarily indicative of the quality of their results. Someone who is better at

---

* People who believe that the U.S. Constitution exists in the workplace are sorely mistaken.

something might very well seem less busy because they are more effective. Results matter more than the time spent to achieve them.[6]

To be sure, some of this is pure vanity, but there's something deeper going on here. Let's say that you faced the following choice at work:

Option 1: Your job is boring and you're clearly out of the loop. You're not copied on important e-mails. Your attendance is not required at key meetings. Every day, you arrive promptly at 9 a.m., take a full one-hour lunch, and leave at 5 p.m. You never work nights, weekends, or holidays. When you're out sick, your company doesn't miss a beat. You're really just going through the motions.

Option 2: You are simply overwhelmed. Your department or organization can't do *anything* without you. You're copied on every e-mail, even—and especially—the pointless ones. Clients, partners, underlings, and management all bug you on your vacation, weekends, and after normal work hours. When you finally leave the office, work follows you.

Ask yourself which option you would honestly select—*and how each would make you feel*. To more people than ever, this is a Hobson's choice. It is Option 2 every day of the week and twice on Sunday.

In reality, most people sit somewhere between these two extremes. It's more accurate to think of these options in terms of a single continuum. Given that, where would you place yourself on it? I'll bet that you lie closer to Option 2 than to Option 1.

Sure, plenty of people check their brains at their office doors— and there's nothing inherently wrong with that. Few, if any, jobs require *all* of an individual's talents and abilities. Others are able to compartmentalize their work. They draw lines while they are off the clock. They aren't afraid to enforce them with their clients, management, colleagues, and partners. These employees are less likely to feel overwhelmed. On some level, they are healthier than Type A personalities: The former can balance work with family, friendships, volunteering, leisure, religion, the arts, and other aspects of life that are important to them.

Pervasive Communication and Self-Actualization

The rise of the Web has ushered in an era of pervasive communications. Fewer of us are willing and able to draw boundaries and then actually abide by them. More of us are becoming overwhelmed. As such, we find it more difficult if not impossible to strike a balance between life and work. We will always prioritize work over the other parts of our lives. Put differently, it seems that we are principally defining ourselves by our professional identities. We humblebrag about our busyness. We embody sentiment expressed by Jack Lemmon's character Shelley Levene in *Glengarry Glen Ross*: "A man *is* his job."*

We want—no, *need*—our careers to do more than provide biweekly paychecks. Our jobs must make us feel important, even indispensable. Many of us want to move up Abraham Maslow's famous hierarchy of needs, displayed in Figure 2.2.

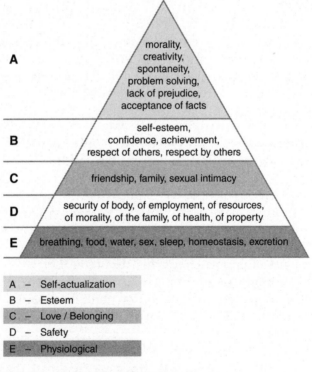

Figure 2.2   Maslow's Hierarchy of Needs

Source: Abraham Maslow, figure provided by author.

---

* For my money, this is one of the five best films ever made.

Again, this doesn't make us bad people, but what are we giving up to become self-actualized at work?

At some level, we have always needed to be needed. This is part of our DNA. However, society and technology have somehow intensified this basic human desire. Sure, we *can* easily unplug, but we usually don't.* Perhaps by always being connected and available, we feel more in control, less helpless, and less detached. Think of our smartphones as digital swords. Maybe they make us feel less threatened by the fact that algorithms, robots, and machines are increasingly performing becoming the work we used to do.

Let's return to this chapter's original question: Is being overwhelmed becoming the new normal?

Yes, but it doesn't have to be.

If we want to feel less overwhelmed, a simple maxim like "Work smarter, not harder" does not even begin to cut it. As a starting point, we need to fully and carefully examine how we communicate at work.

Next

This chapter demonstrated that many employees are beyond saturated at work. This trend shows no signs of abating and has major ramifications for business communication. Even many well-constructed, timely, context-appropriate messages are often not received today because employees are too busy to process them. If you accept that premise, then what does that mean for confusing, verbose, and belated messages that are delivered to already overflowing inboxes?

Part II shifts gears. It is now time to explore the two-fold problem with business communication.

---

* Google "Smartphone Roulette" or "The Phone Stack."

Notes

1. Aimee Picchi, "Why Americans Take Only Half Their Vacation Time," April 4, 2014, www.cbsnews.com/news/why-americans-take-only-half-their-vacation-time.
2. Tom Hodson, Jeff Schwartz, Ardie van Berkel, and Ian Winstrom Otten, "The Overwhelmed Employee," March 7, 2014, http://tinyurl.com/dt-overwhelm. Copyright © 2014 Deloitte Development LLC.
3. Ian Bogost, "Hyperemployment, or the Exhausting Work of the Technology User," November 8, 2013, www.theatlantic.com/technology/archive/2013/11/hyperemployment-or-the-exhausting-work-of-the-technology-user/281149.
4. Sarah Gooding, "Drowning in Data: When News Is Noise," June 15, 2014, https://medium.com/@sarahgooding/drowning-in-data-when-news-is-noise-7ff29278effd.
5. Nicholas Carlson, "The Truth About Those Brutal Descriptions of Working Conditions at Square," May 29, 2012, www.businessinsider.com/the-truth-about-those-brutal-descriptions-of-working-conditions-at-square-2012-5. Read more at www.businessinsider.com/the-truth-about-those-brutal-descriptions-of-working-conditions-at-square-2012-5.
6. Scott Berkun, "The Cult of Busy," March 12, 2010, http://scottberkun.com/2010/the-cult-of-busy.

DIDN'T YOU GET THAT MEMO?

Why We Don't Communicate Good at Work

The lines between work and leisure have been blurring for years. As Justine Sacco learned the hard way, in many instances they have already been obliterated. Technology is no doubt culpable for a great deal of this erosion, but make no mistake: It's a convenient scapegoat. As mentioned in Chapter 2, no one compels us to live in our inboxes.

What if we used new, truly collaborative applications to work smarter, not just harder? What if we drew lines and actually enforced them? What if e-mail wasn't the default mode of business communication? And what if we spoke simpler and without jargon?

Let these questions serve as the starting point for Part II. The next few chapters examine what we say at work, how we say it, and the effects of poor business communication:

- **Chapter 3:** What We Say: Examining Words at Work
- **Chapter 4:** How We Say It: E-Mail Is Dead. Long Live E-Mail!
- **Chapter 5:** Why Bad Communication Is Bad Business: The Unintended Consequences of Mixed and Missed Messages

3

What We Say

Examining Words at Work

Most people who bother with the matter at all would admit that the English language is in a bad way, but it is generally assumed that we cannot by conscious action do anything about it. Our civilization is decadent and our language— so the argument runs—must inevitably share in the general collapse. It follows that any struggle against the abuse of language is a sentimental archaism, like preferring candles to electric light or hansom cabs to aeroplanes. Underneath this lies the half-conscious belief that language is a natural growth and not an instrument which we shape for our own purposes.

—George Orwell, 1946

Orwell is right. New words, phrases, and axioms have *always* made their way into the vernacular. Think about the additions and modifications of just the last 10 to 15 years.

We historically used the word *text* as a noun; up until fairly recently, people never *texted* each other. Pre-Twitter, terms like *tweet, retweet, hashtag,* and *trending* didn't exist.[*] Facebook made *like* a noun and *friend* a verb—and billions of dollars in the process. The *Oxford English Dictionary* (*OED*) formally accepted *Google* as a verb in 2006, defining it as "to use the Google search engine to find information on the Internet." The *OED* 2013 International Word of the Year 2013 was *selfie*. *Blogging* used to be called *journaling*. Netflix has popularized *binge-watching*.

Each of these words is a *neologism,* a fancy word to describe newly coined terms, expressions, or methods of use. There are heaps of others, and many are not tech-related. For instance, the word *cougar* used to exclusively mean "a large American wild cat with a plain tawny to grayish coat, found from Canada to Patagonia." Now, it doubles as "an older woman who frequents clubs in order to score with a much younger man."[†] *Snowclones* like "40 is the new 30" seem to pop up weekly thanks to social media.

I can't speak intelligently about other languages, but English has always been an inherently subjective, very complicated beast. Over its history, English speakers have used many words in wildly inconsistent, diverse, and contentious manners. (This is especially true if you look at the language across countries. Foolish is

---

[*] There's even an online, evolving dictionary at www.twittonary.com.
[†] This is Urban Dictionary's definition.

the soul who believes that American English is identical to British English.)

Even within a particular country, there's no one "right" way to communicate. Try using the same colloquialisms, diction, and pronunciations in North Dakota, Boston, and Mississippi. One person's tomato is another's *tuh-mah-to*. I doubt that your writing and/or speaking style and mine are the same—and that's not a bad thing. It's best not to think of communications as a binary (i.e., good vs. bad). Rather, it's more helpful to view it as a continuum (i.e., clear vs. unclear with degrees in between). To this end, we can take steps to increase the likelihood that others understand us and really receive our messages.

This chapter examines the problems endemic to business communication. After a discussion about the causes of jargon, I'll move to other ineffective and counterproductive business communication techniques.

Jargon: The Cause of So Much Noise

What do you do?

It's a simple question that many professionals have to answer frequently, maybe even daily. If you're at the office, on a plane, or at a conference or networking event, odds are that someone will put that four-word query to you. Unfortunately, many people cannot answer it quickly and in plain English. We've all walked away from introductions confused about what a new acquaintance actually does all day.

What about our professional profiles on public sites? Surely, each of us can craft clear, brief synopses of our careers for the entire world to see, right? Consider a C-level executive at a Fortune 50 company who summarizes her experiences on her LinkedIn profile with this doozy of a sentence:

> A self starting [sic] leader who has launched numerous new marketing strategies, delivers results, embraces change, drives organization and process improvements to deliver business results by significantly improving pipeline management, Sales/ Marketing linkage, brand awareness, consideration and preference to capture mind share and market share growth.[*]

---

[*] See http://tinyurl.com/bad-2bio.

Sadly, buzzword torrents aren't uncommon on—and limited to—LinkedIn profiles and resumes. The following text is taken from the Amazon page of an author and seasoned marketing executive. In his words, he has:

> Spent the majority of his career with a focus on achieving mind-share for his clients and the companies he works for, with 15 years of experience in driving revenues through strategic communications: building value, branding, digital advertising, PR, and cross-platform integration, having worked on both the media and agency sides of the business across multiple vehicles, channels, and digital platforms to amplify brand and customer experiences.*

Go back and read these two self-descriptions out loud. Really, I'll wait. Ask yourself if you truly understand them. I'll bet that, by the 20th word or so, your head will start to spin.

A confusing or poorly worded bio from a marketing or technology professional is one thing. What about content from professional speakers and writers like me? Shouldn't we be able to articulate our messages clearly and without a great deal of technobabble? After all, we communicate for a living, right?

Again, there's no dearth of examples of horrible language from this group either. Exhibit A: In his 2011 book *The End of Business as Usual: Rewire the Way You Work to Succeed in the Consumer Revolution*, Brian Solis scribes the following inscrutable paragraph:

> The *nextwork* sends and receives information at blinding speeds, creating an efficient human switchboard and network that in theory and in practice, outperforms telephone, terrestrial, cell, emergency, and Web networks for the speed and precision at which relevant experiences are shared and re-shared. I call this the new information divide, the delta between an event and the time it's officially reported. It is in this space where today's human network comes alive. Filling the gap is also representative of opportunities and for innovation and engagement. By plugging into the information ecosystem and participating through the creation and curation of information, organizations can augment existing information channels.

---

* See http://tinyurl.com/bad-1bio.

Huh?

Solis's writing style confuses much more than it conveys. Buzzwords such as *ecosystem, engagement, delta*, and—wait for it—*nextwork* make his message impossible to truly comprehend, even after several passes at reading it. There's just no reason to write this way if you really want to invite the reader in.

Let's look at a few more examples of grimace-inducing language:

- "We replatformed last year and switched to WordPress," Bon Appétit digital director Stacey Rivera told Co.Labs.[1]
- "CollabWorks has it right. The next generation of cloud is about people. Their WaaS technology is the middleware to match the right person to the right work at the right time."[2]
- "Believe it or not, I mean, Apple's nearly two years behind, in terms of the leaders, with respect to the form factor."[3]
- "How to Architect a Better Site-Map," the title of a recent article.[4]

Business jargon makes those of us who pride ourselves on speaking as simply as possible cringe. Take *deliverable*, for instance. What does this really mean? What's wrong with *task* or *assignment?* Maybe they became clichés or didn't seem sophisticated enough. Why else would someone invent a fancier word?

Why We Obfuscate

Orwell's quote at the start of this chapter is spot on. The English language may be dynamic, but we control the words we use. No one forces us to write and speak in ways that confuse others.

At the heart of this chapter are two questions:

1. If we can choose to communicate simply and clearly at work, why don't we?
2. Beyond jargon, what else minimizes the chances that others receive our messages?

This section chronicles the reasons that so many people use buzzwords as communication crutches. By understanding why so many of us unnecessarily complicate our messages, we are in a better position to do something about it.

Consultants, MBAs, and the Management "Scientists" By trade, Frederick Winslow Taylor was an American mechanical engineer, but he's not renowned for that. Long before the Bobs in *Office Space*, Taylor was arguably the world's first efficiency expert. In the late nineteenth century, he spent a great deal of time watching factory workers performing manual tasks. Taylor wasn't bored, nor was he a voyeur. He was working, recording everything he saw with his stopwatch. He was on a quest to find the one best way to do each job. That information would further his ultimate goal: to improve—in fact, to maximize—economic efficiency, especially labor productivity. This became the basis for his theory of scientific management.

Taylor passed away in 1915, but his significance in the business world has persevered. For example, in *The Management Myth: Debunking Modern Business Philosophy*, Matthew Stewart describes Taylor's posthumous impact:

> The management idol continues to exert its most direct effect on business education. Although Taylor and his doctrine fell from favor at the business schools as his name became associated with public controversy, his fundamental idea that business management is an applied science remained cemented in the foundations of business school. In 1959, for example, the highly influential Gordon and Howell report on the state of business education called for a reinvigoration of the scientific foundations of business educations.

Over the years, many critics have attacked Taylor's theory. Today you're unlikely to meet one of his acolytes, but Taylor remains an influential if controversial figure a century after his death. Perhaps Taylorism's crowning achievement was that it represented the earliest known attempt to apply science to the field of management. Even now this is an open debate: Is management a true science?

It's a contentious issue with enormous stakes. Corporations pay handsomely for elite management consulting firms such as Bain Capital, McKinsey, Accenture, and the Boston Consulting Group. Ditto for gurus such as Tom Peters, Jim Collins, and Guy Kawasaki. For his part, Collins can command as much as $100,000 for a day-long seminar, not including first-class accommodations. Even junior McKinsey consultants bill upward of $300 per hour.

CEOs pay these exorbitant sums for two reasons. First, hiring a prominent consultancy or guru is widely viewed as safe. Many CEOs continue to abide by the maxim "Nobody ever got fired for buying IBM." Second, experts promise to fix what ails their clients. For this type of coin, management experts are supposed to provide organizations with valuable advice that is guaranteed to work. Can you imagine a team of very pricey consultants concluding a six-month assignment with the words "We're pretty sure that [our recommendations] *might* work?"

Except they often don't, and here's where the "management is a science" argument crumbles. If management really were a true science, then it stands to reason that it would *always* follow immutable laws. For instance, consider chemistry. Water always freezes at 0°C and boils at 100°C at 1 atmosphere. Period. There are never any exceptions.

Where is the management analog?

Keep thinking.

Give up?

It doesn't exist.

Put differently, management is doubtless a critical *discipline*, but referring to it as a *science* is erroneous. Think of it more as a philosophy or, at best, a social science—and there's nothing wrong with that. Unfortunately, a great deal of modern management theory and its practitioners continue to suffer from a scientific inferiority complex. In Stewart's words:

> As with Taylor's purported general science of efficiency, most efforts to concoct a general science of organizations fail not because the universal principles they put forward are wrong— they are usually right—but because they don't belong to an applied science. They properly belong to a philosophy.

Many other books touch on the central theme that even expert predictions are nothing more than coin flips:

- *The Halo Effect: . . . and the Eight Other Business Delusions That Deceive Managers* by Phil Rosenzweig
- *The Witch Doctors: Making Sense of the Management Gurus* by John Micklethwait and Adrian Wooldridge
- *Everything Is Obvious: How Common Sense Fails Us* by Duncan J. Watts
- *The Black Swan: The Impact of the Highly Improbable* by Nassim Nicholas Taleb

Forget trying to predict, manipulate, and manage social and economic systems. Attempting to do this on even an individual level is bound to go awry. For myriad reasons, the same strategy that worked for Company A at one point may fail abysmally when Company B implements it. Diversifying offerings can save one company and ravage another, even if they are in the same industry.

These types of vicissitudes are not very scientific. Even if a team of the world's best management consultants told you that your company ought to "stick to its knitting," adhering to that advice guarantees zilch. This is even truer now than it was 20 years ago. Against this backdrop of rampant technological change, far too many external factors are at play to ensure anything remotely resembling certainty. A trite bromide and 10 point plan will not by themselves yield the desired results. Business is not a laboratory; one cannot hold all other factors constant to pinpoint cause and effect.

This brings us to the liberal use of buzzwords by gurus, management consultants, and MBAs. I challenge you to think of three groups of people who have wrought more jargon on the business community. Scientists create and use sophisticated terms to explain new and complex phenomena. It logically follows, then, that management types will do this as well. In an effort to appear smart and scientific, they have coined phrases like *thinking outside the box, paradigm shift, optics,* and scores more. They have perverted more than their fair share of simple words as well.

Many buzzwords or pithy axioms from management consultants can be explained just as well—in fact, usually better—in simple English. From the consultants' perspective, though, simplicity and clarity pose a significant problem: It makes them appear less smart, less scientific. Maybe they wouldn't be able to charge as much if their advice seemed so obvious.

The Subtle Difference Between Stealing and Reperforming

In late 2008, a prominent hospital in the northeast United States contracted me to solve a knotty data problem. The hospital also brought in a very respected consultancy to work in parallel with me.

I'm normally a pretty happy collaborator but, for audit purposes, the firm and I were each supposed to work independently. I wasn't worried. Although the puzzle was quite vexing, I was quite confident that I'd be able to iron it out without the firm's help.

For reasons I'll never know, the consultancy sent its C-team and soon paid the price. Fresh out of college, its green consultants didn't possess anywhere near the requisite knowledge and experience to solve the hospital's data dilemma; they didn't even fully understand it. They didn't know which questions to ask, much less how to answer them. I was able to spare a few minutes here and there for my counterparts. I gave them answers they should have already known—or at least have Googled. They were walking around blind without canes.

After several months, I had developed a working prototype of the solution and presented it to my client. She was impressed and told me that I was 90 percent of the way home.

Across the hall, however, the consultancy was struggling mightily. Despite billing upward of $6,000 per day, the team was clutching at straws. Hospital management was not pleased; it was getting zero bang for its buck. The pressure was mounting and something had to give.

Backed against the wall, the firm's lead management consultant knocked on my door one afternoon. Rather than just admitting that his firm couldn't do the job it was contracted to do, he took a different path. He told me that his team needed to "reperform" my work.

I asked him what that word meant because I had never heard it before. He kept equivocating and evading my question, as if there was something wrong with me for not understanding it. I felt much more pity than annoyance or anger. It was easier for him to use a bogus word than to cop to the truth: He and his firm were in a world of pain unless I let him copy my homework.

Just to finish the story, I checked with my client. She advised me to turn my files over to the consultancy and I complied. After all, it was her candy store, not mine.

That's enough tormenting management gurus for now. Although some should be incarcerated for their crimes against the English language, it's folly to exclusively blame them for the proliferation of corporate-speak. There are plenty of other reasons that jargon is so pervasive.

Culture and Conformity   Remember Enron?

In 2001, the company employed approximately 20,000 people. It was one of the world's most respected electricity, natural gas, communications, and paper enterprises. *Fortune* named it "America's Most Innovative Company" for six consecutive years. On December

31, 2000, Enron's stock traded at \$83 per share. Its market capitalization exceeded a whopping \$60 billion, roughly 70 times its earnings—an indication of the stock market's high expectations about the company's future prospects.

That was *before* its historic demise, culminating with a formal declaration of bankruptcy on December 2, 2001. Under the surface, a culture of greed, arrogance, and willful ignorance permeated the company. Today it is widely considered the greatest corporate implosion in United States history.[*]

In their superb 2004 book *The Smartest Guys in the Room: The Amazing Rise and Scandalous Fall of Enron,* Bethany McLean and Peter Elkind recount the entire sordid tale. Most instructive for our purposes here, Enron's former president and Chief Operating Officer (COO) Jeffrey Skilling would effectively ask the same question until someone answered it to his liking. That is, if Employee A told him that Enron's risky accounting maneuvers posed a material risk to the company, Skilling would just ignore that underling. He would then repeat the same process with Employee B. Eventually someone would give him the answer he wanted. Skilling chose to hear only what he wanted to hear and to see only what he wanted to see.

There's a very formal-sounding term for that type of behavior: *confirmation bias* or *confirmatory bias.* It is the tendency to favor information that confirms one's beliefs or hypotheses. People display confirmation bias when, like Skilling, they selectively gather, remember, and/or interpret information in a biased way. Skilling's intentional blindness to rampant accounting fraud cascaded throughout Enron. Of the tens of thousands of individuals who worked at Enron throughout its existence, the number of whistleblowers (read: troublemakers) can be counted on one hand. Perhaps most prominent was Sherron Watkins, the company's former vice president of corporate development.

Lest you think that Enron was an isolated example of an organization's culture silencing its employees, consider the recent financial crisis. Some banks allegedly muzzled whistleblowers who saw what was really going on and wanted to speak up. Former Citigroup executive

---

[*] Due to the public backlash over the accounting scandals at Enron, Tyco International, Adelphia, Peregrine Systems, and WorldCom, Congress passed the Sarbanes-Oxley Act of 2002.

Richard M. Bowen III appeared on *60 Minutes* in December 2011 and described the difficulty he faced in getting people to take his concerns seriously. Citigroup may have limited its exposure to the subprime mortgage mess if its senior management had listened to Bowen.

The point here is that, as it pertains to communication at work, many of us are guilty of confirmation bias whether we realize it or not. That's not to say that most organizational cultures are as toxic as Enron's. They're not. Management at the vast majority of large, midsized, and even small businesses, however, is hierarchical and has been for decades.* At some hidebound organizations, criticizing or even questioning a superior is tantamount to subordination. If the CEO gives a bad speech or writes a confusing memorandum, who's going to provide honest feedback? Why cut your own throat? Some cultures are more open than others, but the freedoms that we take for granted as citizens simply do not exist in the workplace. Companies are not democracies. Rank confers privilege, and chief executives are often made of Teflon. Everyone usually tolerates their "quirky" mannerisms and actions. What happens when entry-level employees and even middle management exhibit that same behavior? It's often viewed as completely inappropriate and unprofessional.

Confirmation bias and its cousin *survivorship bias*† are extremely powerful forces in the workplace. Collectively, they explain a great deal of underlings' unwillingness to challenge their superiors' poor communication methods. In many organizations, the pressure to fit in and the concurrent fear not to rock the boat are difficult to overstate, particularly at junior levels. In my experience, new hires typically do one of the following:

1. Quickly, naturally, and successfully assimilate and adapt to their new jobs and cultures. They learn and fully adopt the communication mores expected of them.
2. Initially struggle with their new positions and then modify their language and behavior to fit in. They either realize that

---

* A small number of companies are experimenting with holacracy, an alternative to traditional management structures. Think circles, not a pyramid. In Las Vegas, Zappos is doing this with its 1,500 employees as we speak.
† This is the logical error of concentrating on the people or things that survived some process. We inadvertently overlook those that did not because, quite simply, they're not around to be observed and studied.

something's awry or, more likely, receive feedback from colleagues and superiors that "that's not the way we do things here."

3. Actively defy culture and convention. Much like organ rejection, these mavericks almost always exit the organization after a short period "to pursue other opportunities."

In the early 1960s, the American social psychologist Stanley Milgram conducted a series of controversial experiments on conformity, ones that have been replicated many times since then.* (Most recently, a 2009 episode of the BBC science documentary series *Horizon* revisited them.) Milgram's experiments and their progeny demonstrate that everyday people will often follow the directions, orders, and cues of those in authority, often to disturbing degrees.

Sending hazy e-mails is hardly analogous to thinking that you're giving increasingly painful electric shocks to innocent subjects. Still, for better or worse, there's an overall tendency in many corporate environs to parrot the actions, individual words, aphorisms, and even nonverbal cues of people higher up on the totem pole—in short, to get along. When in Rome, as they say. The bottom line is that bad communication at the top or throughout a culture can be difficult to change. As management guru Peter Drucker bluntly stated, "Culture eats strategy for breakfast."

SEO and the Quest for the Killer Superlative   In the Preface, I referenced CSC's bewildering press release. In crafting it, the company's bigwigs most likely did some research and stumbled upon Cloudant, a competitor that IBM acquired in May 2014. Cloudant sells something called a *Data Platform-as-a-Service*.[5] To that end, I'd bet that at least one CSC exec thought that the company could one-up IBM and Cloudant by offering a *Big* Data Platform as a Service, and a next-generation one to boot! That must be better, right?

The race for the killer superlative faces two related problems. First, what's the point of showing up at the top of Google's organic search results if no one punches in the specific term or phrase that a company has worked so hard to "own"? (See "Google and the Never-Ending Jargon Train" in Chapter 1.) Second, it's actually counterproductive. That is, the vast majority of prospective clients

---

* Watch a snippet at www.youtube.com/watch?v=xOYLCy5PVgM.

don't understand what these technology vendors are trying to sell them. As I wrote in a 2014 *InformationWeek* article, most organizations are justifiably "confused by the incessant noise around Big Data. Social media has given every software vendor a 'platform' to tout its wares."[6]

This goes well beyond Big Data. Chapter 1 covered the extremely competitive race to occupy premium real estate at the top of search engine pages. I'd even wager that, as you're reading this, an employee in marketing or product development somewhere is formulating even more imperious-sounding products and services.

The Classic Mistake: Confusing Features with Benefits   Chapter 1 cited the Pareto Principle (i.e., the *80-20 Rule*) as it relates to SEO. The same law applies to many areas, including the world of IT. One common industry adage is that 80 percent of all users take advantage of a mere 20 percent of any software application's features. Put differently, for any given program, most people don't know what most of the buttons and menu items do. (An interesting corollary exists between software bugs as well. In 2002, Microsoft discovered that fixing the top 20 percent of its most frequently reported issues eliminated a full 80 percent of user errors and crashes.)

Despite this truism, most enterprise software vendors continue to add features to their products irrespective of whether their customers are likely to actually use them. The official term for this phenomenon is *bloatware*, the result of a "tactical arms race to outstrip the competition and meet or exceed specification criteria."[7] Minimalist applications like project management tool Basecamp* are the exceptions that prove the rule. Companies have to name their new products, services, and features *something*. Most understandably don't want to use terminology that is already synonymous with a competing offering.

The Desire to Sound Smart and Important   Somewhere along the line, we all pick up 50-cent words. Some of us even figure out how to use polysyllabic words correctly, if a bit awkwardly. Why not say *utilize* in lieu of *use*? Yes, they mean the same thing, but one seems more sophisticated than the other. Ironically, many effective speakers and writers receive praise precisely because they make things as plain as possible.

---

*Formerly known as *37signals*, the company now goes by the name of its eponymous product.

Inertia: If It Ain't Broke, Don't Fix It   Think about a group, department, division, or company enjoying tremendous success. Perhaps the sales department is regularly exceeding its goals. Let's say that the team uses the same jargon-laden PowerPoint template for its sales calls. Icky words like *repurposing* and *transitioning* appear—multiple times. This offends your English sensibilities.

But here's the rub: Sixty percent of the time, the team closes the deal after giving this buzzword-laden presentation. Oh, and the industry average is not even over 40 percent. Do you really want to make the argument that it's essential for the team to simplify those slides? Why exactly does the team need to communicate differently? What if your conception of a clearer presentation coincides with a lower conversion ratio?

Laziness   Paradoxically, using plain language can actually confuse those who are inured to a certain communications style. When buzzwords are so pervasive within an organization's culture, it often takes a fair amount of effort to swim against the stream. As a result, many overwhelmed knowledge workers just throw in the towel and acquiesce, even if the mere thought of *ideating* or *eating their own dog food* makes them die a little inside. They ignore the feeling that their high school English teachers would disapprove.

The Misguided Belief That Jargon Is Actually Effective   Many horrible communicators are completely oblivious of the effects they have on others. They always use the more impressive-sounding term (e.g., *paradigm* in lieu of *model* and *price point* instead of *price*). These are the managers who tell their employees to "think outside the box" as if it were some grand revelation. I'm amazed at how many times some talking heads can drop terms like *form factor*, *use case*, and *platform* in a three-minute interview.[*]

Was each trying to sound particularly erudite or to come across as a pompous ass? I could have been reading them wrong, but I don't think so. In fact, most seemed to genuinely believe that they were communicating in a natural way, one conducive to others understanding them. None of which changes the fact that they were not.

---

[*] Although often informative, the show *Bloomberg West* frequently parades CEOs and thought leaders who can't express themselves in plain English.

Clarify *This*! The Perverse Desire for Ambiguity   It would be foolish for me to ignore the potential downside of letting others know exactly where you stand and what you want. By being so transparent and coherent, people will know exactly where you stand and what you want.

No, that last sentence was no mistake. I assure you that my editor double-checked it with me. When you make your positions and directions explicitly known, you leave little in the way of wiggle room in the event that you want to flip-flop or, to be more politically correct, "refine your position in light of new facts." "Jargon is our way to grow lazier decision making in corporate cultures," says Kevin Fleming, owner of Grey Matters,[*] a neuroscience-based executive development and coaching firm based in Jackson Hole, Wyoming, and Tulsa, Oklahoma. "We use these words to cover up something. It could also be a way to hide some ambivalence."[8]

Plenty of professionals are intentionally vague for this very purpose. For mostly political motivations, they don't want to be tied to a particular viewpoint. Even when asked very simple one-sentence queries, they respond with a series of empty equivocations. This dance is completely deliberate. They know *exactly* what they are doing.

The Low Bar: Lack of Recognition of the Problem   This section began with the question: If we can choose to communicate simply and clearly, then why is jargon so pervasive?

The final reason is perhaps the most obvious: Many professionals have communicated so badly for so long that they know of no other way. To wit, untold numbers of people have *never* worked in an environment in which communication was particularly effective. Sadly, in many organizations, deficient business communication has become the norm.

The Growing Use of Business Jargon

Jargon and business have always coexisted. Although I wasn't there, I suspect that language purists complained about claptrap and poor business communication at the dawn of the Industrial Age. Perhaps the use of buzzwords could be ignored if only a handful of outliers communicated poorly at work with minimal effects. (Chapter 5 explores the consequences of shoddy business communication.) Maybe we could dismiss jargon if it was declining.

---

[*] I just have to point this coincidence out. *Grey Matter* (singular) was the name of the company that Walter White cofounded on *Breaking Bad*.

Regrettably, neither statement is accurate. In their written and spoken messages, employees are using more jargon than ever. Furthermore, these trends show no discernible ends in sight.

We can attribute these twin rises to the reasons discussed in Part I. The explosion of technology and its aftereffects are driving many profound societal, political, legal, and technological changes—good and bad, intentional and unintentional. I won't review the SEO all-or-nothing game, the ease of starting up, the explosion of mobility, and the other trends examined earlier in great detail here. Suffice it to say we are seeing a surge in business jargon. It's hard to credibly argue otherwise.

If you're still skeptical of this premise, allow me to point out two things. First, the rise of jargon does not affect all employees equally. Perhaps your organization, group, or department operates in a relatively buzzword-free environment. If so, I truly am happy for you. Second, even if the *percentage* of messages containing buzzwords has remained constant, we are receiving more messages than ever while on the clock. It stands to reason, then, that the average professional has to deal with a greater *number* of ambiguous communications than ever.

Let me make this more concrete. Assume that in 2007, 12 percent of the 100 daily messages you received were unclear. Twelve times every day, jargon made your job more difficult in one or more of the following ways:

- You didn't fully understand something and needed to ask the sender for clarification.
- You needed more time to determine what the sender wanted or needed from you. Perhaps you had to ask others for help.
- You made a mistake based on unclear instructions.

Now, in 2015, that *percentage* hasn't moved, but now you receive 150 messages every day. As a result, you have to follow up 18 times daily to understand what others want you to do.

This scenario is happening right now. Global data group Experian reports that inbox volumes are increasing by about 15 percent annually. At that rate, you can expect the number of messages you receive to double in less than five years. (The next chapter will further discuss the never-ending mountain of e-mail that the average knowledge worker must climb.)

The Appendix at the end of this chapter includes what I believe to be some of the most egregious uses of business jargon as well as simple substitutions. (See Table 3.1.) It's by no means a comprehensive list. If it only whets your appetite for bad English, then you're in luck. The Web is a vast place. There's plenty of jargon out there,[*] including an entire dictionary devoted to bad business buzzwords.[†]

The Rise of Numeracy

Before concluding this section, let's revisit Orwell's point about the dynamic nature of language. I am in no way implying that we should avoid using newly accepted words on general principle. Over our lifetimes, some words will be born, plenty will evolve, and a few will even die. We all learn new words, terms, and phrases throughout our careers and lives.

From an early age, we are taught about the importance of literacy. Without being able to read and write, you can only go so far in life. Imagine not being able to read prescription labels. You recognize stop signs, but you cannot read flashing warning signs on the highway. There are too many disadvantages to illiteracy to list here.

Many people believe that Google and spellcheck are making us less intelligent or even stupid. That may be the case, but it's difficult to envision a day when basic literacy will not be essential, especially for knowledge workers. Given technology's tentacles, though, traditional literacy alone is becoming insufficient. The average white-collar job requires greater *numeracy* than ever. No matter how sophisticated gadgets and applications become, that isn't changing anytime soon.

At least for knowledge workers, the days of tolerating innumeracy are coming to an end. This has major ramifications for how we communicate at work. Irrespective of one's title, function, and actual role, the ability to speak intelligently about technology, numbers, and data is becoming increasingly important.

Don't mistake numeracy for jargon.

---

[*] See www.theofficelife.com/download-the-ridiculous-business-jargon-dictionary/.
[†] David Olive published *A Devil's Dictionary of Business Jargon* in 2002.

Does our tech- and data-centric world mean that we all have to become statisticians? Do we all need to break out our scientific calculators and probability textbooks? Should we be prepared to talk about Type I and Type II errors during meetings?* Of course not. However, those who lack at least basic fluency with data and math are limiting their careers.

Beyond Jargon: Other Communication and Language Atrocities

Communicating well at work is not rocket science, but it involves more than simply avoiding jargon. This section details a few of the other ways that people confuse others at work, not anything close to a comprehensive list. The bibliography lists several valuable communication texts. I have focused here on what I believe to be some of the biggest reasons that our messages often lack the desired impact.

Speaking Fouls

When I tell people that I am a writer and public speaker, many people assume that I'm the motivational type. Tony Robbins and Matt Foley of *Saturday Night Live*† quickly come to their minds. Although I've never tried, I don't think that I could convince people to walk on hot coals. I'm not *that* persuasive. I do, however, know a thing or two about addressing crowds of people. I estimated in the middle of 2014 that I've spoken in front of 30,000 people in public settings going back to my days as a grad school teaching assistant.

Whether as a speaker or as an attendee, I attend 15 to 30 public conferences every year, the vast majority of which involve technology. Lamentably, most of the speakers aren't terribly dynamic or even good—and mine is not the minority viewpoint. If I am struggling with a speaker's style and message, I wonder if it's just me. To answer that question, I simply look around the room. It takes about five seconds to determine whether the rest of the audience is engaged. Are the attendees looking *up* at the speaker and listening attentively? Or are they looking *down* at their devices and tapping away?‡

---

* In statistics, committing a Type I error means that you have incorrectly rejected a true null hypothesis. A Type II error means that you have failed to reject a false null hypothesis.
† See www.hulu.com/watch/4183.
‡ To be fair, sometimes people who are looking down are tweeting and/or taking notes.

Never Finishing a Sentence   One of the downsides of these hypercon-
nected times is a spike in attention-deficit disorder (ADD). This is
not confined to Xbox-loving teenagers. Many adults suffer from it as
well and you may well recognize a colleague who appears to exhibit
its symptoms.* Regardless of an official diagnosis, the inability to ever
finish a sentence can quickly confuse an audience and ensure that
the message is not received.

Adult ADD

In 2012, I did some strategic consulting for a financial services company. Call
it Acme Corporation here, although that's obviously a pseudonym. My charter
was to help the organization embrace platform thinking. A few Acme executives had read *The Age of the Platform* and hired me to help put its principles
into action.

After several days of interviews and research on site, I presented my recommendations to a group of Acme senior managers. My presentation went
reasonably well. I wasn't proposing cosmetic changes. As I write in that book,
platform thinking requires a new organizational mind-set, one often anathema to
internally focused business models. I spoke in a simple and jargon-free manner,
offering concrete examples related to my book. (I find that staying exclusively at
30,000 feet rarely works.)

As I expected, the meeting soon evolved into a conversation on not only
what Acme could do, but also how the company should actually do it. Unfortunately, a friendly and well-intentioned director kept derailing the conversation. Let's call him Hank here. He would throw out big ideas and make grand
statements without ever finishing a sentence. Hank's stream-of-consciousness
pronouncements and important-sounding phrases precluded the conversation
from truly progressing; in fact, we regressed.

I stepped back and simply observed the meeting, letting others talk. Given
my role as an external consultant, there really wasn't much that I could realistically do at that point, especially in a public setting. It was obvious to me that
Hank's communication style and overall message only confused others, in effect
making them defensive. Rather than bluntly asking him to finish a thought and
speak clearly, the others in the meeting felt the need to follow his lead. They
feared appearing uninformed, weak, and behind the times. Hank had created
a dangerous dynamic within the meeting and, I can only assume, within the
organization. In truth, Acme and Hank's manager were to blame for enabling it.

---

* See http://tinyurl.com/27v9k9.

Assuming Familiarity With a New Term   Let's say that you attend a conference on a niche topic. It's a safe bet that every attendee has not
heard of each new term, acronym, trend, emerging technology,
company, and concept. The most effective speakers understand this
and, as such, assume very little. They define key terms, even if most
attendees would probably recognize them. A 30-second description
does more than enlighten those who lack familiarity with something;
it also shows the audience that the speaker is willing to establish a
common baseline. A point from the Introduction bears repeating:
the word *communicate* means "to make common." Plenty of speakers
lose their audiences right out of the gate by dropping a boatload of
arcane jargon and obscure acronyms.

General Bloviating

> *Beware of false knowledge; it is more dangerous than ignorance.*
>
> —George Bernard Shaw

There's a world of difference between (a) people with good intentions who choose their words poorly and (b) poseurs who try to appear
vastly more knowledgeable than they are. Bombastic speakers may make
themselves feel smart and important, but listeners usually feel otherwise. Few things inhibit business communications as much as bloviating.

Again, this is nothing new. For centuries, people have spoken
with absolutely zero knowledge of their subjects. There wasn't much
that listeners could do. Not today. In a matter of seconds, listeners
can whip out their smartphones, look up a questionable fact or statement, and call bullshit on modern-day blowhards.

Now, people make honest mistakes all the time, but there's a
world of difference between ignorance and false knowledge, as Shaw
correctly points out. Once people realize that you don't know nearly
as much as you claim, it's exceptionally difficult to earn that trust
back. That toothpaste just doesn't go back in the tube.

What We Don't Say

This chapter has focused on our choice of words. It turns out,
though, that what you *don't* say can have an enormous impact on

whether your message is received. In *Think Like a Freak: The Authors of Freakonomics Offer to Retrain Your Brain*, Stephen Dubner and Steven Levitt write:

> It has long been said that the three hardest words to say in the English language are *I love you*. We heartily disagree! For most people, it is much harder to say *I don't know*. That's a shame, for until you can admit what you don't yet know, it's virtually impossible to learn what you need to.

For cultural, political, and economic reasons, many employees are afraid to say "I don't know" or "I'm not sure." This is particularly acute at the executive level. It's refreshing to hear statements such as these, especially when they are followed by "But I will find out soon and get back to you."

Again, this isn't complicated. Let's say that you're good at your job. You know the answer to a question or problem 90 percent of the time. For the other 10 percent, you have to do some research. Admitting that you aren't sure about what to do next usually doesn't mean that you are incompetent, stupid, or lazy. It just means that you are honest.

Next

Words are a very powerful form of currency, but even the clearest prose is often lost in a maelstrom of messages. We don't communicate in a vacuum. Few people can dispute the utility of e-mail, but no communications tool is equally well suited for everyone all of the time. On the contrary, as a medium, e-mail suffers from significant limitations and often hinders effective business communication. The next chapter explores those problems in earnest.

Notes

1. Neal Ungerleider, "IBM Watson, Cookbooks, And Food's Big Data Future," July 3, 2014, www.fastcolabs.com/3032697/ibm-watson-cookbooks-and-foods-big-data-future.
2. Scott McNealy, www.collabworks.com.
3. Brian Marshall, "Bloomberg West" Interview, August 8, 2014, www.bloomberg.com/video/bigger-screens-and-improved-battery-life-iphone-6-qEsvrDKaS9WIdZhJdZMwDw.html.
4. James Deer, "How to Architect a Better Site-Map," August 6, 2013, http://tinyurl.com/ktagk7x.

5. Josette Rigsby, "Cloudant Expands Data Platform-as-a-Service Infrastructure Globally," May 22, 2012, www.cmswire.com/cms/information-management/cloudant-expands-data-platformasaservice-infrastructure-globally-015715.php.
6. Phil Simon, "Why Big Data in the Enterprise Is Mostly Lip Service," February 18, 2014, www.informationweek.com/big-data/big-data-analytics/why-big-data-in-the-enterprise-is-mostly-lip-service/d/d-id/1113835.
7. "Confusing Features With Benefits," December 17, 2013, http://technicalmarketingdiary.blogspot.com/2013/12/confusing-features-with-benefits.html.
8. Katherine Reynolds Lewis, "What's Hiding Behind the Buzzwords in Job Ads?," February 28, 2012, http://fortune.com/2012/02/28/whats-hiding-behind-the-buzzwords-in-job-ads.

Appendix to Chapter 3

The following table displays some of the worst business jargon and simpler alternatives.

Table 3.1   Simple Alternatives to Horrible Business Jargon[*]

Word or Phrase	Category	Actual Example	Better Word(s)/Phrase and Notes
Action item	Noun	When an employee moves an **action item** from his or her to-do list to yours, simply hand the item back with the words: "No, you figure out how to do it."	Task, assignment, responsibility.
Actionable	Adjective	How can you determine which data will deliver **actionable** insights?	Meaningful, valuable. Note that lawyers frequently use this term because it has a long-standing legal meaning.
Alignment	Noun	Is Your Team Out of Sync? 6 Questions to Spur **Alignment**.	Cohesion.

(*Continued*)

[*] I grabbed these examples from mainstream business sites such as Inc.com, BusinessInsider, and InformationWeek.

Table 3.1   (*Continued*)

Word or Phrase	Category	Actual Example	Better Word(s)/Phrase and Notes
Architect	Verb	So now is the time for customers to **architect** for supplier management in the cloud.	Build, create.
Deep dive	Noun	This person will progress beyond challenging an idea and start a **deep dive** into developing the idea further.	Switch the noun with a verb. How about this? "This person will progress beyond challenging an idea and investigate how to develop the idea further."
Deliverable	Noun	Many people new to marketing expect a career path without concrete **deliverables**.	Objectives, assignments, work products, tasks.
Engagement	Noun	Most so-called employee **engagement** programs are misbegotten, unwieldy, ineffective rolling caravans of impractical or never-going-to-be-implemented PowerPoint presentations.	This one isn't universally horrible. Sometimes it seems appropriate and descriptive. This is one of those instances.
Form factor	Noun	Cell-phone makers largely dropped the curved-headset **form factor** in the late '90s.	Size and shape.
Incent	Verb	Commissions that **incent** people to close the deal may lead them to overpromise on what can be delivered.	Incentivize or encourage.
Learning(s)	Noun	Being proactive about our **learnings** will incentivize the group to focus on the most critical action items and value-add for maximum impact.	Lessons.
Leverage	Verb	How to **leverage** your true talent	*Use* or *take advantage of* is preferred; *utilize* if you must.
Net-net	Idiom	**Net-net**, existing home sales are back with a decisive 4.9% advance in May, shaking off the cold winter decline in January.	Bottom line or brass tacks; often nothing is needed at all.
Optics	Noun	I understand the **optics** of this situation, but despite how it looks, we have not acted inappropriately.	The *appearance* or *how this appears*. Note that the term is entirely acceptable when talking about *fiber optics*.

Word or Phrase	Category	Actual Example	Better Word(s)/Phrase and Notes
Pivot	Noun/ verb	Unfortunately, where we've fallen short in helping the business is taking that data that's captured and making it useful and meaningful in analytics and helping the business to gain visibility and be able to **pivot** and change as the need to change the business model is being brought to bear on the industry.[1]	Generally speaking, *rebranding*, *change*, and *shift* work just fine. (See "transition" in this table.) Still, even swapping out *pivot* wouldn't clarify this complete mess of a 53-word sentence. The sentences contains five "ands." I would break this albatross into at least two shorter, more concise statements.
Paradigm	Noun	The **paradigm** I'm talking about almost always demands a larger number of people playing the game.	Framework, model.
Price point	Noun	Setting a **price point** for goods or services is one of the most difficult decisions an entrepreneur can make.	*Price* is just fine, thank you. Note that some people insist that there's a difference between *price* and *price point*. I have never heard a satisfactory justification of the need for a separate term.
Synergy	Noun	An effective sale is most often achieved between two (or more) people who have **synergy** between them and understand the desired outcome for, not just one, but both parties.	It might be difficult to plug in a different word, but sentences like these can be easily rewritten to avoid this horrible piece of claptrap. In this example, I would replace "who have synergy between them" with "whose businesses complement one another."
Touchpoint	Noun	The guest experience is comprised of many **touchpoints**.	Interactions.
Transition	Verb	What does it really mean to **transition** from employee to founder of a company?	Move or shift. (See "pivot" in this table.)
Use case	Noun	Apple has dictated the **use case** of the iPad with its marketing.	Use. *Use case* is a very specific software development term that today is almost always misused (pun intended).
Value-add	Noun	Radio stations will sometimes throw in website advertising as part of the **value-add** in an advertising contract.	Value generated, value created, benefit.

(Continued)

Table 3.1   (*Continued*)

Word or Phrase	Category	Actual Example	Better Word(s)/Phrase and Notes
Verbage	Noun	As a citizen, teacher, and NASA brat I am used to hearing scientific explanations that are difficult to understand from the agency, but this **verbage** is meaningless.	Should be *verbiage*.
Win-win	Noun	Everybody loves a **win-win** answer to a problem.	Use a combination of adverbs and adjectives instead; *mutually advantageous* or *mutually beneficial*.

Sources: Author and people who honestly believed that these sentences conveyed meaning

Note

1. Gardner, Dana, "Healthcare Turns to Big Data Analytics for Improved Patient Outcomes," December 12, 2013, www.zdnet.com/healthcare-turns-to-big-data-analytics-for-improved-patient-outcomes-7000024237.

4

How We Say It

E-Mail Is Dead. Long Live E-Mail!

> *There is no escape: E-mail is probably the most invasive form of communication yet devised.*
>
> —Nick Bilton

My name is Phil, and I'm a recovering e-mail addict.

Hello, Phil.

It's been three hours since I sent my last e-mail. I've been using e-mail since 1992. In those 23 years, I have sent an insane number of messages. How many? Here's my back-of-the-envelope calculation:

- Approximate days since mid-1992: 8,000
- Average e-mails sent per day: 50*
- Approximate total e-mails sent: 400,000
- Average time spent composing each e-mail: 3 minutes
- Total hours spent composing e-mails: 20,175
- Total days spent composing e-mails: 840
- Total weeks spent composing e-mails: 120
- Total sleepless years spent composing e-mails: 2.3

This exercise produced some interesting statics, but the last is by far the most shocking. I have spent more than *two sleepless years* of my professional life just sending e-mails, and none of this includes the time spent *reading* them. Even if I exclude the e-mails I have penned on weekends, that number only drops to a shade over 1.8 *years!*

If you're curious about how your own stats stack up, I've made it easy for you to find out. Download and play with the simple spreadsheet posted on my website.† Feel free to tweak it however you like.

I've known for a long time that I was addicted to e-mail. I didn't need to run those numbers to prove it. Rather, I can point to a very

---

* This is very much a SWAG, aka *scientific wild-ass guess*. I didn't send too many e-mails while in college.

† See http://tinyurl.com/ps-how-many.

particular incident that led to my moment of clarity, to borrow a
phrase from *Pulp Fiction*.

Curing My E-Mail Addiction, Part I: The Revelation

Headquartered in the bucolic town of Cooperstown, New York, a stone's
throw from the Major League Baseball Hall of Fame, Bassett Healthcare is a
three-hospital network of primary and specialty care providers. The organization
employs about 4,500 people and, in the late 1990s, began pushing the limits
of its legacy enterprise system. In 2000, Bassett purchased and successfully
deployed the Lawson Software enterprise resource planning (ERP) system.

In 2007, Bassett decided to upgrade its time-and-attendance application.
Lawson had launched a new application called Absence Management. This coincided with the eventual retiring—or, in industry parlance, the *decommissioning*—
of its predecessor, Time Accrual.

Bassett needed someone to lead the upgrade and, as it so happened, I was
a very experienced consultant with the Lawson HR suite. I had even helped a
similar healthcare organization perform the same upgrade earlier that year. For
four months in 2007, Bassett contracted me to do the same.

Over the course of my time at Bassett, I worked on-site for four days each
week. I trained employees in the new application, configured it, tested it, created user guides, validated results, loaded data, investigated issues, called in
support requests, participated in meetings, and ultimately hit the switch. You
could say that I was a jack-of-all-trades, a human Swiss Army knife.

Once I activated the new Lawson Absence Management module, there was
no going back. (The specific details aren't terribly important here.) Bottom line:
That bell couldn't be unrung.

Bassett consisted of three disparate legal entities. Because of that and
some system considerations, I had to perform the final data conversion and
system activation three times, each in a separate production or live environment. In so doing, I would be generating hundreds of thousands of transactions that would affect the holiday, sick, and vacation time of more than
4,000 active employees—and twice as many former ones. Adding to the
complexity, I would be activating Absence Management during business
hours. IT certainly wasn't about to revoke everyone's system access just
for me, and therein laid a problem. Because dozens of Bassett's HR and
payroll employees could concurrently access Lawson with me, they could
unknowingly create issues that would complicate or even derail the migration altogether.

I knew that timely communication would be essential for a successful
upgrade, a point that I made during the final few meetings before we went live.

(Continued)

(*Continued*)

It's Go Time

I arrived in the office before 7 a.m. on activation day. I was prepared to face the challenges that lay ahead. Over the course of the eight-hour conversion, I did my best to keep everyone informed, via e-mail of course. I diligently advised Bassett senior management and anyone remotely involved of my progress. My long, incredibly detailed e-mails explained how the last step went, what I was doing now, and my next course of action. In short, I tried to follow the Golden Rule. I wanted people to know exactly what they were and were not supposed to do—and when.

I thought that my e-mails were as clear as possible. In reality, though, I was only confusing people. They simply couldn't handle the volume of detail-laden messages I was sending. At one point, a Bassett employee named Julie visited my desk, unsure about the current status of the migration.

"Didn't you get my e-mail?" I asked, a bit perplexed at how she could possibly be in the dark after my exhaustive communications efforts.

"Which *one*?" Julie chuckled.

At that moment, I had my revelation. Julie was absolutely right. In two words, she showed me the error of my ways. Yes, my heart was in the right place; I was just trying to keep everyone informed—*really* informed. In doing so, however, my actions were having the precisely opposite effect.

Just to finish the story, the upgrade went off without a hitch. Everyone was happy, and I returned to Bassett a few years later to do some additional work.

That experience had a profound effect on me. I realized that I had become an e-mail addict. If I wanted my clients to really understand me, I would have to change my behavior. I needed to send fewer e-mails.

A Communications Dynasty: Explaining E-Mail's Impressive Reign

When was the last time that someone handed you a business card that *didn't* include at least one e-mail address? E-mail has enjoyed a remarkable 20-year reign as the standard medium of business communications. Given our era of massive technological change, e-mail's run is all the more impressive. Blackberrys, fax machines, telexes, intraoffice memos, and other communications stalwarts have all come and gone. E-mail, however, is standing stronger than ever. The reasons covered next explain why.

E-Mail Fulfills a Legitimate Communications Need

Employees have always needed to communicate with their managers, colleagues, and subordinates. Prior to the mainstream adoption of both e-mail and fax machines, organizations spent billions of dollars sending myriad critical business documents that "absolutely, positively had to be there overnight." In fact, that phrase served as the FedEx marketing slogan from 1978 to 1983.[*] Sure, back then you could use other services to send a letter or package for next-day delivery. The very idea of easily and inexpensively sending electronic documents in 1985, though, was about as plausible as using an app like GrubHub to order food from your smartphone in 1999.

No, the rise of e-mail did not put FedEx, DHL, UPS, the USPS, and other overnight carriers out of the courier business. You can't e-mail someone a box of books or office supplies. In addition, certain types of transactions require real signatures on paper documents in 2015. (Banks, lenders, and mortgage companies won't accept digital signatures on the paperwork required to secure a loan, purchase a house, etc.) Compared to letters and faxes, there's little doubt that e-mails represented a fundamentally better way of remitting important messages, documents, and information. No medium could compete with the speed and cost of e-mail.

Lack of Legitimate Communications Alternatives

Think about all of the ways that we can send messages today:

- Snail mail and fax (although the use of each is on the decline).
- Landlines and smartphones (phone calls, text messages).
- Social networks such as LinkedIn, Twitter, and Facebook.
- Pure instant message (IM) clients such as AIM, IRC, Adium, and Yahoo Messenger.
- Video messaging services such as Skype and Google Hangouts.
- Temporal-message applications such as WhatsApp, Snapchat, and myriad copycats.
- Online chat rooms.[†]

---

[*] Technically, it was "When it absolutely, positively has to be there overnight."

[†] Long on the decline, they may be making a comeback. For instance, in October 2014 Facebook introduced Rooms, "a new app that lets you create places for the things you're into, and invite others who are into them too." See http://tinyurl.com/fbroomsz.

- Commenting on blog posts and articles.
- New, publicly available communication, collaboration, and project-management applications such as Asana, Jive, and the like.
- Internally developed programs. (Chapter 8 will introduce Klick Health, a company that has built its own collaborative suite of tools.)

Even 10 years ago, very few of these apps and mediums could be considered mature. Some had yet to be born; others were still in their infancies. On a different level, most large and midsized organizations centrally provisioned laptops and desktops, issuing them to employees as needed. Many if not most IT departments routinely locked down computers, restricting employees from installing unapproved software applications. (Small businesses tended to be much more permissive.) Employees who wanted to use Skype, for example, would often have to open a ticket with the IT help desk. E-mail served not only as the common denominator, but often as the only sanctioned corporate electronic communications medium.

Ease of Use

From the get-go, composing, sending, and reading e-mail wasn't exactly "rocket surgery." Sure, some programs were more user-friendly than others. Lotus Notes,* in particular, rankled many of its users over the years. My employer in 2000, Lawson Software, chose Notes as its default e-mail client. I found it completely unintuitive, slow, and generally maddening. I disliked it so intensely that I downloaded and configured Netscape Mail (another e-mail program) in its stead, neither of which was hard to do. If e-mail had been difficult to configure and use, it's a fair bet that it would not have caught on nearly as quickly in the business world.

Speed

For a long time now, e-mail has been delivered very quickly. Today delivery times are almost always within a minute. Let's say that an e-mail regularly took 15 minutes to routinely reach its recipient. Would that constitute a vast improvement over snail mail? Of course,

---

* Recently rebranded as *IBM Notes*.

but it's a safe bet that employees would consider using fax machines or some other medium for time-sensitive communications.

Reliability, Security, and Privacy

For the most part, professionals can rest assured that nearly 100 percent of their e-mails will be delivered in a reliable and secure manner. As Jay Etchings, enterprise solutions architect at Dell Computer, tells me, "Generally speaking, corporate e-mail is extremely mature, secure, and dependable. People delete messages; systems almost never do."[1]

Beyond those benefits, many of us take solace in the private, one-to-one nature of e-mails. No, we can't stop others from forwarding them at will, but relatively few people do this. Netiquette and the threat of mutually assured destruction (MAD) collectively prevent most of us from forwarding our colleagues' and managers' e-mails willy-nilly. Regardless of why, most of us take comfort in the fact that a message sent to Jack *usually* stays with Jack. It's unlikely that e-mail would have caught fire without that implicit assurance.

The Largely Asynchronous Nature of E-Mail

Most people lump all social networks together when, in fact, there are significant structural differences among them. Each friendship on Facebook is mutual or, if you like, *synchronous.* That represents just a fancy way of saying that connections on Facebook are predicated on each party opting into them. For example, if Badger and Skinny Pete are friends, it's because at some point each *actively* consented to the relationship. The social network can gently recommend new friends to each (and frequently does), but it doesn't compel any two people to "friend" one another. Put differently, Facebook doesn't "auto-friend." Given the potential privacy ramifications of such a move and the subsequent user backlash, that is not going to happen.

On the other hand, Twitter is basically *asynchronous.* Unlike Facebook, a mutual opt-in to consummate the relationship isn't required. As Justine Sacco knows all too well by now, tweets are public by default; they are not confined to a particular audience.* For instance, let's say that Marie follows Jesse on Twitter. Jesse doesn't have to follow her

---

* Again, I am ignoring one's ability to deliberately restrict the audience of a tweet. If you begin a tweet with @philsimon, then it will only be seen in the feeds of users who follow both you and me. Of course, anyone can retweet (RT) anything and remove that restriction with a simple period or quote.

Table 4.1   The Four Different Types of Twitter Relationships

Marie	Jesse	Type of Relationship	Is direct, private communication possible?*
Follows Jesse	Does not follow Marie	One-way follow	No
Does not follow Jesse	Follows Marie	One-way follow	No
Follows Marie	Follows Jesse	Mutual follow	Yes
Does not follow Jesse	Does not follow Marie	None	No

back for Marie to enjoy his witty 140-character observations on life.[†] As a result, Jesse's tweets will appear in Marie's Twitter feed unless she actively mutes him. (The company added that feature in 2014.) Feel free to tweet "at" any Twitter handle, regardless of whether that person or organization follows you. Don't be surprised, though, if that message is not received.

Whereas Facebook relationships are binaries (two people are either friends or they are not), Twitter supports several different types of relationships. Table 4.1 demonstrates them.

Where does all of this leave e-mail? In two respects, the medium is mostly asynchronous. (I'll come back to this caveat shortly). This trait has served e-mail very well over the years. First, to send a message requires no Facebook-like mutual opt-in. Gus can send Walt a message even if Walt has never given Gus explicit permission to do so beforehand.[‡] Unsolicited commercial and bulk messages are called *spam*, but it would be fatuous to equate the terms *unsolicited* and *unwanted*. Whether solicited or not, some types of messages are always welcome. Who *doesn't* want to receive an unrequested but legitimate sales inquiry?

Note that e-mail isn't *completely* asynchronous. IT departments may block certain e-mail domains for different reasons. To this

---

[*] In the parlance of Twitter, this is called a *direct message* (DM). These are also limited to 140 characters and are not shared with the Twitterverse.

[†] In an effort to keep this discussion as simple as possible, I have intentionally ignored Twitter lists. In fact, it's easy to read someone's tweets without following that person on Twitter.

[‡] The astute reader will pick up on these *Breaking Bad* references. They're not accidental.

end, many individuals and small businesses use anti-spam products like SPAMfighter Pro and ChoiceMail. Here's how they work: Based on users' existing address books and e-mail history, the software automatically creates lists of approved senders (i.e., whitelists). Let's say that Steve just met Lydia at a networking event. He wants to send her a message, but he's not on her current whitelist. In this scenario, Steve composes his message and hits the send button. Lydia's whitelist software ensures that Steve's message sits in a type of cyber-purgatory unless and until he takes the additional step of authenticating his e-mail address. By pledging that he's not sending spam, the software releases Steve's message to Lydia. If Lydia accepts the message, then Steve is automatically added to her whitelist. He need not authenticate his e-mail address again.

A second aspect to e-mail's asynchronous nature explains its popularity. Consider the telephone for a moment. Let's say that a telemarketer's auto-dial software cold calls the Schrader residence. No one picks up, and the machine doesn't leave a voicemail message. Who would return such a message? The telephone only works in this case if *both* parties concurrently use it.

Not true with e-mail. (Ignore spam and inboxes that have exceeded their size quotas for the time being.) To be successfully delivered, the sender only needs the recipient's e-mail address. Unlike the telephone, recipients don't need to be on a device in order to (eventually) receive it. They don't need to immediately respond to each message in order for the medium to function. On the contrary, recipients can open and read messages if, whenever, and nowadays wherever they want.

E-mail was *not* designed to ape the functionality of other communication mediums like online chat rooms and IM applications, although far too many people use it for precisely this purpose. Rather, messages just pile up indefinitely in users' inboxes. Recipients can receive, read, and send messages when it's convenient for them. Let's say that Ted wakes up at 2 a.m. and wants to remind Skyler in accounting to send him the P&L by noon. He can go right ahead. Unless Skyler is sleeping next to the phone with new message audio alerts turned on, Ted's e-mail won't wake her up. An employee who is asleep, on a plane lacking Wi-Fi, or with her family on vacation in Belize will still receive all messages when she connects to the Internet and launches her e-mail application.

Portability

In the *Mad Men* days, secretaries took messages for their bosses. They would jot down notes on physical pieces of paper, leaving them on their bosses' desks. (Anyone else remember carbon paper?) Yes, executives could call in and ask, "Are there any messages for me?" In hindsight, this wasn't terribly efficient, but it represented the best that business could do at the time.

E-mail used to tie employees to their office desks, but that hasn't been the case for a long time. Today it follows us everywhere. We only need to connect to the Internet to be able to check our messages. We don't even need to boot up our proper computers and dial in anymore. Thanks to the rise of cloud computing and mobility, we can quickly check our messages from our phones wherever we are. Although many people take this too far, the portable nature of e-mail has been an enormous productivity boon. Imagine having to trudge all the way to the office to check your messages.

Network Effects and Metcalfe's Law

What if you were the first and only person in the world to use e-mail? To whom can you send messages? Who can send messages to you? Nobody. Your e-mail address is effectively pointless and worthless. You *are* the network. Once someone else obtains a working e-mail address, however, that all changes. The two of you now can e-mail each other. E-mail has just become more valuable to both of you. Now imagine that *everyone* has obtained an e-mail address; anyone can send messages to you and vice versa. That network has become tremendously valuable.

Two concepts explain this phenomenon. First, a *network effect* describes the impact that one user of a good or service has on the value of that product to other people. More people mean *exponentially* more potential connections, uses, and value to a network. The classic example is the telephone, presented in Figure 4.1.

Second, Metcalfe's Law states that "the value of a telecommunications network is proportional to the square of the number of connected users of the system (n^2)."[*] For example, a network of 10 users is worth 100 "units." ($10^2 = 100$). If you double the size of the network to 20, its value doesn't just double; it *quadruples* to

---

[*] For more here, see http://tinyurl.com/metcalfex.

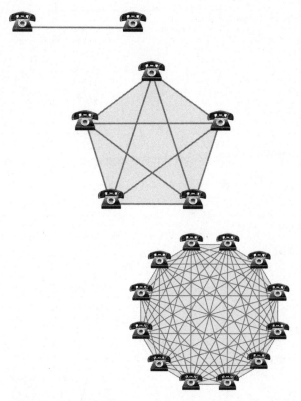

Figure 4.1   Network Effect

400 (20^2 = 400). Figure 4.2 illustrates Metcalfe's Law and exponential growth for a hypothetical communications network.

Techie Stuff: Ubiquity, Interoperability, and Common Protocols

E-mail isn't restricted to employees within the same organization. Unless you have ever worked in IT, you probably don't have the foggiest idea about *how* your company actually processes e-mail messages—and that's very much the point. The vast majority of us don't need to. Behind the scenes, interactions among different e-mail servers and clients are governed by several major e-mail *protocols*. These incoming and outgoing systems of rules effectively manage the exchange of information.[*] Of course, none of this probably

---

[*] IMAP, POP3, SMTP, and HTTP are the most common. For more on this, see http://it.med.miami.edu/x1111.xml.

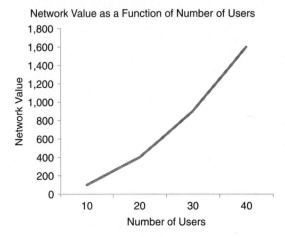

Figure 4.2   Metcalfe's Law in Action

matters to you. You compose, hit send, and *voilà*! The e-mail magically arrives in the recipient's inbox regardless of the organization
for which that employee works.

Think about the interoperability and ubiquity of e-mail in com-
parison to other communications tools. Let's say that you and I want
to chat or IM each other. We will both have to download and install
an application and/or sign up for an online service. That doesn't
get us home, though. We still may be out of luck. Depending on
our company's firewalls and the extent to which IT locks down our
computers, we still may be unable to use these tools to communicate
with each other. What's more, this limitation holds true not just for
us, but also for other partners, clients, and other third parties. (Note
that this restriction has become less effective thanks to the *bring your
own device* movement [BYOD].)

In short, e-mail users don't face the same types of friction typically associated with other communications applications such as chat
and IM. For this reason, e-mail remains wildly popular.

Legitimacy

There's something inherently official about an e-mail, especially one
from management. These messages formalize announcements and
key organizational decisions. E-mail allows us to state our definitive
viewpoints on political matters, to go on the record. They allow us to
say "I told you so" if things break bad. In other words, e-mails serve

as a system of record of sorts. As a medium, it allows us to cover our asses—aka *CYA*.

Failure to Invest in New Technologies

Early versions of productivity suites like Microsoft Office allowed *individuals* to get their work done. Groups of people weren't so lucky—and collaboration and communication usually suffered. Up until recently, Word, Excel, and PowerPoint did not ship with collaborative features "baked in." The latest incarnation, Office 365, offers enhanced communication and collaboration functionality. Lamentably, many organizations have yet to upgrade or roll out similar products to their employees. They continue to run older versions of these productivity stalwarts. Based on phishing and security concerns, organizations such as Oxford University have even blocked employee access to collaborative tools like Google Docs.[2]

Generally speaking, many IT departments at large and midsized organizations have not exactly pioneered new ways of doing things. They tend to be more reactive than proactive. Very few are "early adopters," to steal a term from Geoffrey Moore's classic business text *Crossing the Chasm*. The usual suspects for not adopting new technology include the following:

- Legitimate budgetary restrictions
- Tending to more essential priorities, such as the maintenance and upgrades of enterprise systems, provisioning equipment, staffing the help desk, and the like
- Handling ever-increasing security concerns
- In partnership with different lines of business, a generally terrible record of implementing new systems

Given how important collaboration has become, organizations' general lack of investment in related tools is unfortunate. In the words of ZDNet blogger Dion Hinchcliffe:

> Ironically, given that the workforce is the single biggest investment that most companies make, actual investment in collaboration tools remains as spotty as ever. . . . [C]ollaboration is still considered a "figure it out yourself" process in most organizations, with limited planning and little training in either better ways of collaborating or education on the technologies themselves.[3]

Employee Laziness and Inertia

IT departments have at times been unresponsive to user requests—in this case, the deployment of different and presumably more sophisticated communication and collaboration applications. Let's not pin all of the blame on IT, though. Many employees resist learning new tools, especially if they are overwhelmed with work and messages. Why spend a great deal of limited resources on purchasing, configuring, and deploying a new tool—never mind training—if most employees aren't going to use it? It's a fair question.

E-Mail Nation

Via statistics and an anecdote, I must have major street cred with you by now as an e-mail junkie. You are probably thinking, "You have some serious issues, Phil." After I ran those numbers, I thought so, too. I assumed that I was a much more prolific e-mailer than average, but that's not the case. E-mail management service Baydin recently discovered that the average e-mail user writes 40 messages per day. Most of us don't engage in nearly as many personal conversations during normal business hours.

This makes e-mail the default mode of business communication, and a fair amount of research confirms as much. For instance, in 2013, the Radicati Group released its E-mail Statistics Report, 2013–2017.[*] Among the study's most interesting findings:

- E-mail remains the go-to form of business communication. In 2013, business e-mail accounts totaled 929 million. The number of mailboxes is expected to grow annually at a rate of 5 percent over the next four years, reaching over 1.1 billion by the end of 2017.
- More than 100 billion business e-mails were sent in 2013 *every day*. That number is expected to exceed 130 billion by 2017.

To be sure, these are unwieldy numbers, but what do they mean to you?

In July 2012, the McKinsey Global Institute (MGI) released a report titled "The Social Economy: Unlocking Value and Productivity

---

[*] Access the report at http://tinyurl.com/n6lhq2p.

Through Social Technologies."* MGI found that knowledge workers on average now spend fully 28 percent of their work time managing e-mail. The math here is downright scary: People who work 50 hours per week spend 14 hours stuck in their inboxes. Put in remarkable historical context, a generation ago, professionals spent no time sending and reading e-mails. Today those tasks constitute nearly one-third of their workdays. The McKinsey report recommends that workers use more collaborative tools in lieu of e-mail. In effect, we can "buy back" 7 to 9 percent of our workweeks.

All of this is to say that e-mail has dramatically evolved since its advent in the 1960s as a tool for government types, techies, and wonks. For more than a quarter-century, it remained very much a niche form of communication. Beginning in the mid- to late 1990s, e-mail began its march into—and eventual dominance of—the corporate world. It quickly supplanted the intraoffice memo. Score one for the environment.

Still, its early adoption was anything but smooth. Many VPs employed secretaries to type their e-mails for them; these bigwigs clearly did not want to be self-sufficient. Back then, storage costs were considerable. In response, IT departments typically restricted the size of employee inboxes to now laughable levels. A message sent with a 3-megabyte attachment would typically bounce back.

Most corporations, nonprofits, and small businesses quickly realized that e-mail was becoming an indispensable internal and external communications tool. Business was willing to pay for fast, reliable, secure e-mail, and software vendors responded. As a result, the reliability of the medium has significantly improved from its early days. Sure, with rare exception, messages sometimes inexplicably vanish, perhaps because of a glitch in the matrix. Spam filters sometimes incorrectly flag messages before they reach their intended recipients. Most organizations have relaxed their message size limits, if not altogether eliminated them. Data storage has never been less expensive.

Yes, spam remains a problem, Bill Gates's proclamations about its impending demise notwithstanding.† Sometimes e-mail accounts are hacked. Everyone (including yours truly) has mistakenly replied to everyone copied on an e-mail instead of just to the sender—and

---

* Read the study at http://tinyurl.com/cpdceyz.
† Gates famously predicted in 2004 that spam as we know it would be cured by 2006.

eaten a fair amount of crow for doing so. Beyond that, the novelty of sending around time-sucking chain e-mails has thankfully waned. We now have social networks and blogs to share jokes and stories that once routinely contaminated our inboxes.

The overall e-mail experience is qualitatively better and smoother than it was 15 years ago. To be sure, though, it continues to suffer from some profound problems. Let's look at them.

How We're Working Isn't Working

Devoting an entire chapter to the perils and limitations of e-mail may leave the reader with the impression that I despise e-mail it. In fact, nothing could be further from the truth. Hearing from a friend puts a smile on my face. For people like me, e-mail is a very valuable business tool. I'd even call it *indispensable*. Despite its limitations and the often-maddening insistence of so many people to ignore better collaboration tools, I would have a really difficult time working in a world sans e-mail. I suspect that I'm not alone.

Let me make this as clear as possible:

> The problem isn't e-mail. The problem is how we use it.

One could write a long book about the sentiment behind those two pithy sentences. By no means do they apply only to e-mail. In the technology world, there's an oft-invoked axiom for this type of phenomenon: *PICNIC*. It stands for "problem in chair, not in computer."

It's easy to blame software applications for exacerbating business communication. For instance, Microsoft PowerPoint often takes a bad rap, but it's a perfectly serviceable application. In fact, it is my presentation tool of choice. (I find its Presentation View to be exceptionally useful.) As much as we may like to criticize it, PowerPoint does not automatically generate dozens of inscrutable slides and force its users to read off of them. The problem lies in how we use it. Prezi, Keynote, and other presentation applications may offer slightly different bells and whistles, but they don't change poorly designed slides.

E-Mail's Cross-Purposes

We have long since solved e-mail's nascent problems: reliability, dependability, and interoperability. None of which alters the fact that e-mail remains a fundamentally limited medium, and sending more messages only exacerbates its limitations. Most germane here is that an increase in the number of e-mails often enhances the extent to which workers feel overwhelmed. Employees frequently use their inboxes as catch-alls for absolutely everything work-related and even some nonwork purposes. In doing so, they conflate several often overlapping but fundamentally disparate types of communications, including:

- Group work-related messages (i.e., announcements)
- Individual work-related messages
- New and existing work-related projects, issues, and tasks
- Comments and udpates to existing work-related projects, issues, and tasks
- Important personal communications (e.g., messages from significant others)

We've conditioned ourselves to use our inboxes as de facto to-do lists for our professional and personal lives. As such, it's entirely rational for us to check in frequently, if not constantly. This goes double during deadlines, and when employees fear for their jobs. How *else* are employees supposed to answer essential questions such as the following:

- What do I need to be doing *right now?*
- What *else* do I need to do?
- What's the status of a current task, project, or issue?
- Does my team or manager need anything else from me?
- Are there any *other* problems of which I need to be aware?
- What *else* needs fixing?
- Is anything going on with my kids?

> When we cram everything into e-mail, it becomes far less useful as a communications medium.

We're just getting started with e-mail's limitations.

E-Mail Often Lacks Nuance and Emotional Depth

For relatively straightforward matters, e-mail just plain works. Can you send me the URL to that product? Here's that photo of the gang from our golf trip. E-mail is ideal for these types of discrete interactions. But what about an issue or problem that requires considerably more tact, nuance, and sentiment? Here e-mail often fails us.

Writing for *Harvard Business Review*, Anthony Tjan, managing partner of venture capital firm Cue Ball, lists a few of the medium's obvious problems. When trying to resolve sensitive matters over e-mail or text, Tjan writes that:

- E-mail prolongs debate.
- E-mail and text often promote reactive responses, as opposed to progress and action to move forward.
- It is hard to get the emotional intelligence right in e-mail.[4]

These are all major problems, but let's focus on that last point for a moment. Put differently, text-based communication mediums such as e-mail suffer from significant semantic limitations. A great deal of research has confirmed that emotions and subtext are often missed and misinterpreted in e-mails.

For instance, consider the findings of one particularly eye-opening 2006 series of studies by two psychologists, Justin Kruger, PhD of New York University and Nicholas Epley of the University of Chicago.[5] One group of participants read messages with a certain tone (e.g., sarcasm, humor, or gravity). Kruger and Epley asked the second group to discern the readers' intent via voice and, separately, via text. At the beginning of the experiment, nearly 80 percent of the participants believed that, irrespective of the medium, others would be able to accurately detect the tone their messages.

Listeners correctly picked up on sarcasm and humor more than 75 percent of the time, a number in line with earlier participant expectations. With e-mail, though, the results were quite different. As Louise Dobson of *Psychology Today* wrote about the study:

> Participants were only able to accurately communicate sarcasm and humor in barely half—56 percent—of the e-mails they sent. What's worse, *most people had no idea that they weren't making themselves understood.* [Emphasis mine][6]

This second finding is arguably more troubling than the first, and it begs two questions: Why is the message so frequently lost on

messages and work fell by 10 points—the equivalent of missing a whole night's sleep. Even more remarkably, this is more than double the four-point fall caused by smoking marijuana. Yes, constantly checking e-mail lowers our intelligence and concentration more than toking does. "This is a very real and widespread phenomenon," Wilson said. "We have found that this obsession with looking at messages, if unchecked, will damage a worker's performance by reducing their mental sharpness. Companies should encourage a more balanced and appropriate way of working."[8]

Research by Gallup in 2013 affirms the finding that e-mail is a major source of distraction on the job. Its "State of the American Workplace: Employee Engagement Insights for U.S. Business Leaders" report examined the American workplace from 2010 through 2012. Nearly seven in ten Americans have difficulty focusing on one thing at a time. Knowledge workers are easily distracted during the day, especially by e-mail.[*]

Few learned people would dispute the fact that incessantly checking and sending e-mail inhibits deep thought. Let's say that you're trying to solve a tricky issue, writing some code, or revising a marketing plan. Which of the following is more conducive to a successful outcome: Constantly sending and responding to e-mails or unplugging for a considerable period of time? Much of my best thinking takes place at the gym when I am decidedly unconnected.

Don't get me wrong. Today's workers cannot be compared to seventeenth century farmers. Rare is the crisis-free professional workplace in which schedules never change. With technology, the fleas come with the dog. I don't know too many people who fastidiously plan their day, week, or month well in advance—and actually stick to those plans. Change happens faster than ever, but there's a problem: Our brains are just not wired for chronic multitasking. It's silly to think that there are no mental, personal and emotional costs to juggling so many balls at once. Deadlines, key tasks, and goals are bound to fall through the cracks.

E-Mail's Largely Unknown Legal Issues

The burnt hand teaches best. Justine Sacco learned three important lessons the hard way:

1. Twitter has become a *very* public town square.

---

[*] Read the entire study at http://tinyurl.com/yygallup.

its recipient? And why doesn't the sender realize this? The answ
are part human and part technological.

These schisms are certainly not deliberate. That is, few of us int
tionally obfuscate when we communicate and, more specifically, wh
we e-mail our bosses, colleagues, and subordinates. After all, *we* co
pletely understand what we're trying to convey. (Do you know man
people who would rate themselves as *poor communicators*? Neither d
I.) And it's not text per se. Kruger and Epley astutely note that wri
ten communications (e.g., pencils, typewriters, and the like) predate
e-mail by centuries. Letters, telegrams, and memos have historically
not engendered widespread confusion and distortion. So what is it?

Epley believes that there's something fundamentally different
about e-mail, something that actually lends itself to frequent misunderstandings. In his words, the problem is "the ease with which we
can fire things back and forth. It makes text-based communication
seem more informal and more like face-to-face communication than
it really is."[7] I would put text messages in the same boat, as they simu-
late conversations.

All of this is to say that, despite our intentions, e-mail often fails
us as an effective communications medium. It has happened to everyone at one point or another; no one bats a thousand. Unbeknownst
to us, the key emotional components of our messages often elude
recipients. Whether the messages in our e-mails are *fully* received and
understood basically comes down to a coin flip. Relatively few of us
realize the extent to which we're gambling when we rattle off e-mails.

E-Mail Is Often Wholly Inefficient

Even ostensibly simple tasks can become logistical nightmares over
e-mail. Try scheduling a meeting with people from different organizations in this way. Go back and forth with your help desk trying to
diagnose a problem. Reverting to e-mail for these types of activities
wastes a great deal of time. Often, those involved in these "conversations" quickly become frustrated.

Our E-Mail Obsession Makes Us Dumber

In 2005, Dr. Glenn Wilson, a psychiatrist at King's College London
University, conducted a fascinating study on the effects of e-mail. In
80 clinical trials, he monitored the IQs of workers throughout the
day. Wilson's discovered that the IQs of those who tried to juggle

2. Some thoughts are best left unsaid and certainly unwritten.
3. Never before have private vs. public and personal vs. professional lines been blurrier.

Sacco expressed a very unpopular *personal* opinion on a public social network. For that, she quickly paid the ultimate *professional* price. Other than issuing an apology, Sacco kept mum. Perhaps she consulted a lawyer, but she ultimately did not sue Twitter for its role in her termination. I suspect that every judge in the country would have laughed her out of the courtroom. Like most Americans, Sacco was an at-will employee. (See "What's Holding Us Back?" in Chapter 2.) As such, IAC was well within its rights to axe her. The vast majority of organizations would have done the same thing. Sacco's personal actions on a public network didn't exactly help IAC's reputation.

This begs the question: What about an employee's professional communication on private networks? U.S. courts have generally ruled that employees enjoy "reasonable" privacy rights while using company-owned telephones. Those same rights, however, do not apply to e-mail.

If this bothers you, then you can blame politicians and judges, folks who generally can't keep up with contemporary technology. "Employees enjoy no expectation of privacy when sending personal e-mails from corporate accounts," writes Jon Hyman, a partner in the Labor & Employment group of Kohrman Jackson & Krantz.[9] Of course, no law can prevent employees from sending public, offensive, and objectionable messages—and being justifiably fired for doing so.

E-Mail Fosters Unhealthy Internal Competition

In many organizations, employees avoid silence at all costs. For one, it equals consent. Beyond that, failing to respond to an e-mail is tantamount to not working, not being important. As a result, a single e-mail often results in a veritable maelstrom of replies. This is particularly true in big corporate environments. What's more, escalating a situation by "cc-ing" an executive practically guarantees a litany of politically charged responses. It's as if first prize goes to the first reply, quality or content be damned. Everyone has to chime in.

Look back at a recent long e-mail thread from your current job or a previous one. Did it quickly clarify matters? Or, as is so often the case, did it cause more problems than it solved?

E-Mail Is (Too) Private

Privacy may be dying, but plenty of conversations should still be restricted to two people: the sender and the recipient. The downside here is that key decisions, documentation, explanations, discussions, knowledge, and facts often remain trapped in myriad individual inboxes across corporate America. A great deal of this one-to-one information rightfully belongs in *relatively* public, internally searchable, many-to-many forums.

The benefits of using alternatives to e-mail are multifold. Most employees are used to self-service by now. They have learned how to navigate websites, even sloppily designed ones. Why not make it as easy as possible for them to rapidly find what they need? Why bombard new hires with blizzards of e-mails on their first day? Valuable tidbits often go missing in that type of "exchange." Even if everything is included in those torrents, will employees be able to quickly find key information?

E-Mail Search Can Be Lacking

Consider this mathematical paradox. As of this writing, we use Google to search more than 30 trillion Web pages.* Searches typically take far less than one second, and we usually find exactly what we want—*or at least what we think we want.* Yet many of us struggle to find a key conversation, document, or e-mail in an inbox of only 2,000 or 20,000 messages.

Without question, recent improvements in e-mail search help us find what we need. Applications and Web-based services like Gmail contain far superior search capability than their nascent counterparts of the mid-1990s ever did. Let's be honest, though: It is often difficult for us to instantaneously access much of the content contained in e-mails. Folders, flags, filters, tags, keywords, and restricted searches by date range can help. Rare are the people, however, who can always and instantaneously find what they need in their inboxes.

---

* It's an astonishing number. For more, go to http://tinyurl.com/30freakingT.

Timing and the Folly of the Urgent E-Mail

Because of its place as the Cadillac of corporate communications, countless employees send urgent e-mails and expect immediate or rapid responses. Sure, those e-mails are almost guaranteed to success-fully travel through one or more company's servers to their intended recipients. But what if the recipients are not checking their inboxes at that very moment? Or what if recipients are working their way up their queues? Somehow, typing "urgent" in the subject line for many people represents a sufficient means of dealing with a crisis.

E-Mail Easily Overwhelms Us

I have never met anyone who has complained about not receiving enough e-mail, and I'd bet that you haven't either. There's a simple reason for this: Just about all of us get way too many of them. Don't take my word for it, though. Let's look at some data.

No Mas: The Biggest Reason That People Opt Out of E-Mail Lists

Build your e-mail list.

We've heard that mantra for years. The Web is rife with posts titled "25 Clever Ways to Grow Your E-Mail Marketing List."[10] You'll get no argument from me on the importance of knowing who your customers are, but e-mail lists are double-edged swords.

Launched in 1998, Constant Contact provides a raft of marketing and online survey tools. The company serves more than 600,000 small businesses, nonprofit organizations, and member associations. Most people have received at some point a newsletter with the company's logo at the bottom.

In 2012, the company wanted to determine why list subscribers opted out from its members' e-mail lists.* It asked 1,400 consumers that very question and discovered the following:

- 69 percent of respondents said that they received too many e-mails from the business/organization.
- 56 percent of respondents said that the content is no longer relevant.
- 51 percent of respondents said that the content wasn't what they expected.

In other words, the most-cited reason for unsubscribing is that recipients felt overwhelmed. As Figure 4.3 shows, the rationale is similar for Facebook unlikes.

(Continued)

---

* Read the whole study at http://tinyurl.com/n24dg79.

(*Continued*)

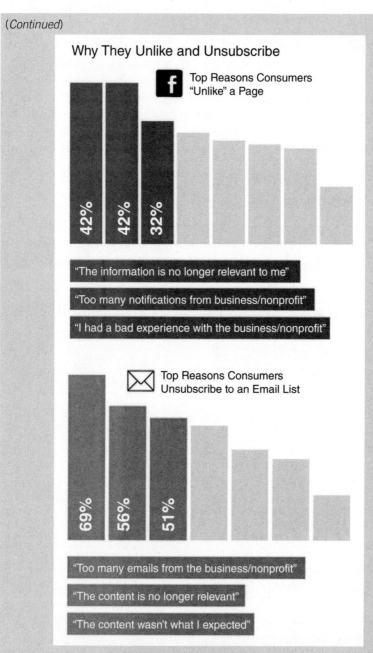

Figure 4.3   **Why and How Consumers Like and Subscribe**

Source: Constant Contact

This research is in keeping with the general trend of declining click-through rates (CTRs)[*] for e-mail marketing campaigns. Bombarding subscribers and customers with Facebook status updates, tweets, and e-mails is certainly easy and cheap. Less certain, though, is whether it represents an intelligent marketing strategy. The data indicates that this method is often counterproductive.

E-Mail Is Often an Inappropriate Medium

A few years ago, one of my clients took issue with a few things I said at a conference. Neil (not his real name) sent me an e-mail indicating his displeasure with my actions. I generally don't try to make enemies, and that rule certainly applies to my clients. I immediately dialed Neil and left a message on his voice mail. Without being defensive, I said that I had received his message and thought that it was best for us to talk.

A few minutes later, Neil sent me yet another e-mail. Yes, he had received my message, but he was intent on having this "conversation" over e-mail. I probably didn't score any points by replying that we needed to actually, you know, talk about this. Call me old-fashioned, but certain conversations need to take place in a more personal way.

Much Better Collaboration and Communication Tools Exist

Forget for a minute all of the reasons mentioned up to this point about e-mail's inefficacy in many situations. All of them could be excused if no one had bothered to build a better communications mousetrap, but nothing could be further from the truth. There has never been a wider variety of user-friendly, affordable, secure, and mobile tools that let people work smarter. (Chapter 8 will have much more to say about this topic.)

---

[*] Put simply, the *CTR* is a way of measuring the success of an online advertising campaign for a particular website. It can also gauge the effectiveness of an e-mail campaign by the number of users who clicked on a specific link. Along with open, bounce, and abandonment rates, marketers can theoretically determine what's working and what isn't.

What's *Really* Inhibiting Employee Productivity?

In 2013, I attended an interactive one-day event for one of my clients with 40 other thought leaders in New York City. The agenda was fairly loose: We participated in a wide array of discussions on tech-related topics. These included Big Data, cloud computing, and "platforms" (never a precisely defined term these days).

I agreed with much of what was said, but some level of discord was inevitable. Try to get 40 people to agree on *anything*. One attendee's particularly objectionable lamentation got my goat: "Employees would be so much more productive if better tools existed." I could not have disagreed more, and it didn't take me long to say as much.

The no-tools argument is wrong on many levels. First, it contradicts a little thing called *reality*. Long gone are the Web's early days. Back then most professionals relied on e-mail. Nascent sharing tools like knowledge bases and intranets simply didn't catch on. Sure, e-mail remains the killer app, but it just doesn't need to be that way.

In *The Year Without Pants: WordPress.com and the Future of Work*, Scott Berkun describes how the roughly 200 employees at Automattic (its parent company) rarely use e-mail. They must work in the same office, right? No, quite the contrary. Employees work remotely in more than 80 countries across the globe. Instead of e-mail, they opt for tools like Skype, Internet Relay Chat (IRC), a WordPress theme called *P2*, and other collaboration tools.

I can name oodles more: DropBox, Jive, Smartsheet, Slack, HipChat, Asana, and screen-sharing tools like Join.me allow us to be vastly more productive while we're away from the office. Far superior collaboration tools exist relative to 15 years ago. It's not even remotely debatable.

Second, the fallacious argument completely ignores both organizational culture and the human side of the equation. If you extend this line of thought to its logical conclusion, employees are just waiting for that one über-useful tool to come along. When it does, they'll immediately adopt it in droves and become 10 times more productive. They'll unlearn bad habits and force IT departments to buy and deploy the new tool.

Again, the history of technology suggests otherwise. There's *always* an adoption curve. Is our general lack of collaboration a function of deficient technology or something else? It's the latter. Many of us are too busy, too lazy, and/ or too stubborn to learn new ways of doing things. In the early days of the Web, truly collaborative tools were in hindsight a bit lacking, but that hasn't been true for a very long time.

The contrast between the way the average consumer and employee communicates today could not be more pronounced. Whereas the former has adopted a bevy of new tools, the latter still tends to rely almost exclusively on—you guessed it—e-mail. Others share this feeling. Consider the words of Conrad Bayer, co-founder and CEO of sales-automation company Tellwise:

> We are seeing a revolution in many areas of business communications, including the messages between buyers and sellers. Sales professionals have been stuck on e-mail but the modern buyer has evolved. Today's buyers prefer communicating on multiple devices and channels. The days of "one size fits all" have long passed. The seller needs to move beyond e-mail. By communicating through more productive and collaborative tools, sales professionals will be more successful.[11]

Of course, much like simple and clear language, new tools by themselves do not guarantee that our messages will be received; they merely increase the chances.

Next

This chapter has described the dual problems with contemporary business communication: the prevalence of confusing language and the reliance on e-mail. This begs the question, what happens when our messages aren't received?

The next chapter answers that query in spades.

Notes

1. Personal e-mail from Etchings, on August 7, 2014.
2. http://tinyurl.com/k3z6hcq.
3. Dion Hinchcliffe, "Digital Collaboration Goes Deeper, Gets Lightweight and Intelligent," May 23, 2014, www.zdnet.com/digital-collaboration-goes-deeper-gets-lightweight-and-intelligent-7000029818.
4. Anthony Tjan, "Don't Send That Email. Pick up the Phone!," November 1, 2011, http://blogs.hbr.org/2011/11/dont-send-that-email-pick-up-t.
5. www.apa.org/monitor/feb06/egos.aspx.
6. www.psychologytoday.com/articles/200604/avoiding-email-catastrophe.
7. www.apa.org/monitor/feb06/egos.aspx.
8. "E-mails 'Hurt IQ More Than Pot'," April 22, 2005, www.cnn.com/2005/WORLD/europe/04/22/text.iq.

9. Jon Hyman, "Do Employees Have Any Privacy Rights in Personal Emails Sent From Corporate Accounts?," March 14, 2013, www.workforce.com/blogs/3-the-practical-employer/post/do-employees-have-any-privacy-rights-in-personal-emails-sent-from-corporate-accounts.

10. Andy Pitre, "25 Clever Ways to Grow Your Email Marketing List," March 28, 2012, http://blog.hubspot.com/blog/tabid/6307/bid/32028/25-Clever-Ways-to-Grow-Your-Email-Marketing-List.aspx.

11. E-mail exchange with Bayer, on August 18, 2014.

5

Why Bad Communication Is Bad Business

The Unintended Consequences of Mixed and Missed Messages

Think twice before you speak because your words and influence will plant the seed of either success or failure in the mind of another.

—Napoleon Hill

Generally speaking, business communication leaves more than a bit to be desired. Messages are frequently not received, much less fully understood. To propose solutions at this point, though, would be a bit premature. Even if you concede that the use of language and e-mail isn't ideal, are you supposed to make major changes in communication in your organization just because I say so? In other words, what are the effects of others not receiving our messages?

On a macroeconomic level, the precise monetary figure of bad business communication is impossible to quantify. We can only guess. The McKinsey Global Institute report referenced in Chapter 4 is not shy with its estimate. Its authors concluded that widespread use of social technologies could vastly improve communication and collaboration and yield savings of nearly $1 trillion.

Perhaps nowhere is poor business communication more evident than on discrete projects. (See "From Organizations to Projects: The Evolution of Work" in Chapter 2.) When organizations implement new systems, adopt new processes, and develop new methodologies, employees often find themselves removed from the comfort zones of their day jobs. Their responsibilities change; they often have to do two jobs for the duration of these projects. For these reasons, things invariably fall between the cracks.

The Project Management Institute (PMI) understands this all too well. In May 2013, the PMI released its annual "Pulse of the Profession" report.* Its findings confirmed what many of us have long suspected: Poor communication significantly increases the risk of project failure and often derails large projects altogether. Specifically, "$135 million

---

* Read it at http://tinyurl.com/qaal7xx.

is at risk for every $1 billion spent on a project. Further research on the importance of effective communications uncovers that a startling 56 percent ($75 million of that $135 million) is at risk due to ineffective communications." In a similar vein, PricewaterhouseCoopers LLC, Forbes, and Towers Watson have all performed extensive work on the extent to which deficient communications impedes successful projects.

One Size Does Not Misfit All

At a micro level, communication breakdowns cause myriad problems at work and exacerbate others. The inability to effectively communicate results in all sorts of inefficiencies, misunderstandings, gaffes, squabbles, missed opportunities, and outright disasters. That's not to say, though, that one size misfits all. The effects of unclear messages vary considerably by individual, organization, group, department, and industry. For reasons far beyond the scope of this book, different organizations and people handle things in very different manners. It's entirely possible, for instance, that your organization routinely overcomes dubious internal communication practices. It engages in risky behavior but routinely succeeds despite itself. (Sustained success with this type of approach, of course, is highly improbable. Organizations can only defy the odds for so long.)

This is analogous to smoking cigarettes. At this point, few people doubt that cigarettes really are bad for you. Still, not everyone who regularly smokes develops lung cancer. My grandfather puffed two packs every day for 50 years and lived to be 94.

As you read this chapter, think about the following questions:

- How many misunderstandings could have been averted at your organization if two colleagues had simply engaged in a five-minute in-person conversation or videoconference over Skype?
- Have you ever walked away from a meeting confused? You didn't know what to make of your manager's instructions to "find new actionable value-adds at different price points going forward."
- How many application or software problems could have been solved with a quick phone call and a simple screen-sharing session rather than a 10-message exchange?
- How many projects in your organization failed mainly because of internal and/or external communications issues?

- Have you ever overlooked a truly critical e-mail in your never-ending inbox?
- Have you ever been unable to do your job because key documents languished in a colleague's inbox or on his hard drive—and not a secure medium that all team members and colleagues could securely access?

I'd be shocked if you didn't answer *yes* to at least a few of these questions. For my part, I've seen plenty of poor communication with all sorts of organizations over my career. In point of fact, my hands aren't entirely clean. I've occasionally contributed to the problem by e-mailing too frequently. (See "Curing My E-mail Addiction, Part I: The Revelation" in Chapter 4.)

Message Not Received

Perhaps the most pernicious effect of poor business communication is also the most obvious: Our intended audiences neither receive nor understand our messages. We all have seen the following scenarios play out.

Why Others Ignore Your Perfectly Clear Message

Your company has just launched a new product, press release, and extensive social media and marketing campaigns. Immediately afterward, its website goes down. Your worst professional nightmare has just come true.

You suspect that these two events are not coincidental. Perhaps the cause of the outage is a distributed denial-of-service (DDoS) attack. After all, these are hardly infrequent these days. Content aggregator Feedly experienced several of these in June 2014. Cybercriminals unsuccessfully tried to extort the company's management and took down the popular site for several days.* Millions of its users were affected.

You do some digging. You determine the cause of the attack and the solution. You write the clearest e-mail possible with that information and dutifully send it to the right people at your company. You then go back to work.

Twenty-four hours later, your company's website is still down yet no one can figure out why. People are furious. Would-be customers go to the site and

---

* See http://tinyurl.com/x-feedly.

only see 404 errors.* Your message wasn't received because the people capable of—and responsible for—website hosting haven't had time to check their e-mail. They're too busy trying to fix the problem!

Decreased Clarity, Credibility, and Trust

On my Twitter profile, I describe myself as *an occasional grouch*. When it comes to workplace communication, my two biggest pet peeves are the misuse/overuse of e-mail (especially when a five-minute conversation would solve an issue) and the proliferation of faux and contrived terms.

Now, I'll be the first to admit that I can be a bit persnickety when it comes to language. (Don't get me started on the word *platform*.) Forget the semantic pet peeves of English teachers, curmudgeons, and grammarians for the moment. There's increasing evidence that abstract and perplexing language isn't just annoying; it inhibits trust.

In 2010, psychology professors Jochim Hansen of New York University and Michaela Wänke of the University of Basel in Switzerland published a study that confirmed what many of us have known intuitively for a long time. Hansen and Wänke discovered that people are more likely to think you're lying if you use abstract language rather than concrete terms and phrasing. In their words, "Statements of the very same content were judged as more probably true when they were written in concrete language than when they were written in abstract language."[1] To use the authors' ironically clunky term, *linguistic concreteness* offers major benefits.

"Jargon masks real meaning," says Jennifer Chatman, management professor at the Haas School of Business, University of California at Berkeley. "People use it as a substitute for thinking hard and clearly about their goals and the direction that they want to give others."[2]

Lost Sales

Salespeople fail to close deals for all sorts of reasons. To claim that communication is the sole or even main reason for many lost sales would be dramatically overstating things. For instance, a product costs $300,000

---

* Everyone has seen one of these at some point. To refresh your memory, the 404 Not Found error means that the Web page was not found.

but the prospective client's budget is only $100,000. Clear communication won't bridge that gap. Issues often arise when two parties are feeling each other out: Does the product or service do what the prospective client requires? Here, communication can be essential.

What Exactly Are We Buying Here?

The mid- to late 1990s represented the heyday for many enterprise technology vendors, not to mention the consultants implementing their products. Chief executives spent untold billions of dollars buying and deploying systems that were supposed to unleash massive savings, discover valuable insights, and transform their businesses. The major categories of software included:

- Enterprise resource planning (ERP)
- Customer relationship management (CRM)
- Business intelligence (BI)

By the early 2000s, these product categories had matured considerably. Chief Information Officers (CIOs) knew exactly what they were buying and why. Despite that, the batting average on these implementations was deplorable, a topic that I discuss extensively in *Why New Systems Fail*.

This doesn't bode well for the many chief executives who don't understand what software vendors are trying to sell them. Confusing marketing coupled with a relative dearth of client understanding are inhibiting the adoption of truly important technologies such as Big Data. Quite a few software vendors lose potential sales because their websites and sales reps can't explain in plain English to prospective clients what their product actually does.

Severed Relationships and Burnt Bridges

Throughout the 2000s, I frequently worked with third parties to secure consulting gigs. Large organizations are generally more comfortable hiring independent contractors via respected IT service firms. As a result, I would usually deal with recruiters and other liaisons who took a 25 to 30 percent cut. Most freelancers and independents looked at recruiters' fees as a necessary cost of doing business.

To be sure, many recruiters would do exactly as they said. Of course, others some were unreasonable, and a few were downright flaky. I can remember two in particular who were extremely demanding. Although we had no prior relationship, from the get-go they expected me to drop whatever I was doing. Because of their clients' urgent needs, they needed me to immediately hop on a call.

I would generally comply, especially if I wasn't currently on an assignment. After all, I wanted the work. I discovered with these two recruiters, though, that communication was a one-way street. I would follow up with them about updates and only hear crickets. Three or four months later I would finally receive a terse e-mail with bad news.

After being burned a few times, I chose to ignore these recruiters' allegedly urgent e-mails and phone calls. Amazingly, they didn't take the hint. They were clearly oblivious to how unprofessionally they had behaved. Other recruiters would keep me informed as events unfolded, and I preferred to do business with courteous and respectful types.

I rarely deal with recruiters these days but some journalists are clearly cut from the same communications cloth. I can think of several who expected me to churn out very specific content for them under tight deadlines. After sending them what they required, they would immediately go missing. In the days and weeks that followed, my subsequent e-mails and voice mails remained unanswered. I would check Twitter. They were still alive, actively tweeting.

A few years later, the same communication-challenged reporters would magically reappear with new requirements and deadlines. Some didn't remember our prior history. Others sheepishly made vague promises that things would be different this time, but I wasn't going to fall for that again. I didn't want to put the work in and have them mysteriously vanish. I ignored their queries.

Cutting Your Own Throat: Unprofessionalism Personified

In the early spring of 2014, I independently arranged a book tour to promote my previous book *The Visual Organization.* Over a four-day period, I spoke at nine venues in San Francisco, one of the most expensive cities in the world. I could justify the cost, though. I figured that the juice was worth the squeeze. I spoke at eBay, Autodesk, Netflix, and other prominent organizations. I only requested that each organization adhere to two reasonable requests:

1. Buy a decent number of discounted copies of the book.
2. Record the talks and let me post them online.

A few glitches aside, the book tour was a success.* The talks went very well, and I will probably repeat the process to support *Message Not Received.*

(Continued)

---

*A woman from a very prominent company canceled four days before I was scheduled to speak there—via e-mail no less.

(Continued)

One of my stops was at Visier, an HR analytics start-up a full 50 miles from my hotel in San Jose. The folks seemed excited to host me, although the company lacked the budget to buy any books. I waived that requirement and even brought a few signed copies for my primary contact and the CEO. Rather than give a talk to the company's small employee population, we agreed to record an interview with its marketing head and an independent videographer. I discussed the importance of the very problem that Visier's product ostensibly addresses. The video wouldn't be a commercial, but it would serve as excellent content marketing for the company.

The interview went well and I told my contact to let me know when the video was ready. I was pleased.

From Enthusiasm to Crickets

May arrived and I still hadn't heard anything from Visier. I sent my contact a few messages. She was neither rude nor apologetic. In a very matter-of-fact kind of way, she informed me that they were swamped with other priorities. I made a note to follow up again in June. At that point, my contact changed her story: She claimed that there were problems with the video. I told her that I understood. After all, things don't always go according to plan. I politely asked her to keep me apprised.

By July, I was still in the dark. I tried not to be pushy, but I wanted to put the video on my site and Visier had agreed to let me do just that. I called her and asked for an update. I quickly sensed that she didn't want to speak with me. Without being very specific, she said that the video was unusable. Plus, she said that she didn't think I had wanted it anyway.

I was baffled. I asked her two questions:

1. If that were true, why would I have gone to Visier in the first place?
2. Given how many times I had followed up with her in the last three months, how could she possibly be under that impression?

She equivocated and answered neither question. I asked her to send me the native video file. How hard could *that* be? (Perhaps my own excellent video guy could resurrect it, even at my own cost.) She demurred and I decided that it was time to circumvent her. I dialed the CEO and left a voice mail. I expressed my desire to briefly speak with him about the situation. An hour later, he replied with a terse e-mail advising me that Visier was not interesting in pursuing this "project."

I wasn't upset about the video file being corrupted, if that indeed was the case. Things happen. I was miffed at Visier's shoddy communication after I walked out of its office. I vented to a few friends in private, but I didn't bash the company on Quora or Twitter.

Given how Visier's personnel comported themselves, what would you do if you were in my shoes? Would you ever refer prospective clients or employees to the company in the future? Would you give it props on one of the sites for which you wrote or on social media networks? Me neither. Moreover, as a start-up in a very crowded area, Visier's actions are downright perplexing. The interaction left me with the following questions:

- Doesn't the company need all of the help that it can get?
- Wouldn't the interview help it generate leads?
- Why turn a potential advocate into a potential detractor?

More professional and timely communication from its employees may not have salvaged the video. Still, it could have preserved or rescued a potentially fruitful business relationship.

This story illustrates one of the key points in this book: Bad communication is bad business.

Poor Execution and Strategic Blunders

Automation and routinization are changing many jobs and eliminating others. Although they are hardly ubiquitous, artificial intelligence and machine learning have never been more pervasive in the workplace. That's not to say, though, that employees don't need to regularly exercise discretion. Even call center reps who often read from scripts can't completely check out during work. (I should know. I spent a year after college working at SONY Electronics as a customer service rep.)

The need to make judgment calls is much more pronounced at senior levels. Most people in corner offices maintain profit and loss (P&L) responsibility. This is perhaps the single largest reason that they are compensated so well. For better or worse, a single executive decision can affect all of an organization's employees, customers, investors, and partners. As the following story shows, senior leaders far too often cannot clearly articulate their strategy and/or vision to their lieutenants. The consequences can be grave.

Communication, Ambiguity, and the Role of Luck

I used to work at a global healthcare company and saw the following scenario play out over the course of a few months. Note that the names used here are pseudonyms.

(Continued)

(*Continued*)

The president (Richard) issued a series of directives to his leadership team. His staff had to significantly to improve his unit's financial results. Costs needed to be cut. Although Richard fancied himself a clear communicator, he spoke vaguely about "toughness," "accountability," and "hitting the numbers." He assumed that everyone knew exactly what he meant, but Richard omitted critical parts of the message, including:

- Which numbers? Was it important to hit profit targets, growing revenues, cutting expenses, or some combination?
- Was he open to different alternatives?

Richard's ambiguity caused two of the regional heads to interpret his message very differently. One saw this as an inflexible edict while the other saw the opportunity for flexibility. As such, each lieutenant took a different approach and told his team to follow divergent paths. Their presentations at the next business review meeting manifested this stark contrast.

The first division head (James) stayed truer to Richard's specific edict to cut costs in his region. He provided a fairly standard financial analysis of what could be cut or restructured. James and his team knew that many of his recommendations would be painful. As he presented his plan, the dialogue turned confrontational. James was playing defense the whole time, defending his numbers and responding to claims that he was playing it too safe. He failed to force any meaningful discussion of unintended consequences or the opportunity for innovative approaches.

The other regional head (Tom) took Richard's edict in a different direction. He asked his team to develop two approaches. He recognized the necessity of cutting costs, but he also saw other options. Tom directed his leadership team to identify two scenarios:

1. Reaching profit goals simply by cutting costs while highlighting any resulting unintended consequences and risks to the business
2. Providing a blended solution that identified alternative approaches to increase revenues, coupled with responsible expense reduction

In either case, Tom's approach would virtually ensure that his region met its goals.

The resulting discussion was more balanced. Compared to James, Tom was in a better position to control the conversation and influence Richard's thinking. Tom fielded tough questions from a position of strength. All expense reductions made sense, no draconian cuts took place, and the region exceeded its plan.

Because of Richard's ambiguity, James misunderstood his message. The company squandered opportunities to consider better ideas, alienated several key leaders, and ultimately missed earnings targets. In the end, James's region ended up missing its numbers. Several leadership changes followed. James never fully recovered and left the company within a year and Richard wasn't too far behind him.

Judgment is always required, especially at the executive level. However, a vague communications style benefits no one.

Najeeb Ahmad is a founder and principal of Pennington Human Dynamics, a leadership performance consultancy.

Lower Productivity

Many professionals have come to terms with the demises of traditional 9-to-5 jobs and 40-hour workweeks. Some struggle with planning their personal lives because they are *always* on call. Employees who are constantly interrupted and unable to manage their time are under severe stress. As a result, they are more likely to listen to recruiters' phone calls. Perhaps most important from the organization's perspective, overworked employees are less productive.

When we are stressed out, we are much less apt to enter what Mihaly Csikszentmihalyi calls *flow* or a state of "optimal experience." In his eponymous book *Flow: The Psychology of Optimal Experience,* the author describes the genuinely satisfying state of consciousness that artists, athletes, musicians, and even everyday employees can reach. Flow results in deep enjoyment, creativity, and productivity. Michael Jordan called it "the zone." Employees cannot enter this state—never mind remain there—if they stop what they're doing to respond to text messages and e-mails every 10 minutes.

Writing for *The Huffington Post,* Deborah Lovich and Grant Freeland of the Boston Consulting Group (BCG) discuss how they combatted their company's growing turnover problem. In researching the issue of work-life balance, Lovich and Freeland discovered:

> The big problem wasn't so much the long hours and incessant travel. Our consultants expected that when they joined BCG. Rather [it] was the complete lack of predictability or control we had over their daily lives.
>
> When consultants woke up in the morning, they literally had no idea how many hours they would be putting in that day. When asked in the morning how long they expected to work that day, they underestimated by up to 30 percent.[3]

To its credit, BCG took drastic steps to alleviate the issue. The company effectively forced its employees to completely unplug for periods during the week—consequences be damned. Not surprisingly, its turnover rate dropped. Most organizations, however, turn a blind eye to this issue, usually to their employees' and their own detriments.

Inefficiency, Waste, and Severed Relationships

Speaking of relationships, a trusted vendor or partner can be extremely valuable, especially because everyone is so busy today. Great peace of mind stems from handing off work to third parties with the full knowledge that it will be done correctly and on time. By the same token, many organizations waste a tremendous amount of time and money by not being able to articulate their needs. Consider the following story.

The Indefinable Sizzle Factor

Web design and marketing companies like ours have to be comfortable with some degree of ambiguity. We frequently have to translate vague and conflicting information from clients into solid requirements. Our teams must then deliver them. A misinterpreted word or phrase can result in thousands of dollars of design or development time. It's imperative that everyone is on the same page if we want to keep our projects on time and under budget. Design projects are particularly difficult because aesthetics are so personal. "Minimalist" or "cutting edge" usually means different things to different people. As a result, designers must translate and synthesize random bits of information. In the end, they must produce concepts consistent with clients' visions.

Here's the story of our most frustrating communication breakdown in recent history. Individual and company names have been changed.

A few years ago, ABC Agency contracted us to design an application skin for a client (Generico) launching a new product in a very tight time frame. During the sales process, we sent samples of other application skins we had designed for our other clients. Everyone seemed pleased with our team's design abilities, and we were excited to tackle the project.

We worked with ABC to develop mood boards that identified colors, fonts, imagery, and other applications that Generico liked. We then set about designing the first round of concepts. We sent the design concepts over to Jerry, our contact at ABC, before they were shown to Generico. Jerry's reception, however, was lukewarm. "These designs just don't sizzle," he said. We asked for more specific feedback, but Jerry was unable to tell us what wasn't "sizzling." Since we had used the approved mood boards for inspiration, we were a little stumped. Still, we went back to the drawing board and tried another round of concepts.

Again, Jerry was disappointed. He insisted that we had to do something to make the design "sizzle" more. We were dumbfounded. We asked Jerry and ABC for more examples of apps that fit this description. We tried to understand the difference between what we had produced and what ABC thought had "sizzle factor." We spent hours on the phone trying to understand each other, but we just couldn't seem to speak the same language. We also repeatedly asked to speak directly with the client, Generico, to make sure something wasn't being lost in translation, but ABC insisted on protecting the client from "too much communication."

Our designer (Barry) had never failed to please a client throughout his nearly 20 years in the field. As such, the situation particularly frustrated and upset him. Barry was losing sleep. We all had stomachaches. While we tried to please ABC, we were neglecting our other clients, not to mention our families.

Finally, after about two weeks of beating our heads against the wall, I made the executive decision to sever our relationship with ABC. I was worried that if we continued on our current course, the entire project would be at risk and everyone involved would end up suffering in the long run. The breakup conversation wasn't fun, but we felt immediate relief.

Since then, we've been much more cautious about starting creative projects with agencies and other third parties. We try to minimize the number of people giving design direction and feedback on a project. We also take more time to clarify the fuzzy words that clients use to describe their design preferences. Finally, we divide projects into smaller chunks to give us an escape hatch if we need it.

Marisa Smith is the Head Brainiac at The Whole Brain Group, a Web design and social media firm based in Michigan.

Increased Risk of Project Failure

Generally speaking, organizations, departments, groups, and individuals communicate better when it's business as usual. When following standard operating procedure, employees are more likely to receive and understand each other's messages. They know the proper channels to follow and when to escalate issues. In short, they know what's expected of them, especially if they've been on the job for a while and the organization has codified its processes.

All of this changes when employees leave their comfort zones. In my days implementing enterprise systems, I routinely saw deficient communication among salespeople, clients, and consultants. On many key projects, the left hand rarely knew what the right one was doing. This often resulted in omitted or misinterpreted system requirements, missed deadlines, budget overruns, dissatisfied clients, and even the occasional lawsuit.

Consider Healthcare.gov, an IT failure of epic proportions. Launched on October 1, 2013, the website immediately experienced myriad technical problems. Postmortems on the debacle manifested what many seasoned IT professionals instinctively knew: There appeared to be little in the way of actual communication and collaboration among the nearly 50 different consulting firms and software vendors involved with the launch.

The Effect of Bad Communication Channels

The following names are pseudonyms.

Enterprise software systems don't install themselves. They also don't automatically ingest data, build their own models, or integrate with existing systems. Those tasks require people, who need to communicate well if the system is to be built on time, to spec, and under budget. If the communication channel is bad, then the project is at risk.

When I consulted on these kinds of projects all parties involved followed defined processes. Upper management on both the client and consultant sides would meet early on to gather requirements. Requirements were turned into task lists. In turn, those tasks were then broken down into support tickets and assigned to the appropriate person. It sounds orderly and everyone certainly intended it to work that way. In reality, though, it meant that we were unequipped to handle anything that couldn't be turned into a support ticket.

On one notable project, a customer we'll call Upton-Perry hired my firm (ABWH) to build a system to detect fraudulent accounts. Everyone handled their tickets perfectly, except the team responsible for developing the statistical model: mine. Upton-Perry's data made no sense. It didn't take long for my team and me to fall behind. Accounts were assigned mutually incompatible statuses. The defined signals for opening and closing accounts were present for only a subset. Every model we built surfaced approximately half the accounts as highly suspicious. Even under very corrupt business practices, this was very unlikely.

I assigned support tickets to Upton-Perry, noting accounts with unusual activity. They filled out a spreadsheet indicating whether each account seemed unusual and then assigned the ticket back to me. All of the accounts we flagged were marked "normal." Again, this was unlikely even under exceptionally honest business practices. Everyone did everything right, yet nothing worked.

In the end, Upton-Perry paid $2 million for a system it never used. The man-hours that ABWH burned building the system cost approximately the same. Factor in opportunity cost and ABWH probably lost an additional $1 million it could have earned working with a different customer instead.

Why? During the project's postmortem, we discovered that the transactions we were told to look for resided in a completely different system from the one we were given. As one of their database programmers (a person we had never met before) said, the data we were using was "wholly inappropriate." Perhaps, but we had no opportunity to get the right data. The teams and the customer had no means of actually communicating with each other to determine the real issue.

ABWH's management assumed that the model was the problem because the delayed tickets always involved my team. My statements about missing signals fell on deaf ears because they fell outside of existing system parameters. The ingestion teams had followed their checklist. Upton-Perry was responding to alerts. I requested that we share information and solve the problem as a group. Management at Upton-Perry considered this time wasted.

Ultimately, the project metastasized bad communication by restricting how we could communicate with one another. We had all agreed to a procedure in a vacuum. That same procedure proved unworkable in real time. Even worse, neither side recognized the need for a fix. Employees who followed the process simply could not address the real issues because their communication practices didn't allow them, *even when they did everything right.*

Lydia Barman, PhD, is a statistician with 15 years of experience in software development and government contracting. She currently works for a large software company that specializes in statistical consulting.

Other Long-Term Employee Issues

Say what you will about a system or project failure. When a website like Healthcare.gov crashes or a product simply doesn't work, anyone with a modicum of common sense can tell. That isn't necessarily the case with business communication. It often suffers from the appearance of functioning well when, in reality, nothing can be further from the truth.

Many of the problems caused by ineffective business communication ossify over time. This is the equivalent of death by a thousand cuts. Employees might not quit en masse over a single confusing e-mail, boring meeting, or stressful project. Still, these incidents move many average knowledge workers closer to their breaking points. Many if not most workers are already saturated with information, messages, responsibilities, and work. Poor business communication only piles on. It often induces higher turnover and lower employee productivity, morale, and performance.

Net Effect: A Vicious Cycle

Perhaps the most pernicious effect of most contemporary business communication is that it often begets even worse communication. In doing so, it creates a vicious cycle of dysfunction. Habits like commonly using jargon and sending excessive e-mails become ingrained in an organization's culture. Simpler and more effective communication methods are rejected. Intra- and intergroup barriers are created and only grow taller. The organization creates unnecessary friction, ultimately inhibiting its performance.

Next

The last three chapters have covered a great deal of ground. As a whole, Part II described how confusing language and an overdependence on e-mail generally inhibit effective business communication. The cumulative effects of this failure cannot be ignored. They include lower employee productivity and morale, duplicate efforts, inefficiencies, project failures, easily avoidable gaffes, internal political squabbles, and forgone sales and business opportunities.

It is now time to move on to the solution. Fortunately, all hope is not lost. Better business communication is well within our grasp.

Notes

1. Jochim Hansen, and Michaela Wänke, "Truth from Language and Truth from Fit: The Impact of Linguistic Concreteness and Level of Construal on Subjective Truth," November 12, 2010, http://psp.sagepub.com/content/36/11/1576.
2. Max Mallet, "The Most Annoying, Pretentious and Useless Business Jargon," January 26, 2012, www.forbes.com/sites/groupthink/2012/01/26/the-most-annoying-pretentious-and-useless-business-jargon.
3. Deborah Lovich, and Grant Freeland, "How Our Team of Always-On Consultants Learned to Unplug," November 20, 2013, www.huffingtonpost.com/grant-freeland/how-our-team-of-alwayson-_b_4311318.html.

PART

III

MESSAGE
RECEIVED

P art II explained the two problems exacerbating business communication. Part III provides solutions. It's time for us to embrace simpler language and superior tools. I'll introduce three progressive organizations that have moved from theory to practice. They have slayed the e-mail dragon once and for all.

This part includes the following chapters:

- **Chapter 6:** Don't Call It a *Paradigm*: Guidelines for Effective Business Communication
- **Chapter 7:** Words and Context: Building a Solid Communication Foundation
- **Chapter 8:** Life Beyond E-Mail: How Progressive Organizations Are Using New Tools to Enable More Effective Collaboration and Communication

6

Don't Call It a *Paradigm*

Guidelines for Effective Business Communication

> *The ability to express an idea is well nigh as important as the idea itself.*
>
> —Bernard Baruch

Imagine that your mother is undergoing what should be a routine appendectomy. You are not a doctor but the hospital has agreed to let you watch the procedure. All appears to be going well, although you're a bit lost. You've never even heard of the words the staff is using: *gastrointestinal tract, pneumoperitoneum,* and *peritoneal cavity.*

All of a sudden, an unexpected, life-threatening complication ensues. Two surgeons discuss the best way to deal with it. They move around the room quickly, speaking in a rapid-fire style replete with a shorthand you can't begin to follow. You are justifiably scared for your mother's well-being, but you take some comfort in the fact that the members of the surgical team are effectively communicating with one another. They understand these polysyllabic medical terms even though you don't.

This story illustrates that there are times in which speaking in everyday English is not desirable or even possible. This book stresses the merits of simplicity in language in business contexts. At the same time, though, there is no one right way to communicate.

English as a Second Language: When to Speak Lawsonese

Like many occupations, implementing enterprise systems sometimes involves engaging in extremely technical conversations. One particularly vivid example comes to mind.

In 2002, I consulted for a leading educational organization in Pittsburgh, Pennsylvania. A colleague and I were talking about the best way to solve a particularly vexing Lawson Software data problem. The discussion necessitated an advanced understanding of the inner workings of Lawson's applicant tracking system and its admittedly esoteric nomenclature.

About 15 minutes into our snappy dialogue, I chuckled and remarked that, at this moment, we had to be the only two people on earth talking about this arcane subject. He agreed. To an outsider, we must have appeared to be speaking a foreign language, even though my colleague and I completely understood what the other was saying. A few minutes later, the two of us figured out a viable solution. Not once did either of us say, "What are you talking about?"

Sometimes it's completely normal, beneficial, and even necessary for people to communicate in manners that others would find abstruse. In the words of Friedrich Nietzsche, "Style should be suited to the specific person with whom you wish to communicate." Airline pilots, doctors, lawyers, and others who work in specialized fields often don't have time to make things plain to laypersons. In fact, there's no need. Relying on shorthand saves valuable time, but only when the other parties speak the same language. These types of discussions, however, are largely ineffective with general public. Too often, we forget that truism at work. As a result, communication suffers.

This short chapter offers some general guidelines to promote effective business communication. These protocols are subject to two caveats. First, they are not universal. In each case, some pretty big exceptions exist. Second, they only increase the chances that a message is received. They guarantee nothing.

Language

Buzzwords are toxic. They significantly lower the chance that your audience will receive and understand your message.

Embrace simple language.

For every person who is impressed by your use of jargon, 10 more either don't really understand you or think that you're bloviating.

Don't mistake an audience's silence for understanding.

The more potentially confusing the topic, the greater the need for clarity and simplicity.

If you need to explain a complicated issue, then your message is much more likely to be received if you use the simplest possible terms.

If you're not sure if your audience will understand a term or phrase, either don't use it or make sure to define it and properly explain it.

Back in my HR days at CapitalOne, I used to teach sexual harassment classes. Attendees would often ask, "Will I get in trouble if I do X?" I explained that there was no list of commandments. I couldn't possibly name all of the things that employees could and could not do at work. I would, however, give them what I thought was a good general rule of thumb: If you're not sure about whether something is appropriate, don't do it.

The same rule applies with the use of newfangled terms. If you're not sure whether your audience will understand a word or phrase, either use something else or carefully define and explain it.

E-Mail

Aim for Inbox Zero.

You may never get there, but it's a worthwhile goal.

In lieu of using your inbox to read articles and blog posts, use an app like Pocket or Evernote or an RSS Reader.*

You will be more focused on actual messages, not content.

After three e-mails, someone needs to pick up the phone.

Refuse to engage in e-mail conversations.

Frequency, Quantity, and Use

Increasing the length of the message lowers the chance that the audience will receive and understand it.

No, everything can't be compressed into a sound bite. As a general rule, though, less is usually more.

The greater the number of discrete communications you send, the greater the chance that you will overwhelm and alienate your audience.

Try to make your point in a single e-mail or, better yet, a phone conversation.

Use something other than an e-mail application for task management.

You're in trouble if your inbox also serves as your to-do list. You'll inadvertently check your messages while trying to add, complete, or update a task. As Mike Vardy writes on LifeHack:

---

* Examples include Feedly, NewsBlur, and The Old Reader. You can even use HootSuite.

The barrier to using a task management application is often because people "feel" or "think" they can use their e-mail application to manage their tasks with folders and the like. You can try, but you won't be nearly as effective or efficient. I challenge you to use a separate piece of software (or, if you're using Outlook, use the To Do component) to manage your tasks rather than using your e-mail application to manage your tasks. Stick with it through the initial adjustment, and I bet you'll see your workflow improve.

No matter what e-mail app or service you use, unless you put the discipline and boundaries in place when it comes to using this valuable communication tool, you're doing it wrong.

So what's the e-mail problem? It's not the technology; it's the people using the technology. And until we fix that e-mail will always appear . . . broken.[1]

Timing

Use e-mail as a last resort if you need an immediate answer or response.
Exhaust all other methods first.

Slow down. Fight the competitive urge to be the first to respond to a group e-mail or communication. Ask yourself if an immediate response is really required—or any response, for that matter.
E-mail usually begets more e-mail. In particularly political environments, failing to instantly respond to an e-mail chain sends the message that you're slacking off, out of the loop, or not important. As such, there's a tendency for everyone copied on an e-mail to chime in with their thoughts, no matter how mundane and superfluous they might be.

Is this reaction certainly understandable and even natural? Of course. We frequently accede to the pressure to respond immediately. In the corporate world, employees who think about an issue run the risk of being perceived as doing nothing. But here's the rub: It shouldn't be. There are tremendous benefits to contemplation, especially on thorny issues. In the words of Jonathan Smallwood, a cognitive neuroscientist at the University of York, in England:

> Idle mental processing encourages creativity and solutions because imagining your problem when you aren't in it is not the same as reality. Using your imagination means you are in fact rethinking the problem in a novel way.[2]

Depending on the context, there's nothing wrong with doing nothing.

Selecting a Communications Medium

Ask yourself these three questions:

1. What's the goal of the communication?
2. Who's your audience?
3. What's the best mode to communicate your message?

If others will likely need access to the information in the future, then e-mail is the worst possible medium.

Search within e-mail applications has certainly improved over the last 15 years, but a great deal of the valuable content within messages and attachments resides in the inboxes of individual employees.[*] It might as well be on the moon. If that employee is out of the office, asleep, or otherwise unavailable, it's virtually impossible for others to access the information.

Conversations started on Facebook, Twitter, LinkedIn, and e-mail are often best moved to a phone, Skype, or a coffee shop.
Many topics should be discussed in person.

After you escalate a conversation from e-mail to the phone, stick to your guns.
If you leave a voice mail after exchanging a series of e-mails or text messages, you've effectively said, "Let's talk—for real." The recipient may "respond" to your voice mail with a text message or e-mail. This is a trap.

Don't let someone avoid an in-person conversation. Make it clear that you need to actually talk to—or meet with—that person. A terse, four-word reply of "We need to talk" usually gets the point home. By reengaging via text or e-mail, you are taking a step back. You are implicitly saying that those mediums are acceptable forms of communication.

Handling the Fallout

Ignore as many of these guidelines as you like. Make up your own.
Different tools and communication styles work for different people.

---

[*] Not to mention a veritable gold mine of data about data (i.e., metadata).

Expect blowback. Some people will not adhere to your guidelines.

Decide how you're going to handle them.

Don't be afraid to politely invoke your new communications guidelines.

Old habits die hard. Depending on your audience, you may have to tread lightly. Other times, you can guide or even dictate the format of the conversation.

Next

This chapter introduced several high-level principles designed to promote effective communications at work. The next two are more tactical in nature. They provide more specific advice about how we can maximize the probability that our messages are received. Chapter 7 provides tips on using language. Chapter 8 introduces some new communications tools and, more important, profiles three progressive companies that are actually using them.

Notes

1. Michael Vardy, 'Mike, "The Real Problem with Email," August 22, 2012, www.lifehack.org/articles/technology/the-real-problem-with-email.html.
2. Kate Murphy, "No Time to Think," July 25, 2014, www.nytimes.com/2014/07/27/sunday-review/no-time-to-think.html.

7

Words and Context

Building a Solid Communication Foundation

If you can't explain it simply, you don't understand it well enough.

—Albert Einstein

Some people know what they want to be when they grow up from an early age. Not me. I changed careers several times. Up until six years ago, I called myself as a *systems consultant*. With the notable exception of the lovable Martin Prince on *The Simpsons*,[*] does any kid plan on becoming one?

It's fair to say that I kind of fell into the field, using the process of elimination to make the best out of an undesirable professional situation. In 1997, I was doing pure HR work. It was anything but ideal for me, and I needed to find something else. I couldn't realistically make a clean break, though. I had to play the long game.

A Trip Down Memory Lane

From 1998 to 2000, I worked at Merck in a hybrid capacity. I spent about 60 percent of my time on a global PeopleSoft project and the other 40 percent doing more traditional HR work (recruiting, compensation, and general administration). Put mildly, I was much better at—and interested in—the former than the latter. After leaving Merck, I worked at Lawson Software as a full-blown systems consultant. My rationale for gravitating toward this type of work was simple: I liked it. I was good at it. In 2002, I decided to hang out my own shingle. I believed that I was disciplined enough to handle the challenges of self-employment.

In Chapter 3, I listed my issues with management gurus. (See "Consultants, MBAs, and the Management 'Scientists.'") I'll be the first to admit, though, that consultants are often whipping boys for issues that are far beyond their control. Toss in frequent travel and untenable situations, and it should be no surprise that annual

---

[*] See http://tinyurl.com/qzvmgpx.

turnover at most consulting firms hovers around 20 percent.[1] The profession is certainly no picnic, regardless of who signs your checks, and I scraped my knees more than a few times early in my career.

I could handle the data and technology issues entailed in migrating my clients from one complex enterprise system. Since the age of 12, I have known my way around a computer. I graduated from Carnegie Mellon University, and my technical skills have always been strong. Even the poets at CMU learn how to code. (In September 2013, the site HerCampus.com ranked it the geekiest school in the nation.* Go Tartans.)

In those early days, though, I struggled with the nontechnical aspects of the job (i.e., the warm and fuzzy side). I hadn't yet learned that technology is inherently political. I wrestled with delivering bad news to my clients and dealing with internal corporate politics. As a result, I found myself in the middle of my fair share of kerfuffles. It didn't take me long to realize that some degree of conflict was par for the course in the consulting and technology worlds. Over time, I improved my communications skills, and my clients and colleagues were less likely to shoot the messenger (me).

The shooting metaphor has endured for centuries for one simple reason: We do it all the time. It's easy to criticize even an empathetic bearer of bad news, never mind a callous one. No, there's not an easy way to announce a mass layoff, but we can maximize the chances that our messages will be received. As a starting point, we can choose our words judiciously and deliberately.

This chapter begins with a look at the world of words and then offers some general communications tips.

The World of Words

If you still doubt the power of words, consider the following story from Robert B. Cialdini's best-selling book *Influence: The Psychology of Persuasion*. The author describes a famous study conducted by Harvard psychologist Ellen Langer:

> A well-known principle of human behavior says that when we ask someone to do us a favor we will be more successful if we provide a reason. People simply like to have reasons for what they do. Langer demonstrated this unsurprising fact by asking a small

---

* See http://tinyurl.com/mgpscwh.

favor of people waiting in line to use a library copying machine: *Excuse me, I have five pages. May I use the Xerox machine because I am in a rush?* The effectiveness of this request-plus-reason was nearly total: Ninety-four percent of those asked let her skip ahead of them in line. Compare this success rate to the results when she made the request only. *Excuse me, I have five pages. May I use the Xerox machine?* Under those circumstances, only 60 percent of those asked complied. At first glance, it appears that the crucial difference between the two requests was the additional information provided by the words "because I'm in a rush." But a third type of request tried by Langer showed that this was not the case. It seems that it was not the whole series of words, but the first one, "because," that made the difference. Instead of including a real reason for compliance, Langer's third type of request used the word "because" and then, adding nothing new, merely restated the obvious: *Excuse me, I have five pages. May I use the Xerox machine because I have to make some copies?* The result was that once again nearly all (93 percent) agreed, even though no real reason, no new information, was added to justify their compliance.

Something tells me that a request shrouded in jargon would not have had anywhere near the desired effect. *Excuse me, I have five pages. May I use the Xerox machine because my manager has empowered me with blue-skying a value-added new paradigm going forward?*

The Perils of the Single Sentence

To communicate better at work, start by recognizing that, while writing is subjective, your choice of words matters. Arguments are often better and more clearly expressed as several sentences, not as a single mega-sentence. For instance, Patty McCord used to serve as the chief talent officer at Netflix. Today she runs her own consulting shop. In 2014, she gave a presentation on HR at Netflix for the *Harvard Business Review*. Here's an excerpt from one of her opening slides:

> The actual company values, as opposed to the nice-sounding values, are shown by who gets rewarded, promoted, or let go.[2]

I wholeheartedly agree with the sentiment, but terrible English muddies the message. Circuitous sentences like these with superfluous clauses are downright confusing. Why not split the single, run-on sentence into two or more comprehensible ones? And why not lose the passive voice while we're at it? How's this instead?

> Any company can espouse obvious dictums like "people and culture matter." In reality, though, an organization demonstrates its actual values not through its words, but by its actions: promotions, reward systems, and how it handles employee exits.

Using two or three sentences usually yields greater understanding than a single one does. Table 7.1 presents another example of a confusing mega-sentence.

Table 7.1   The Perils of the Single Sentence

Bad Phrasing	Better Phrasing
Bernard Marr's book *The Intelligent Company* outlines how companies and managers can become more intelligent by creating a culture that focuses on the things that matter the most and by making decisions based on real facts rather than fiction and gut feel.	In his new book *The Intelligent Company*, Bernard Marr outlines how companies and managers can become more intelligent. They do this in two ways. First, they create a culture that focuses on the things that matter the most. Second, they make decisions based on real facts rather than fiction and gut feel.

Don't cram too much into one sentence or bullet point.

Get Active: Minimize the Passive Voice

You probably have heard the expression "Mistakes were made." Although its roots lie with Ulysses S. Grant in 1876, today more people are familiar with it in the context of Richard Nixon and the Watergate scandal. It serves as a type of non-apology; one that admits wrongdoing without *really* admitting it. The passive voice intentionally deflects blame. If you want others to truly understand your messages, though, use the active voice as much as possible. Table 7.2 presents a few examples of this simple trick.

Table 7.2   Passive vs. Active Voice

Bad Phrasing (A)	Better Phrasing (B)	Word Difference (A-B)
Ideas are just a multiplier of execution.	Ideas simply multiply execution.	3
This task needs to be performed by John.	John needs to do this task.	2
What he's doing is breaking down barriers and changing the company for the better.	He's breaking down barriers and changing the company for the better.	3
It was determined by the committee that the report was inconclusive.	The committee determined that the report was inconclusive.[3]	3

Short and Simple: Nail the Opening

You never get a second chance to make a first impression. It's a cliché, but not without reason. With so much content on the Web on even the most arcane of topics, nobody can watch every video, read every blog post and article, and follow every expert on social networks. To this end, it's never been more essential for the opening salvo of a speech or article to make an immediate impact.

Think about how each of the following articles begins:

- "The NY Post case-studied our company's approach of harnessing social media energy through internal social media platforms that benefit the employer and foster a more engaged workforce."[4]
- "In 2012, Dave Morin was a tech industry celebrity."[5]

With no other information, which of the two articles would you prefer to read? I'm betting on the second. The author is Nick Bilton, a *New York Times* columnist and the author of the excellent book *Hatching Twitter.*

That clunky 27-word first sentence comes from Eliyahu Federman, author of an article titled "Internal Social Networks Increase Workplace Productivity" on the popular website Social Media Today. Federman serves as the Senior Vice President and Chief Communications Officer of deal site 1SaleADay.com. He may understand the value of "enterprise social networks," but he could certainly use some pointers on how to draw readers in. I doubt that he's heard of *tl;dr.*[*]

---

[*] Slang for *too long; didn't read.*

Synonyms: The Sexy Syllable Savers

Effective communicators often use shorter words in lieu of longer ones whenever possible. This is even more important with new and potentially vexing topics. Unfortunately, many people ignore this general guideline. For instance, consider the article "Surviving & Thriving in the Current Risk Management & Regulatory Environment" by Bill Kramer on the website Wall Street and Tech.[6] That title is a bit of a mouthful, and it's common for websites these days to also include relatively pithy article subtitles. These subtitles can increase the odds that viewers will stick around and become readers, and maybe even subscribers. In this case, the article is subtitled, "How financial institutions can leverage compliance initiatives to improve their business with a 360-degree view of the customer."

Leverage compliance initiatives to improve their business with a 360-degree view of the customer? Say that five times in a row.

Before continuing, note that Kramer does not appear to be a full-time reporter. According to his bio, he serves as the senior vice president of product management at Linedata Lending & Leasing. I mention this tidbit because, as I know from my stint at writing for Inc.com, contributors often have very little input into the titles of their posts. Site community managers and editors use tools like Google's Keyword Planner* to maximize ad revenue, page views, time spent on site, and "shares" (e.g., retweets and Facebook likes). See anything missing from the list? Readability is a key omission.

Instead of that verbose subtitle, how about this one?

How financial institutions can use compliance initiatives to improve their business with a 360-degree view of the customer.

Better, let's keep trimming. How about this eight-word sentence instead?

Use compliance initiatives to better understand your customers.

Again, less is almost always more for these types of articles. Use your words and syllables sparingly. By shortening and simplifying the article's subtitle, the phrase *compliance initiatives* no longer seems like utter gibberish. On the contrary, now it seems really important. After all, they might help businesses understand their customers better! The reader is now more prone to think, "Maybe I *should* read that article."

---

* Keyword Planner is "a free AdWords tool that helps you build Search Network campaigns by finding keyword ideas and estimating how they may perform." See https://adwords.google.com/KeywordPlanner.

Are you stuck for a good synonym?* Check out the Visual Thesaurus† and the new thesaurus.com. The latter lets users filter by a synonym's relevance, complexity, and length. I regularly use both of these sites myself.

Here's a final tip on synonyms: Use them! I've seen four-sentence paragraphs with eight uses of the word *platform*. I've heard executives drop the phrase *Big Data analytics* and *cloud-based solutions* in just about every sentence during a five-minute interview. For the listener, this quickly gets repetitive. Try to find suitable substitutes. Doing so will make you sound more intelligent, learned, and less robotic. More important, others will be more apt to receive your message.

KISS as Often as Possible

Think back to Einstein's words at the beginning of this chapter. (If you haven't figured this out by now, I enjoy a good quote.) Here's another gem by the American poet Charles Bukowski: "The shortest distance between two points is often unbearable." There's no shortage of businesspeople who have either not heard this sage advice or routinely ignore it. They communicate in ways that make things as complicated as possible and, sadly, that's exactly how they like it.

KISS is the well-worn acronym that stands for "keep it simple, stupid." Simple communication is almost always better than its complicated counterpart. If someone asks you a convoluted question, you can rarely go wrong by responding with the shortest and most straightforward answer possible. Remember this even if there's much more depth to a particular issue, as several examples in the next section will show.

Think of KISS as a general rule for effective business communications, not an absolute one. We know that certain conversations must be technical and esoteric, at least as far as the general public is concerned. Put differently, just because you *can* complicate your message doesn't mean that you *should*.

Mind Your Acronyms

In the classic 1987 film *Wall Street*, ambitious young stock trader Bud Fox (Charlie Sheen) looks at himself in a mirror, adjusts his tie, and says, "Life all comes down to a few moments. This is one of them."

---

* Not bad alliteration for a geek, eh?

† See http://www.visualthesaurus.com.

After months of cold calling, Fox is minutes away from pitching billionaire investor Gordon Gekko (Michael Douglas). Fox knows that he'll only get one bite at this apple; he'd better make the most of the opportunity. What he says—and how he says it—will go a long way toward determining his future.

We often forget this lesson at work. The following story illustrates the perils of launching a series of acronym bombs,[*] especially in the first minute of a pitch or presentation.

Acronym Soup + Magic Numbers = Utter Confusion

I've been on the receiving end of tens of thousands of pitches for new start-ups. Some are amazing. Many suck. I have a strong point of view that the first minute matters the most. You have 30 seconds to tell me what you do and then another 30 seconds to tell me why I care. It doesn't matter whether we are in an elevator (in which case you might need to talk faster to get it all within 30 seconds), a demo day presentation at an accelerator, my conference room, or a walk around my hometown of Boulder, Colorado. Start with the punch line, but speak in that language known as English. Yeah, I know all the buzzwords and acronyms, especially the three-letter acronyms (TLAs) for most of the stuff I invest in. My brain needs some time to warm up.

Consider the following intro to a pitch that I recently received. Have someone read this to you so you actually hear it. This will make it even more difficult to absorb.

> *Fugly* (a pseudonym) is a SaaS-based BYOT company aimed at helping the F1000 comply with HIPAA for their ACA compliance. We've quickly turned on 10 customers with a total MRR of $53K, an LTV of $250K, CAC[†] of $100k, and a magic number of 1.2.

My response to this terrible word soup was "So, what do you do?" Largely based on its presentation, we passed on investing in the company.

Brad Feld serves as the Managing Director at Foundry Group. He has penned several books, including the award-winning *Startup Communities: Building an Entrepreneurial Ecosystem in Your City.*

---

[*] For what I think is an amusing comic on acronyms starring yours truly, check out http://tinyurl.com/phil-comic.

[†] *CAC* stands for customer acquisition cost. LTV (loan-to-value ratio) is a lending risk assessment ratio that financial institutions and other lenders examine before approving a mortgage.

Think about it. If a morass of acronyms will confuse an experienced and successful investor like Feld, what does that mean if you are pitching someone with lesser credentials? Using excessive jargon and acronyms to sound impressive is likely to have the opposite effect.

Embrace the Power of Questions

Rather than saying that "our product does X," why not ask—and answer—a simple question about fulfilling a genuine need? In his book *A More Beautiful Question: The Power of Inquiry to Spark Breakthrough Ideas*, Warren Berger stresses the importance of asking, not telling. Questions often serve as extraordinarily powerful communication vehicles.

Table 7.3 shows three one-sentence, jargon-filled company descriptions. In the second column are question-based analogues. Which ones make you yawn? Which ones make you want to know more?

The verbose descriptions in the left-hand column don't exactly lend themselves to understanding. Aside from being considerably shorter, the descriptions on the right are much more evocative. They make the reader wonder, What if? Through relatively simple questions, they engender understanding.

Table 7.3 Confusing Company Descriptions and Simpler Alternatives

Confusing, Feature-Laden Approach	Simpler, Question-Driven Approach
Alleantia is an Internet of Things (IoT) company supplying an HW and OS-independent software platform for implementing native Web and mobile monitoring and control applications for any kind of device and system.	Want to develop apps for the Internet of Things? Alleantia lets you do just that.
Appticles is an online platform suited for content creators (bloggers, small and medium publishing houses, but also data-driven enterprises) that enables them to effortlessly reach their mobile audience by packaging their existing content into cross-platform mobile Web applications.	Wouldn't it be cool to quickly reach your audience no matter where they are? Appticles is just the thing for you.
Pocket is a cross-platform app that seamlessly enables the sharing of valuable social-media content.	Want to easily store articles on the fly to read at a later date on any device? Meet Pocket.

Source: Company descriptions aggregated by DataFox.

Be Precise

In his controversial 2014 book *Flash Boys: A Wall Street Revolt*, Michael Lewis recounts the story of high-frequency trading firms spending untold billions of dollars to shave microseconds off of trade-execution times. Lewis's riveting account of the world of high-stakes automated trading tangentially touches on something I've seen countless times in my career: the conflict between business folks and technology folks. In one particularly resonant passage about a brilliant but irksome Russian programmer named Zoran, Lewis writes:

> His first few months on the job, Zoran drove everyone nuts. Lacking a market crisis, he proceeded to create a social one. They'd tell him about some new feature they had thought to introduce into the system and ask, "Will this make the system harder to manage?" To which Zoran would reply, "It depends on your definition of 'harder.'" Or they would ask him if some small change in the system would cause the system to become less stable—to which Zoran would reply, "It depends on your definition of 'stable.'" Every question he answered with an uneasy chuckle, followed by some other question. A rare exception came when he was asked, "Why do you always answer a question with another question?" "Clarity," he said.

Most techies can empathize with Zoran's plight. When it comes to technical matters such as developing apps, deploying systems, and writing code, businesspeople often fail to provide sufficient clarity and precision. This is particularly acute when those "from the line" don't fully understand new technologies. The consequences of a missed requirement or bad design are lost on them. For my part, I've seen this movie many times before. Here's one of those times.

That Report

In 2008, I consulted for New York & Company (NYCO), a women's wear-to-work retailer with headquarters in Manhattan. During the nine months on which I helped NYCO implement Lawson Software, I built more than 500 reports and 50 databases. Every day, I was swimming in data. At any given point, I was working on several dozen items that touched interdependent data sources, interfaces, and key systems.

(Continued)

(*Continued*)

Yet, for the first few months of the project, most NYCO employees would ask me about the status of "that report." This would confuse me. I would make light of the question, usually with a jocular response like "Oh, yeah . . . the one with the numbers. *That one.* What about it?"

Eventually, the NYCO folks came to appreciate my need for precision. I'm no mind reader. I couldn't help them unless they helped me first. Because I assigned unique names to my reports, my clients knew that I would understand that AR-123 analyzed accounts receivable. PR-345 listed employee overtime wages by state. It would have been silly for me to apply generic labels such as *payroll report* or *finance report*.

NYCO employees started putting their questions to me in the context of specific reports. After that, our communication became much more streamlined and effective, and my productivity skyrocketed. I no longer had to answer their preliminary questions with questions.

Keep Verbing and Nominalizations to a Minimum

We should *partner* on that.

He's *transitioning* into a new role.

The company is *pivoting* to a different model.

At some point, the nouns *partner, pivot,* and *transition* became verbs—as have many others. Some of these neologisms work better than others, but most reek of obfuscation. This practice is called *verbing* and has earned the ire of language mavens for centuries. Consider an editorial in Britain's *Guardian* newspaper 20 years ago. It implores English speakers to cease engaging in this "filthy" habit and forever end a practice that has:

> seemed increasingly to be defacing the English language: the pressing of decent defenseless nouns, which have gone about their business for centuries without giving the mildest offence or provocation, into service as verbs, sometimes in their original form but quite often after a process of horrible mutilation.

Writing for the *New York Times*, Henry Hitchings takes these *nominalizations* to task. He correctly points out that many people "associate [these terms] with legalese, bureaucracy, corporate jive, advertising or the more hollow kinds of academic prose. Writing packed with nominalizations is commonly regarded as slovenly, obfuscatory, pretentious, or merely ugly."[7]

I can't stop you from desecrating "defenseless" nouns. Just be mindful of the considerable drawbacks of verbing. It is far from universally liked, and it is often unnecessary.[*]

Communication Context, Awareness, and Technique

This book so far has attempted to establish that the use of jargon contravenes effective business communication. It is generally ill advised. Making a concerted effort to avoid buzzwords by itself, however, should not be mistaken for communicating well. There's more nuance to it than that. If we want others to *really* receive our messages without a raft of follow-up questions, quizzical looks, and Google searches, then we need to apply a little discretion. This is especially true when we're communicating with individuals and audiences for the first time.

Put differently, business communication does not take place in an empty semantic forest. Content may be king these days, but context is close behind. We would do well to consider the situational factors surrounding our messages. They can be more important than the messages themselves.

Note that I am intentionally cherry-picking some of the most useful, *general* communication tips about context and audiences. It's difficult to list hard-and-fast rules because so much hinges on any audience's makeup. For instance, consider material that might be considered way too technical for a Society for Human Resource Management (SHRM) event. That same message may very well be standard operating procedure at a geek-laden security conference like DEF CON or Black Hat.

Finally, I am well aware of the extensive works of others on the art of presenting. Authors such as Dale Carnegie, Garr Reynolds, and Nancy Duarte are just a few who have written extensively about the subject. Beyond public speaking, there's no shortage of highly informative guides to grammar and business writing. Two of my favorites include *Eats, Shoots & Leaves: The Zero Tolerance Approach to Punctuation* and *Action Grammar: Fast, No-Hassle Answers on Everyday Usage and Punctuation*. It would be impossible to condense volumes of sage wisdom on these topics. I'm not even going to try.

---

[*] A friend of mine invited me to his birthday party via Facebook a few years ago. The title of the event: "Paul Is Transitioning to 30." *Sheesh.*

Unless You're Absolutely Sure, Assume Nothing

Imagine taking an advanced college-level calculus course on differential equations without any background on the subject. You'd be lost. Fortunately, every course syllabus contains prerequisites, even if nothing is required. Calculus III typically requires the successful completion of Calculus I and II. Somewhere along the line, many speakers forget the benefit of providing advanced knowledge.

One of the best ways to quickly lose your audience is to assume familiarity with a key term or acronym. This happens far too frequently. For instance, at a conference I attended a few years ago, an executive kept using obscure acronyms. After about the twentieth one, I raised my hand and asked her, "What do ABC and XYZ mean?" I didn't care if I appeared ignorant in front of the 200 attendees; I was trying to follow her and just couldn't. It turns out that I was not the only one in the dark. Later that day, several individuals privately thanked me for asking my question. They didn't know what those acronyms stood for either.

The Novelty of Asking

You probably haven't heard of *Hadoop*.* If not, don't fret. You're certainly not alone. Most people who write, speak, and work in the data world have known about it for years. Put simply, Hadoop and frameworks like it allow organizations to store, access, and interpret enormous amounts of data. Companies such as Amazon, Facebook, Google, Netflix, and Yahoo handle petabytes of mostly unstructured (read: not Excel-friendly) data. New and powerful technologies like Hadoop are at the core of these companies' internal operations.

In May 2014, I spoke to 300 employees of a library system in Minnesota about Big Data, the subject of my prior two books. Rather than assuming that everyone or even most people had heard of Hadoop, I simply asked the question. Fewer than 30 people raised their hands—around 10 percent of the attendees.

Equipped with that new information, I explained at a very high level why these successful companies use Hadoop and its ilk. I also provided an everyday example. (I asked them to imagine that they were all computers and I was doing a Google search.) As I spoke, I looked around the room. People were nodding their heads. I was truly communicating. Just about everyone appeared to be receiving my message.

---

* There's much more to it, but Hadoop is an open-source software framework for storage and large-scale processing of datasets on clusters of commodity hardware.

By no means does this anecdote make me exceptional. It just means that I am aware of the fact that my audience may not possess the same level of knowledge on certain topics that I do. Foolish is the speaker who makes that mistake. Why does a conference organizer hire speakers in the first place? After all, aren't the ability to effectively confer new concepts and offer a fresh perspective high on the list? Speakers need not avoid acronyms and industry-specific terminology altogether. It usually takes about 30 seconds to proffer a brief definition and explanation of a key term.

Recognize That One Size Does Not Fit All

Using jargon is perhaps the single easiest way to ensure that a message is not received. A close second, though, might be ignoring the different ages, backgrounds, communication styles, and sizes of your audience. Nobody can concurrently deliver a different message to 10 diverse people in 10 different ways. As the following stories will illustrate, whenever possible, it behooves us to customize our messages and even segment our audiences.

Technical Proficiency   Although most white-collar employees these days are computer-literate, levels of comfort and knowledge on technology matters often run the gamut. Some jobs require a detailed knowledge of technical esoterica. Others necessitate only a cursory understanding of certain topics.

One Problem, One Solution, and Two Conversations

In 2004, I did some consulting for South Jersey Gas (SJG), a utility that provides safe, efficient natural gas to more than 300,000 customers in southern New Jersey. SJG had purchased Lawson Software and intended to supplant its legacy enterprise systems. SJG needed help and hired me through a third party to work my magic.

Toward the end of the project, the team discovered a potential showstopper: The Lawson employee overtime calculation program (PR132) did not work the way that SJG required. Note that SJG could not just skip running PR132; organizations are legally obligated to pay overtime to their nonexempt employees. It's federal law. What to do?

Upon making this discovery, the project manager immediately called a meeting to discuss options and hopefully determine the best course of action. Its two options were:

(Continued)

(*Continued*)

1. To postpone the go-live date until someone could develop an acceptable alternative to calculate overtime. This was a very expensive proposition.
2. To customize PR132.

Customizing any batch program* like PR132 is a risky gambit for several reasons. First, doing so violates standard vendor support contracts. Second, payroll programs are sequential and interwoven. (You can't calculate overtime until employee hours have been loaded.) Tweaking one program may inadvertently break another. Finally, even if the revised calculation works for the time being, a subsequent upgrade or vendor patch may break it, wreaking havoc throughout the organization and exposing it to legal issues.

My manager told me about the two options under consideration. I suggested a third way—one that would avoid the perils of customizing the program while theoretically keeping us on track. I could build a Microsoft Access database that would do the following:

- Take the data generated by PR132
- Modify the data according to SJG's specifications
- Reload the data into the system

I also mentioned that I could do all of this in such a way that required zero technical skill and database knowledge from SJG's payroll and IT folks. They could just type in a date, hit a button, and let my Access database take care of the rest. My manager loved the idea. He told me to build the prototype while he sought approval from the project's steering committee.

My suggestion wasn't anything extraordinary. Consultants and IT professionals routinely build these types of extract, transform, and load (ETL) processes for their clients.

SJG senior management concurred and quickly signed off on the fix. Afterward, I had to explain to two very different SJG employees what I had done: Paul, the database administrator (DBA), and Carol, a very friendly but admittedly technology-challenged woman who worked in the benefits department. Both were in the room when I realized that there was no way that I could effectively tell them what they needed to know at the same time. I asked Carol if she wouldn't mind getting a cup of coffee and returning to my office in 10 minutes. She did so.

I explained to Paul in very specific terms the new ETL process. I reviewed the technical documentation with him. I explained the affected database tables and fields. Paul reviewed my checklist and asked a few pointed questions. He had to fully understand what to do—and when—for thousands of people to be

---

* Batch programs in enterprise systems are extremely powerful. They create, modify, and/or delete data. All else being equal, simple listings are much less dangerous to tweak, as they only pull records from existing database tables.

paid properly. After all, consultants aren't around forever. After 10 minutes, Paul shook my hand and said, "Thanks, I got it. This is *exactly* what I needed."

Carol returned a few minutes later and asked what was going on. At a very high level, I explained the database and what it did. She squinted and asked me, "There's more to this, right?" I replied, "Absolutely. I'm happy to tell you about it if you like." "No," she said with a smile. "This is perfect. Thank you."

I knew at that moment that I had become a pretty good consultant. I not only suggested a viable solution to a critical issue, but I also built it and communicated it effectively to two very different types of people. Most important, in each case, the message was received. If I tried to have that conversation with both Carol and Paul in the room, I would have failed miserably. A detailed, step-by-step, technical discussion would have satisfied Paul but confused and, in all likelihood, irritated Carol. A high-level, generic explanation about moving data around would have placated Carol but left Paul wanting and, even worse, unable to do his job.

Age Differences I knew from working with Carol and Paul that they were roughly the same age. Of course, in the context of my time at SJG, that didn't really matter. It didn't change the fact that I had to deliver my message in very different ways. I suspect that I would have had a more difficult time, though, if one was significantly younger than the other. More generally, it's silly to apply a one-size-fits-all rule to communicating with people of different generations.

Communicating Employee Benefits

It used to be easier to "know your audience." Dale Carnegie's work suggests that you should know what your audience is interested in before you start. Nelson Mandela stressed the importance of speaking the audience's language, not your own. Linda Flowers emphasizes that you know what the audience already knows—and *how they feel about it*.

All of this is great advice, but it's not enough today. For most of these experts' careers, the organizational communication options were fairly straightforward: paper, face-to-face, or on the phone.

Ultimately, these ideas remain on target as they highlight the importance of the audience over the author or presenter. For example, my goal isn't about what I want to write, but rather about what I want you to understand from that writing. These ideas are important, but you also have to know how to get your ideas in front of your audience. You can't just focus on the human aspects of what they will think when they receive your communication. You need to manage a

(Continued)

(Continued)

constantly shifting set of communication tools (everything from a letter to a virtual reality site) and the broader reach of your communication when everyone in the world can often see what you write, say, or do.

I recently had the chance to work with the Certified Equity Professional Institute (CEPI) on a guidebook for communication about employee stock plans. Many employees do not take advantage of their companies' stock purchase plans, even when offered at a discount. Often the employees say they didn't know or didn't understand their choices. The companies and employees can both lose in this situation. The company loses because employment benefits aren't yielding the expected results. Employees who miss out on valuable investment opportunities lose as well.

In our research at the CEPI at Santa Clara University, we found that Facebook and transportation company Norfolk Southern were both successful in their communications. Employees generally understand their choices.* Not surprisingly, given very different employee bases, these two companies communicated in very different ways.

Many of Facebook's employees are working in their first proper jobs. (As of this writing, the average employee age is 26 years old.) As such, many have limited knowledge of corporate benefits. The company uses a variety of tools to communicate with its employees, including:

- A private Facebook group devoted to information about their equity programs
- A moderated Wiki (all employees can edit the online site, but HR staff keep an eye on the answers)
- Some e-mail for personal responses
- Hardcopy for job offers or performance summary letters that talk about equity compensation

Norfolk Southern offers equity to its nonunion employees. Most of the employees with equity in the company are over 55 and start out with limited understanding of stock plans. The company relies heavily on a third party to handle benefit-related communications. Employees learn about their benefits via e-mail, online tools, and other documents, although they also receive hardcopy summaries every quarter. The company does not rely upon social media to communicate about benefits, although it does for marketing.

Facebook and Norfolk Southern both understand their audiences. They know which technologies will allow their messages to reach their employees. They have each organized their internal communications to keep information current in a way that suits their needs.

Terri L. Griffith, PhD, is the author of the award-winning book *The Plugged-In Manager: Get in Tune with Your People, Technology, and Organization to Thrive.*

---

* Read more on the research at http://tinyurl.com/nas8yw4.

Size Matters Examples like Griffith's underscore the fact that 20-somethings and AARP members rarely speak the same language. Ask a typical 60-year-old man if he's heard of Snapchat or Vine. The need to fine-tune our messages, however, isn't restricted to factors like the average age of an audience. Effective communicators recognize that the dynamics of speaking to a large group of people can differ dramatically from those of smaller, more intimate crowds. As the following story illustrates, while you may ultimately deliver the same message, you might need to refine your presentation style.

Shape Shifting

Let's say that you're preparing a presentation, meeting with some new clients, or even thinking about writing a book. The first question you should ask is, Who's my audience? But that question requires more than a one-word answer. For most people, the first answer to the audience question is: everyone. Of course. My message is universal. Everyone should be interested in what I have to say. I'm an important person!

But in fact that question should serve as the beginning of an exploration of the exact circumstances of your audience—who, what, when, where, and why—everything about them you can determine.

Why should you care? After all, isn't it a matter of integrity to say the same thing to everybody? Yes and no. The message, fundamentally, has to be the same. But the shape that it takes may need to be entirely different. Would you use the same words to describe World War II to a group of six-year-olds as you would to a group of adults?

Beyond age group, social characteristics, demographics, and all the rest, size matters—and in ways that you might not expect. I recently had the chance to speak to 5,000 salespeople at an annual gathering of the company's entire sales force. I was excited; it was the largest audience I had ever spoken to. And I was invited to talk about storytelling—my favorite subject.

Now, I knew going in that big audiences are different from small ones in two important ways. First, they want to laugh more than small audiences, so you need to give them a chuckle or two from time to time. Second, because of the sheer physics of sound waves, they react more slowly than a small audience. I also knew that I had to slow down and give them time to react.

I did my research. I talked to the event organizers. I interviewed everyone who they would let me talk to about this sales force and the company it represented. It turned out that I was facing a tough crowd. The team had just come

(Continued)

(*Continued*)

off a disastrous year—after a series of bad years. They were demoralized and uncertain about the future. Just coming in with jokes about salespeople would have been unsympathetic, even tasteless.

I had to find a way to make them laugh, but they weren't in a laughing mood. What to do? I settled on self-deprecating humor. I talked about my own experience years ago as a spectacularly bad rookie salesperson trying to sell testing software to academic institutions.

The audience ate it up. They had all been there, but it was safe to laugh at my misfortunes as proxies for their own tough years. We all ultimately got on the same wavelength. We talked about how sales needed to change from focusing on the features of a product to focusing on storytelling. This would give meaning to the relationship between the customer and the product.

Keep in mind the *differences* among audiences when you get ready to shape your message for a particular occasion. The message stays fundamentally the same, but the packaging must vary, sometimes considerably.

Dr. Nick Morgan is the President of Public Words Inc. His latest book is *Power Cues: The Subtle Science of Leading Groups, Persuading Others, and Maximizing Your Personal Impact* (Harvard Business School Press, 2014).

Know When To Be Specific—Really Specific

With the exceptions of general checkups, most people visit their doctors for a particular reason. Your shoulder hurts or you're getting migraines. If you want your physician to fix what ails you, you had best be specific. Simply saying "I don't feel well" helps neither the doctor nor you.

The same principle applies when you're communicating. It's critical to be explicit, especially when communicating with technical individuals. To paraphrase Tom Cruise from the movie *Jerry Maguire,* help them help you. IT help desk folks, consultants, and developers can't read minds.

However well-meaning they are, general statements such as "The report doesn't work" are typically not very helpful. When diagnosing a problem, provide as many specifics as possible: dates, steps, and specific file names. Better yet, take screenshots. Record a video. Replicate the error. Share your screen as you try to access a Web page or run a report. You'll be glad that you did. Your problem will probably be solved in a fraction of the time needed via e-mail.

Get Visual, But Not Too Visual

Compared to raw data, the human brain can more quickly and easily make sense of information that is represented in a visual format.* Especially at first, introducing an idea via a simple illustration can go a long ways toward effectively communicating it. Beyond actually conveying your message and increasing the chance that others will receive it, including a visual element serves as an important signal to your audience: You are willing to take the time to put it in there. By making the effort, attendees are much less likely to tune out than if you had just used text.

Don't get too figure-happy, though. Slides with nine separate visuals or complicated flowcharts should remain in technical manuals; they are sure-fire ways to put your audience to sleep.

Silence: The Art of the Pause

Many professionals avoid pauses at all costs. Perhaps they fear that others will bolt for the door the moment they stop talking. In group settings, silence might result in someone else stealing the floor. This approach is in direct contrast to many of the world's best entertainers. Jazz musicians know that the space between the notes is just as important as the notes themselves. The most accomplished comedians understand the value of occasionally saying bupkus. Jerry Seinfeld, Ricky Gervais, Dennis Miller, Kevin Hart, George Carlin, and scores of others have all used silence strategically and for maximum effect over their careers. In fact, certain jokes bomb *without* pauses.

Most of us don't play the trumpet or make people laugh for a living, but there's much to be said for pausing and carefully thinking about our words and messages prior to responding. Faced with internal or external pressure to react, we often fail to fully process and think about the best or right response. In his book *Wait: The Art and Science of Delay*, Frank Partnoy describes how many ER doctors are predisposed to taking immediate action, even if that immediacy may ultimately harm the patient. It's counterintuitive, but *inaction* is often the smarter move (i.e., pausing until more information is available). There's a case to be made for saying to our physicians, "Don't just do something! Stand there!"

---

*There's a good deal of science behind this. If you're curious, Google "pre-attentive processing."

Other Tips

Here are a few other tips to maximize the chance that others receive your messages:

- **Rehearse.** Actors, comedians, and musicians who are committed to their crafts watch themselves and refine their acts. Why should businesspeople be any different? Chris Rock famously hones his act by performing unpublicized gigs at small clubs, trying out completely new material that often fails to get a single chuckle. The best public speakers practice; they don't get up there and "wing it."[*] The members of my favorite band (Rush) all rehearse individually before gathering for formal group rehearsals. In the words of drummer Neil Peart, "I start rehearsing for a tour on my own before getting together with the whole band."[8]
- **Review your past talks, posts, and e-mails.** Ask yourself if your communication is really improving. Every few months, look at a random sample of your old blog posts, e-mails, and/or talks. You'll always notice slight imperfections, but your general concern should be whether you are becoming a more effective communicator.
- **Solicit honest feedback.** After their talks, most speakers volunteer to sign books. I can't speak for others, but no one waiting in line for 15 minutes to get my autograph has ever told me that I sucked. This is the very definition of *confirmation bias*. (See "Culture and Conformity" in Chapter 3.) If you only listen to those who like and/or agree with you, you're unlikely to improve your communication skills. Ask people for their honest advice on how you can communicate more effectively, and be prepared to receive constructive feedback.

Next

Simple language tends to convey understanding. By itself, though, it's insufficient to ensure that our messages are received. Contrary

---

[*] One of the most hackneyed and derided ways to begin a talk starts with, "I was thinking about what I was going to say last night. . . ."

to what many people believe, sending an e-mail is not our sole communications option. There are other, more effective mediums. The next chapter explores many of them, as well as progressive companies that understand the benefits of adopting these new tools.

Notes

1. Charles Batchelor, "'Up or Out' Is Part of Industry Culture," April 20, 2011, www
.ft.com/cms/s/0/d42434b2-6b69-11e0-a53e-00144feab49a.html#axzz3AJb6DzTd.
2. Patty McCord, "How Netflix Reinvented HR," Jan-Feb 2014, http://hbr.org/
2014/01/how-netflix-reinvented-hr/ar/1.
3. Mark Nichol, "7 Examples of Passive Voice (and How to Fix Them)," February
3, 2011, www.dailywritingtips.com/7-examples-of-passive-voice/.
4. Eliyahu Federman, "Internal Social Networks Increase Workplace Productivity,"
January 28, 2013, www.socialmediatoday.com/content/internal-social-networks-
increase-workplace-productivity.
5. Nick Bilton, "After a Fast Start, a Fading Path Looks to Reinvent Itself, Again,"
June 29, 2014, http://bits.blogs.nytimes.com/2014/06/29/after-a-fast-start-a-
fading-path-looks-to-reinvent-itself-again.
6. Bill Kramer, "Surviving & Thriving in the Current Risk Management &
Regulatory Environment," July 23, 2014, www.wallstreetandtech.com/
compliance/surviving-and-thriving-in-the-current-risk-management-and-
regulatory-environment/a/d-id/1297528.
7. Henry Hitchings, "Those Irritating Verbs-as-Nouns," March 30, 2013,
http://opinionator.blogs.nytimes.com/2013/03/30/those-irritating-verbs-as-
nouns.
8. Michael Parillo, "Neil Peart: Taking Center Stage," November 21, 2011,
www.moderndrummer.com/site/2011/11/neil-peart-2/#.U-q3foBdW-l.

8

Life Beyond
E-Mail

How Progressive Organizations Are Using New Tools to Enable More Effective Collaboration and Communication

> *I continue to get further away from the usual painter's tools such as easel, palette, brushes, etc.*
>
> —Jackson Pollock

In the Preface I mentioned that I used to work for the consulting firm CSC in the mid-2000s. On my first engagement for my new employer in February 2004, I consulted on a massive system implementation for a 13-site hospital system based in the mid-Atlantic United States. Call it *Vamanos Health* here, although the name is a pseudonym.[*] A brief trip down memory lane will show the sea change that has taken place regarding project management and collaboration tools.

Communication and Collaboration Circa 2004

Vamanos signed a $5 million contract with CSC to provide consulting services supporting its new enterprise system. The CSC team consisted of six full-time individuals, including a partner, technical and functional consultants, and proper project manager (PM). We descended on Vamanos's headquarters from different locations across the country every Monday morning. We left every Thursday afternoon barring some type of crisis.

Replacing disparate back-office systems at more than a dozen hospitals has never been a small endeavor. (I'll just leave it at that here.) This was the antithesis of a weekend hackathon in which sleep-deprived, T-shirt clad Millennials throw ideas and code against the wall, eventually producing a working prototype. Vamanos was a truly corporate assignment. Everyone participated in weekly meetings and conference calls to discuss the state of the project, known issues, proposed solutions, status updates, upcoming deadlines, and the like.

As was the norm with this type of consulting gig at the time, our PM relied heavily on Microsoft Project, the most popular project

---

[*] It's also a another *Breaking Bad* reference.

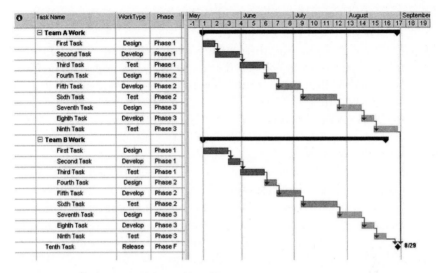

0	Task Name	WorkType	Phase	May				June				July				August				September
				-1	1	2	3	4	5	6	7	8	9	10	11	12	13	14	15	16	17	18	19
	⊟ **Team A Work**																			
	First Task	Design	Phase 1																	
	Second Task	Develop	Phase 1																	
	Third Task	Test	Phase 1																	
	Fourth Task	Design	Phase 2																	
	Fifth Task	Develop	Phase 2																	
	Sixth Task	Test	Phase 2																	
	Seventh Task	Design	Phase 3																	
	Eighth Task	Develop	Phase 3																	
	Ninth Task	Test	Phase 3																	
	⊟ **Team B Work**																			
	First Task	Design	Phase 1																	
	Second Task	Develop	Phase 1																	
	Third Task	Test	Phase 1																	
	Fourth Task	Design	Phase 2																	
	Fifth Task	Develop	Phase 2																	
	Sixth Task	Test	Phase 2																	
	Seventh Task	Design	Phase 3																	
	Eighth Task	Develop	Phase 3																	
	Ninth Task	Test	Phase 3																	
	Tenth Task	Release	Phase F																		8/29

Figure 8.1   Generic Microsoft Project Gantt Chart

Source: Microsoft

management application at the time. The program tracked project schedules and generated Gantt charts, a tool developed by Henry Gantt in the 1910s still in use today. A generic Microsoft Project screenshot is presented in Figure 8.1.

That massive *.mpp** file served as the epicenter of the project and the consultants' professional lives. Unless that master file contained the most current information, bad things would happen to Vamanos, CSC, and everyone involved. Budgets would be exceeded, deadlines would be missed, issues would go unreported and unresolved, people would be tased, and heads would roll. As a result, a decent percentage of our time involved keeping the master file accurate and up-to-date.

On a warm June evening, the entire team sat down over dinner at our hotel's restaurant. It was time for a five-hour power session. We reviewed each of the nearly 800 tasks that had to be completed. The laborious process went as follows:

1. The PM would read the task or set of tasks.
2. The person responsible would explain why X was only 60 percent finished and when it was likely to be completed. Follow-up questions might include: Was the deadline still realistic?

---

* This was the Microsoft proprietary file format for Project files.

Did other contingent tasks need to be moved? How would this affect everything else?

3. The other five members of the team would sit idly by until it was their turn to speak. (A consultant from Poland was there to simply listen. He said fewer than 10 words during the four-hour dinner.)

4. The PM would update the master file.

5. Repeat until finished.

By 10 p.m., red wine never tasted so good. I went to bed a few hours later feeling numb—and not from the vino.

In retrospect, that session was tantamount to an annual visit to the dentist's office—painful but necessary. For this type of consulting engagement back in 2004, this was standard operating procedure. How else could we efficiently communicate and collaborate with one another? Microsoft Project was certainly useful, but by no means perfect. Its chief limitation at the time the inability of concurrent users to work on individual files. By way of background, Microsoft conceived of Project in the mid-1980s, long before the explosion of the Web. As such, only one user could maintain and update the master file at a time. Although it did allow for exporting and subsequent importing of tasks, that process was neither foolproof nor terribly efficient, especially compared with today's Web-based tools.

As I look back at that project more than a decade ago, I'm fascinated at how far technology has come. The Web has changed just about everything, including how organizations and people *can* communicate with each other, manage projects, and get work done. (Of course, the mere existence of these tools means very little. Whether employees actually embrace new ways of working and communicating is a separate matter.) A raft of much more collaborative tools makes it easier than ever to communicate and to get work done.

If you're still hell-bent on using Microsoft Project, go right ahead. The latest version (available under the Office365 umbrella) is Web-based. As such, it facilitates true collaboration more than its antecedents, although the product's marketing copy could use some work. From the Microsoft site, Project allows its users to "effectively evaluate ideas or measure the strategic contribution of competing requests to determine alignments and streamline project initiation."* Huh?

---

* See http://tinyurl.com/new-ms-proj.

Judging by that clunky language, it appears as if the same communications team wrote the aforementioned Ballmer and Nadella memos.

At present, Project allows users to concurrently update tasks in real time. If you want to use another application for project management, you're not limited to Microsoft products. The world is your oyster, a point that the forthcoming case studies make in spades.

The Benefits of Old Tools

The preponderance of this chapter involves new technologies and applications that enable better business communication. It introduces progressive organizations whose employees understand the vital role that technology can play in this regard.

Before continuing, however, remember that even the most powerful technology does not guarantee—or even enable—effective business communication. Sometimes, as the following story manifests, it's best to *regress*—to use a simpler and more mature medium.

Shhh! Why Amazon Starts Senior Meetings with 30 Minutes of Silence

Despite Amazon's two-decade presence as an e-commerce juggernaut, much has remained mysterious about the company's inner workings—and that's just how CEO Jeff Bezos likes it.

At least Amazon is consistent. It routinely rankles investors by stubbornly refusing to provide specific numbers on Kindles sold, Prime memberships, revenue derived from its cloud-computing business Amazon Web Services (AWS), and the like. In an age of diminished privacy, Amazon is bucking the trend.

In this vein, Brad Stone's 2013 book *The Everything Store: Jeff Bezos and the Age of Amazon* shined a much-needed flashlight on some of the formerly opaque aspects of the company, its history, and its culture. No, Stone didn't have Bezos's blessing and carte blanche.[*] By an order of magnitude, though, it is the most comprehensive and detailed look at one of today's most powerful and truly iconic companies.

Most germane for our purposes, *The Everything Store* reveals how Amazon senior executives conduct their staff meetings—that is, how its leadership team communicates. Stone's research uncovered two fascinating nuggets.

(Continued)

---

[*] MacKenzie Bezos, Jeff's wife and a novelist, wrote a particularly scathing review of the book questioning Stone's research and reporting. Read it at http://tinyurl.com/oor4seh.

(*Continued*)

First, one seat at the conference table remains perennially vacant. Internally, this is nicknamed *the empty chair*. In it sits the theoretical customer, "the most important person in the room." This is not idle talk. Say what you will about Amazon; no one can question its commitment to customer service.

Second, meetings frequently start in silence—or, to be more precise, with everyone in attendance reading quietly for 30 minutes. PowerPoint isn't just discouraged; it is banned altogether. Bezos told Charlie Rose in a November 2012 interview that he considers the application "easy for the presenter, but difficult for the audience."[*]

In Bezos's view, slides generally communicate very little real information—primarily bullet points and simple numeric data. In their stead, Amazon execs write and actually read memos capped at six pages. These memos serve as the starting point for discussion at senior meetings. The necessity to communicate thoughts clearly (read: in full sentences and paragraphs) requires presenters to think in an almost-philosophical manner. In other words, these detailed memos "force a deeper clarity."[1]

As is usually the case, Bezos is on to something:

Deep thought is not only possible at work; it's desirable and even essential.

As you read this chapter, keep that thought in mind.

Much like using new language, deploying new tools in a vacuum is rarely wise. Before the majority of individuals, groups, and organizations can really take advantage of new technologies, they have to admit that the status quo is untenable. Sadly, the maxim "if it ain't broke, don't fix it" remains alive and well in many workplaces.

E-Mail Detox

As discussed in Chapter 4, e-mail suffers from many inherent limitations. Despite that, it isn't going away anytime soon, nor should it. Sure, technology has both caused this problem and offers part of the solution. I have learned, though, that the real cure requires looking inward and making personal changes.

---

[*] Watch the full interview at http://tinyurl.com/bezos-12.

Curing My E-Mail Addiction, Part II: Changing Behavior and Fallout

No one can overcome an addiction unless he or she recognizes the problem. This is why interventions are often necessary. Alcoholics and drug addicts fail to see the behavior and changes that have become so clear to their loved ones. I realized that I was addicted to e-mail, but what was my next step?

I started thinking long and hard about why I sent so many e-mails. I read some books. *Hamlet's BlackBerry: Building a Good Life in the Digital Age* and *The Tyranny of E-mail: The Four-Thousand-Year Journey to Your Inbox* stand out. I even took "Revive Your Inbox," an online self-help course of sorts, a 21-step program.*

These steps were helpful. Given my predisposition to new bells and whistles, however, I thought that I could use more technology to solve my problem. What digital tchotchkes would help me manage the deluge of messages I receive every day? I explored a range of complementary tools, apps, and services that would help me intelligently manage my messages. Some worked well. RightInbox, AwayFind, and Boomerang for Gmail showed immediate promise. Others were unmitigated disasters. Unroll.me took control of my inbox—and not for the better.

The Second Revelation: It's On Me

Ultimately, I discovered that even the most useful tools are only Band-Aids. Blame the Indian, not the arrow. *I* was the problem, not e-mail. I had to adopt an entirely different mind-set, not just new Gmail extensions. Rather than looking outward, why not look inward? What was I doing wrong?

No one forced me to check e-mail and respond immediately. I *chose* to reply to messages. If I do that immediately for each message, then I was effectively conditioning others to expect more of the same. It's all very Pavlovian.

I started detoxing. I was intent on stopping this cycle–or at least trying. I intentionally left my phone at home while going to the gym to resist the temptation to quickly check my e-mail while at a red light.

At first, this was downright weird but, after awhile, I started to get used to it. There was also some fallout. A few people sent me confused messages because I hadn't responded within an hour as I usually did. Growing pains were inevitable.

Over the past few years, I have sent fewer e-mails. When possible, I rely on other forms of communication like those discussed in the remaining part of this chapter. E-mail is *not* the only communications tool or, depending on the circumstance, even the ideal one. Getting others to recognize its limitations, though, has admittedly been difficult. (Some of my friends drive me bonkers.) This will take time.

---

* See http://tinyurl.com/email21step.

If Not E-Mail, Then What?

New applications, technologies, and services have made it easier than ever for us to effectively communicate at work wherever we are located. There are oodles of extremely useful productivity, project management, communication, and collaboration tools. Table 8.1 provides some examples.

Table 8.1   Useful Communications, Collaboration, and Productivity Tools Other Than E-Mail

Main Category	Popular Tools	Notes
Communication and Collaboration	JiveX, HipChat, Slack, Yammer, GetSatisfaction, Salesforce Communities, Lithium, Discourse, Drupal Commons via Acquia, Microsoft Office365, SharePoint, IBM Verse, Convo, Facebook at Work	Some of these are designed for large and midsized enterprises; others are geared toward small businesses.
Digital Signatures	PDFPen, RightSignature, DocuSign, SignEasy app	Why print, sign, scan, and e-mail? Just drop in a digital signature.
Distraction Prevention	WriteRoom, Q10, OmmWriter, WriteMonkey, FocusWriter	Of course, you can always just close your browser or unplug from the Internet. Admittedly, this is tough if you're researching a nonfiction book like I usually am.
E-mail Management	RightInbox, Boomerang, ActiveInbox, Scheduling via MS Outlook, AwayFind, Mailbox (acquired by DropBox), InboxPause	I gladly pay $50 every year for the premium version of RightInbox. I love the ability to schedule messages and have others return to my inbox.
File Transfer and General Productivity	DropBox, DropBox for Business, Box.net, GoogleDocs, WeTransfer, FaxZero, SugarSync, Hightail	Sending 30-MB attachments via e-mail is insane these days whether your company's IT department restricts it or not.
Instant Message	Google Chat, Adium, Skype, IRC, iChat, Proteus, Instabird, Facebook Messenger	Some of these are single-protocol applications; some support multiple protocols. (See Chapter 4.)
Project Management	BaseCamp, Podio (now part of Citrix), Asana, Flowdock, Omnifocus, Trello, Microsoft Bitrix24, Phabricator, Zimbra, Smartsheet, Todoist, Quip	I used to use Do.com until the company shut its doors. I have since converted to Todoist. It has changed the way I work for the better.

Table 8.1 *(Continued)*

Main Category	Popular Tools	Notes
Reading and Content Management	Evernote, Readability, Pocket, RSS Readers like Feedly and The Old Reader	You're more likely to fully read, understand, and remember an article or blog post if you read it outside of your inbox.
Scheduling	YouCanBookMe, Doodle, Calendly	These are enormous time-savers.
Screen Sharing	Join.me, WebEx, GoToMeeting	The freemium version of Join.me is good enough for me.
Task Management	DropTask, Todoist, GetFlow, HiTask, Outlook Task functionality	
Text Expansion and Keyboard Shortcuts	TextExpander, Typinator, TypeIt4Me, aText	TextExpander is one of my three favorite Apple programs. Its shortcuts save me hours every week.
Voice Recognition and Dictation	Dragon, TalkTyper, Tazti	
Writing/Grammar	Hemingway Desktop, Ginger (app)	These take different approaches than your standard spellcheck functionality.

Let me point out a few things about this new wave of communications tools. First, Table 8.1 is not remotely comprehensive. New ones come and go on almost a daily basis. I can't keep track of them all. So many apps, so little time.

Second, although I put them in single buckets, in reality many apps fall into multiple categories. For example, DropBox is primarily known for easy file sharing, but you can do so much more with it. As of this writing, more than 300,000 business apps connect to Dropbox.* Let's say that 99 percent of them are either redundant, immature, not very good, simply not useful, or some combination thereof. That leaves 3,000 potentially beneficial tools. Choice abounds, and one size need not fit all. Different people may use the same application in slightly or totally different ways—or they may use different ones altogether. This is not 1998; there are fundamentally more collaborative mediums than e-mail.

Next, the time savings and value of new communications tools almost always exceed the sum of their parts. Look at what happens when we use applications in conjunction with one another. For

---

* See http://tinyurl.com/o6mrb97.

instance, if I'm in front of my MacBook Pro, I often sign a document e-mailed to me as an attachment as follows:

- Download the document.
- Open it in PDFPen, an application that lets me edit PDFs.
- Drop in my digital signature.
- Add supplemental text fields like date or employer identification number (EIN*) via TextExpander short codes.
- Save the document in DropBox.
- Shoot a quick instant message (IM) to the sender with a Drop-Box link to the document.

If I'm holding my iPad, I'll use a similar process with the SignEasy app. If this seems like a great deal of work, ask yourself how long it would take you to print out the document, manually sign it, scan it to your computer, and e-mail it back. And what if you're not near a printer or a scanner?

Most of the productivity and collaboration tools in Table 8.1 can be used in isolation—and with some benefit. For instance, writing is usually a solitary exercise. Grammar-improvement apps like Hemingway and Ginger are designed for individual users. These are not collaboration and communication tools per se.

Many of the apps and services in Table 8.1, though, are virtually ineffectual unless other people use them as well. (See "Network Effects and Metcalfe's Law" in Chapter 4.) To make them work and prevent our colleagues from reverting to e-mail, we have some work to do. This is where our habits, organizational culture, and technology collide.

In "How To Train Your Internet Friends," Jon Mitchell of Read-WriteWeb writes:

> Computers are inanimate (so far). We are responsible for the way we use them. The problem is not that we have too much technology. It's that we've trained each other to use it badly. If we want better communication, the first thing we have to do is communicate better.[2]

---

* This is also known as a *Federal Tax Identification Number*. The government uses these to uniquely identify a business entity. Think of it as an organization's social security number.

We complain about the e-mail deluge, yet we effectively enable it by checking our messages constantly and replying as soon as they arrive. This perpetuates the vicious cycle. What's the solution? In a word, *don't*.

Easier said than done, right? It may not be possible or even desirable to completely cut the cord with e-mail. As the following companies have learned, however, it need not rule our professional lives.

True Communication and Collaboration in Action

A simple list of e-mail alternatives is instructive but, in the end, unsatisfying. Just knowing about the existence of tools like Yammer, Slack, Asana, and JiveX, for instance, may not help you conceptualize how your organization would benefit from using them. In other words, it's time for me to show you, not tell you. Natural questions at this point include the following:

- How have organizations adopted new collaboration and communication tools?
- Have they been successful?
- What have they learned from deploying them?
- What challenges have they faced in deploying them?
- What results have they seen?

This chapter concludes with three case studies on how diverse organizations have embraced these new communication and collaboration tools.

Slaying the E-Mail Dragon: Klick Health

Founded in 1997 by Peter Cordy, Leerom Segal, and Aaron Goldstein, Klick Health is the world's largest independent digital health agency. Its products and services help leading biopharmaceutical companies bring lifesaving therapies to market, particularly for serious and degenerative conditions. As of this writing, the company employs 400 people across the globe. Headquartered in Toronto, Canada, the company employs teams in Chicago, New Jersey, New York, Philadelphia, and San Francisco. Based on its clients' needs, though, Klick employees (aka *Klicksters*) could be anywhere. This arrangement has far-reaching implications for internal communication.

Impetus

Credit Klick's progressive management for recognizing two things early in the company's existence. First, if Klick was going to succeed, employees would need to use an application that would promote true collaboration and communication. Second, an e-mail program was *not* that application. Klick correctly views e-mail as only a marginal improvement over the traditional office memo.[*] As its current CEO Leerom Segal frequently says, "E-mail is the ultimate tool for letting *other* people prioritize your day for you." Truer words have never been spoken, but Klick is the rare company that walks the talk—and has now for more than a decade.

For two reasons, Klick's development and production teams proved to be the most vocal e-mail opponents. First, in the early 2000s, client-service employees (CSEs) would constantly e-mail their technical brethren, effectively assigning them tasks in the process. As a result, individual production staff and related teams could quickly lose track of what they actually need to do. Sound familiar? To this day, many people use e-mail to manage their tasks.

Second, the CSEs began annoying the technical team. CSEs would send developers e-mails requesting work. Of course, the developers were already swimming in messages. Because they did not respond immediately, CSEs would often walk over to the developers' desks minutes later. CSEs would tap technical team members on the shoulder and innocently ask, "Did you get the e-mail I just sent?"

As a communications medium, e-mail caused many more problems than it solved, but what to do? Leerom and Aaron found inspiration from IT help desk ticket systems. Generally speaking, these follow the same basic process:

1. A user calls with an issue.
2. If the help desk employee can't resolve that issue, he or she opens a case and either accepts it or assigns it to a different employee.
3. The case is marked as *open* and remains that way until it's resolved.
4. Work, steps, and updates are recorded within the individual case—*not* in an all-inclusive inbox.
5. When the case is resolved, it is marked *closed*.

---

[*] E-mail terminology (cc/bcc) dates back to the paper memo.

Klick implemented the same system for its technical team to complete development tasks. The process was simple: A CSE who needed something done created a ticket. The system would assign that ticket to a member of the technical team. Once an issue was resolved and had been marked *closed*, whoever created it would verify its resolution. To institutionalize the process, Klick introduced—*and enforced*—a new, simple, and powerful rule: no ticket, no work. Technology by itself accomplishes nothing.

This new process worked swimmingly well. Accountability, quality, and efficiency improved. Much to Klick's relief, the technical team's agita plummeted. Against that backdrop, the company expanded the system throughout the entire organization and christened it Genome. It provides users with key information on each issue: context, relevant conversations, the ability to prioritize, status, and accountability.[*] In other words, unlike e-mail, Genome facilitates effective communication and collaboration.

How Genome Improves the Work Experience

It's wrong to think of Genome as a single-purpose communications tool. It's not a walkie-talkie. It's better understood as an enterprise operating system powered by a suite of robust applications. Let me explain.

In most organizations, employees waste valuable time trying to find key documents. How many times have you created a spreadsheet or presentation when someone else had already done so? Regrettably, you didn't know that. While we're at it, how many project issues have remained undetected until it was too late?

Klick designed Genome with these concerns very much in mind. Genome captures as much client and institutional knowledge as possible, none of which would happen if Klicksters didn't use it so extensively. Although some things remain confidential, most information is particularly well suited to this transparent, Wiki-like environment. The data for each project resides on easily searchable homepages and related Wiki for anyone to see.

Finder

Klick has grown considerably from its founding. Its Toronto office alone consists of four floors. As team members travel among them,

---

[*] Tasks were assigned to only one person.

they swipe in and out using their security badges at each door. When Klicksters need to physically find their colleagues, they use a quick search utility called Finder. Employees simply log into Genome, hit a few keys on their keyboards, and type in colleagues' names. Genome reveals each employee's relative location within the building, as well as other information, such as who's traveling, who hasn't arrived at work yet, who's in today but currently out of the office, and who's on a beach.

How is this possible? Klick employees book all of their travel and vacation through Genome. Employees can access this information via an iOS app on their own phones. Through Finder, Klicksters save a great deal of time by not trying to track down people who are otherwise engaged. As we'll soon see, though, this is just the tip of the iceberg.

Weekly and Project 360s

The company is particularly interested in digitizing the subtle, nonverbal cues that might help detect project issues before they occur. Its Weekly360s serve as central repositories of information. They include project reviews, status updates, and individual goal tracking.

Every week, project team members complete two-question 360 reviews. Employees rate the project as blue (awesome), green, yellow, or red. (The latter three designations require brief explanations.) Klicksters comment at the project level rather than the task level. "This lets everyone involved in the project participate in the same feedback regardless of what they're adding to it," Jay Goldman tells me. Goldman serves as the company's Managing Director of Sensei Labs.* "Genome automatically solicits feedback from employees who have booked more than six hours of time to the project in that week."

Klick is attempting to encode employees' gut feelings on projects, tasks, and issues. In some ways, Genome is the antithesis of a social tool. These 360 reviews serve as safe environments in which employees can be completely honest about issues. Through a bit of social engineering, Klick incorporates essential feedback mechanisms into

---

*Launched in June 2014, Sensei Labs helps biotech companies evolve into more mature commercial entities.

Additional Information
■ **Keith Liu** 4 days ago at 4:09 PM Client let us know that their POLARIS study results will be published earlier than expected, so they would like to add three key messages with that content. They're okay with a slight delay in timelines. Review Concerns: ! timeline
■ **Mike Caron** Jul 21, 2014 8:45 AM
■ **Jay Goldman** Jul 14, 2014 4:58 PM Good news! Client really liked the designs. Thanks Creative team!
■ **Keith Liu** Jul 14, 2014 1:37 AM Client has signed the SOW!

Figure 8.2   Genome Weekly 360 in the Project 360 Module

Source: Klick Health

its data-driven process. These serve as excellent early warning systems and minimize the chance that projects go off track. An example is shown in Figure 8.2.

Andrew Woronowicz, Genome's Director of Business Process & Systems, recalls the origin of Genome's Project 360. In his words:

> A project was going off the rails, and everyone knew it. Some of us talked about it. Some of us escalated it. These tiny pieces of information didn't add up to a cohesive story. Also, it was very easy to trust feedback from the project leadership and never ask anyone else. After all, they should have their finger on the pulse of the project, right? Well, it turns out very few people truly understood how messed up things were, but everyone individually knew that some things were messed up. After that project, Klick introduced P360s. They give everyone on the project a voice in the conversation. They collate that information and those conversations into a single story. What's more, by giving your "gut feel" on a specific status, you can essentially pull the

handbrake on the project. You call all of the necessary people into a room and make sure your specific concerns are being heard. We can then find an appropriate resolution.

Teachable Moments and Klick Academy

Klick is constantly looking for what it calls *Teachable Moments*. By way of background, the company uses Genome in conjunction with data on employee work history and experience. Put together, the company can identify the precise moment at which Klicksters would benefit from training. The company delivers this education in a way that is customized to each employee's exact needs.

Like most Genome modules, Teachable Moments have served Klick well. At most companies, reporting systems flag issues *after* employees have made mistakes, if at all. Teachable Moments allow Klick to identify opportunities to improve employee performance and skills proactively and as they happen. Employees don't view Genome as an annoyance; they look at it as a truly useful tool and source of information.

"U.S. companies spend well over $130 billion per year on training, less than 30 percent of which is actually retained," says Goldman. "That has to be one of the worst returns on investment on record. Instead of a traditional, one-size-fits-all approach, we believe in just-enough-just-in-time-just-for-you learning. We deeply personalize it to each member of our team."

Klick collects and analyzes a wide variety of project and employee data via Genome. As a result, the company can identify the precise moment at which an employee should receive training. This increases its overall quality, not to mention employee knowledge retention, productivity, and performance.

Teachable Moments often trigger online learning via Klick Academy. Genome connects Klicksters in need of additional training with the company's best internal experts in different subjects. For example, consider a first-time project manager. Genome might *automatically* present her with the following:

- Klick Academy videos recorded by the company's subject matter experts
- A list of colleagues who can help
- Extra checklists and guardrails

Chatter

Chatter is an activity feed that captures and displays all of Klick's happenings.* It streams on the right-hand side of *every* Genome page. An example is presented in Figure 8.3.

Klick designed, developed, and deployed Chatter in a manner consistent with other Genome modules—as an experiment. The company did not know if Chatter would take root, much less how. Yet Klick proceeded anyway, an approach that most mature organizations would never have even considered. If successful, Klick knew that Chatter would naturally evolve and expand. Perhaps it would meet needs that the other Genome modules did not address. Much

Figure 8.3   Klick Daily Chatter

Source: Klick Health

---

* This should not be confused with the Salesforce.com product of the same name.

like Twitter, what began as a way of sharing simple status updates quickly became something much bigger. Today Klicksters share all sorts of content with each other, including:

- Links and videos to common interests
- Photos from the road to bring teams together
- Genome news and social good tracking activity to keep everyone informed
- Featured Kudos (read: employee praise). Klick looks at what it calls its *positivity ratio* of posts to Chatter as a quick gauge of its overall morale.

News

Many organizations tightly control their official newsfeeds. Not Klick. The company takes a much more transparent approach to communication. In much the same way that any employee can post to Chatter, the Genome newsfeed is open to every Klickster. Any employee who wishes to share information can do so. This encourages social interaction within posts and across departments and groups. In this way, Genome helps break down traditional organizational silos.

Klick sends its newsfeed to large LCD displays throughout its office hallways.* Items surface in both the News tool (for archival and continued reading purposes) and on Chatter for conversation. Users can also comment on and/or like the feature.

Dynamic Dashboards

Access to relevant, timely information has never been more essential. To this end, Dynamic Dashboards serve as Genome's most important tool. Klicksters use these every day to help prioritize their goals. The dashboards provide employees and their managers with the freedom to define anything as a goal as long as Genome can track it. This last part is essential. Dashboards account for just about everything work-related: milestones, deadlines, and goals at the individual, group, department, and company levels. This is displayed in Figure 8.4.

---

* Google does the same thing at its headquarters with filtered, real-time search queries. Employees and visitors are amazed.

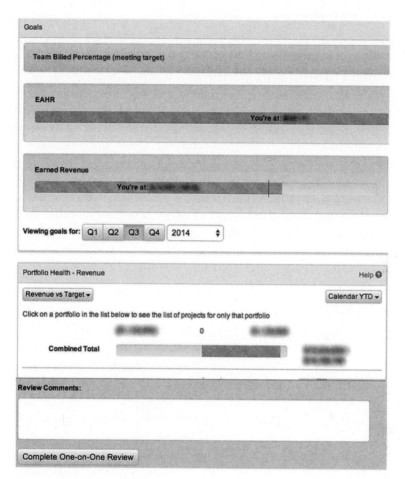

Figure 8.4   Genome's Goals Dashboard
Source: Klick Health

Genome is able to automatically balance all employee priorities. Employees can easily view their most essential tasks and goals—and when they need to be completed. Genome constantly updates employee goals based on the most current information. Klicksters understand that dashboards will help them manage their professional lives. Managers can then strike the right balance between flexibility and goal setting.

Despite Klick's revolutionary tools, in a way the company is no different from any other. Sometimes company priorities change, and employees must adjust their goals accordingly. Dynamic Dashboards automatically flag potential issues. In so doing, they help minimize project risk, surprises, and the chance of failure.

Genome assists with performance management as well. It looks at annual employee and team objectives for the entire year, not just for a specific period. Beyond adding a level of neutrality, this helps fight the bias that plagues annual performance-review cycles: the most recent failures and successes are the easiest to recall. (This cognitive bias is known as the *primacy* or *recency effect*.) Finally, it provides employees with constant, near-immediate feedback. In this vein, Klick has a leg up on other organizations: Its employees fully understand the criteria and peer groups against which they will be evaluated. They are rarely surprised at bonus and raise time.

How many organizations can say *that* about their employees?

Lessons and Next Steps

Klick has eschewed a set-it-and-forget-it approach with Genome. For more than a decade now, the company has enhanced its enterprise operating system. In so doing, it has learned some valuable lessons that would behoove all organizations.

Perhaps most important, Klick has embraced an organic or bottom-up approach to development. Management doesn't force developers to dilute or pervert Genome. Remarkably, the technical team is allowed to resist and, if necessary, *even decline* executive requests. Although that balance can be difficult to maintain, it is nevertheless an essential one. Consider the downside: A impotent development team beholden to the whims of detached chief executives usually churns out mediocre tools that relatively few rank-and-file employees actually use.

Second, Klick underscores the benefits of lean and agile development methods.* (We'll see this as well with Sidecar, the following case study.) The Genome team builds each module and feature in the smallest way possible. Klick can then test a feature's effectiveness *before* launching it throughout the entire company. Klick's employees ultimately decide its fate, not its senior management. To this end, collecting data and using feedback mechanisms are essential. As

---

* This is in stark contrast to the Waterfall or "big bang" methodology.

W. Edwards Deming once famously said, "In God we trust; all others must bring data."

All Klicksters are responsible for effective communication and collaboration, not just employees in IT and/or HR. No department makes broad decrees. Through News and Chatter, Klick fosters an environment that is conducive to innovation, discovery, improvement, and iteration. For example, all users can comment on Chatter posts and suggest new features by using the #dogfood hashtag. This causes Genome to automatically create a ticket for its development team. (No e-mails are required.) At Klick, Genome development is *never* finished.

Finally, nothing in Genome is sacred. Klick is completely willing to retire and kill features—and even entire modules—that just aren't working. The company practices what it calls Digital Darwinism. Unused and underperforming features are expensive to maintain, so why let them live?

Results

To understand just how much Klicksters use Genome, look at the following usage data:

- More than 1.4 million unique pages
- More than 638,000 tickets (tasks)
- More than 6,400 projects
- More than 6,500 Kudos (peer recognition posts)
- More than 50 unique tools

Figure 8.5 presents a more visual look at this data.

To be sure, one cannot attribute Klick's success exclusively to its development and use of a powerful communication tool. Ultimately, all companies need to offer a product and service that customers will actually pay for. Still, it's impossible to ignore the impact of Genome at Klick. It's no coincidence that the company has grown at the remarkable annual rate of 30 to 60 percent for each of the past 17 years.*

---

*For more on the Klick story, see *The Decoded Company: Know Your Talent Better Than You Know Your Customers.*

Figure 8.5   Klick Activity Over the Past Year
Source: Klick Health

Keep Calm and Jive On

It's fair to say that urban transportation is in the midst of a revolution. In January 2013, car-rental company Avis paid a reported $500 million for ZipCar, the world's biggest "car club" service. Although they face fierce resistance from taxi drivers and significant regulatory hurdles, Uber and Lyft also sport sky-high valuations. Google's driverless cars aren't ready for prime time yet, but that day may be coming sooner than many people think. Brass tacks: The options for many city dwellers to get around will be vastly different in five to ten years.

It's not difficult to understand why change is needed. Traffic is the scourge of many cities. It's neither cheap nor convenient to own a car. Some residents in New York and San Francisco pay upward of $600 per month for the privilege of parking their automobiles. Never mind the other costs associated with car ownership: gas, insurance, tolls, and monthly payments or depreciation. Public transportation and car rentals are still viable options. Thanks to apps, GPS, and smartphones, though, an exciting new alternative in recent years has made significant inroads: ridesharing.

One of the most promising ridesharing communities is Sidecar. Its app matches drivers with spare seats in their cars to passengers in need of instant rides in real time. Currently operating in 10 cities in the United States, its hundreds of drivers have facilitated more than a million rides as of this writing. Based in San Francisco, the company began operating in 2012. According to CrunchBase, it has raised more than $35 million in funding from Union Square Ventures, Lightspeed Venture Partners, Google Ventures, and others.[*] This includes a recent round of $15 million closed in September 2014.

Impetus for Change

On two levels, the ultimate success of a business like Sidecar hinges on effective communication. First, allow me to state the obvious: Unless it quickly matches a prospective driver with a passenger, a ride never happens and the company makes no money. Soon after its founding, Sidecar built, tested, and launched two apps: a consumer-facing one and a driver-facing counterpart. After that, the company began tweaking the other, equally essential, side of the communications coin: facilitating better, faster, and more streamlined communication among drivers and employees.

At the onset, Sidecar employees and drivers initially communicated via relatively primitive methods: e-mails and private, region-specific Facebook groups in Los Angeles, Boston, DC, Chicago, Seattle, and San Francisco. As the company grew, it didn't take long for these low-cost, quasi-public, and general communication methods to break down. (This is usually the case.) Sidecar's temporary solutions started becoming permanent problems, to borrow from Craig Bruce's wise observation. The Facebook-centric method severely limited communication and collaboration at Sidecar on several levels:

- *All drivers needed to create an account with the social network, but not everyone wanted to do that.* This is certainly understandable given Facebook's sketchy privacy record. Plainly, no Facebook account meant no access to private Sidecar Facebook groups. This was an enormous problem.
- *Each private Facebook group was a nightmare to administer.* By definition, the social network makes private groups nearly impossible to find. Drivers would have to friend each other.

---

[*] See www.crunchbase.com/organization/side-cr.

Sidecar had to manually cull lists of its drivers, wasting valuable time in the process.

- *Facebook frequently and surreptitiously changes News Feed.* Sidecar could not ensure that messages sent to its drivers would be received briskly or even at all. The company had zero control over the placement of its messages.
- *On a related level, Facebook content is ephemeral.* Its News Feed emphasizes the most recent updates, not the most critical ones.
- *Search within private groups is severely lacking.* There was then— and is as of this writing—no simple, efficient way for group members to find relevant content. (The only option is endlessly scrolling—hardly ideal on smartphones.) In the case of Sidecar drivers, this included things like Saturday night hotspots (i.e., potential customers).
- *Sidecar management could not easily extract driver data.* The company could not discern what, when, and how its drivers were communicating; it was limited to what Facebook allowed the company to see.
- *How could Sidecar know that valuable content shared would remain private?* Perhaps Facebook would use this information to serve up ads to drivers on competing products and services? (Uber is extremely aggressive in recruiting new drivers.)

Sidecar's management knew that it had reached the point of no return. To continue progressing, the company needed to buy or create its own contemporary communications platform.

"Building a community is like building a product," Sidecar's Maria Ogneva tells me. She serves as the company's Head of Community. "You need to embrace lean methods." Ogneva spearheaded the search for a new communication and collaboration tool. There's no shortage of related applications and services these days. She knew that its new application would have to be all of the following:

- Global, local, and deeply collaborative
- Mobile
- Easy to use
- Flexible and agile
- Already integrated into existing systems—or easy to do so

After evaluating a variety of options, the company selected Jive Software. Jive had recently released its new cloud-based communications tool (JiveX).[*] Social Edge Consulting handled its initial development and implementation.

JiveX met all of Sidecar's essential needs. In the words of Mike Fraietta of Social Edge Consulting:

> One of the beautiful things about the new collaborative tools like JiveX is that they allow companies to have the best of both worlds. Companies can blend bottom-up and top-down development approaches. The applications are easily customizable, and information can flow freely through the community to those who need it.[3]

Sidecar's nontechnical employees found JiveX to be intuitive to use, customize, and deploy. They could easily add functionality. No coding was necessary; they only needed to drag and drop.

Deployment

Within a month after signing a contract, Sidecar was up and running with JiveX. The company christened its community *The Garage*, a screenshot of which is shown in Figure 8.6.

Communication is essential these days—*especially about communication*. Sidecar advised its drivers that The Garage was launching well ahead of time. "We gradually tapered off communication via Facebook groups," Ogneva says. "We pointed people back to The Garage and answered their questions there." Rather than relying on private individual e-mails, the company encouraged drivers to use its new forum to engage in public conversations. This did several critical things. It captured valuable content that would otherwise sit either on Facebook or in e-mail inboxes. Second, it reinforced the fact that The Garage was not a temporary management fad; it would serve as the company's new communications hub for the foreseeable future. Finally, it minimized the frustrating and interminable back-and-forth e-mails that plague so many companies.

As Klick did with Genome, Sidecar intelligently rolled out The Garage in stages. In so doing, it learned valuable lessons along the way. By way of contrast, "big bang" deployments often fail. Resistance

---

[*] For more on Ogneva's software-selection methodology, see http://tinyurl.com/nzdpwed.

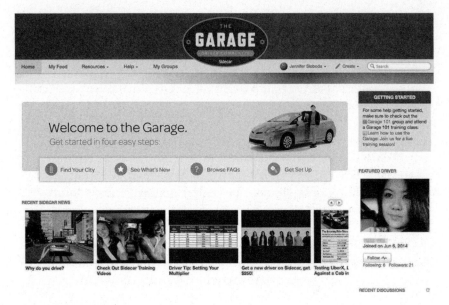

Figure 8.6   The Garage

Source: Sidecar

to The Garage and JiveX was essentially nonexistent. For one, it met the vast majority of the drivers' needs. Beyond that, the Facebook private group method was, to put it mildly, a mess.

"We were pretty reliant upon e-mail and Facebook, but our system wasn't working. All of the information used to live in those messages," says Ogneva. "Now, all of our drivers' content goes into The Garage. People access it in a much more organized way than before."

From the get-go, Sidecar took advantage of many of JiveX's native features. First, the company highlights the best, most relevant information to its drivers. It even profiles particular creative, insightful, and helpful community members. The Garage provides Sidecar drivers with real-time news, product announcements, status updates, tips, and messages on their smartphones. Drivers can spend more time where they should be: in the field. No one has to report to a corporate office to receive updates or access critical information. When a new Sidecar driver signs up, JiveX automatically provisions a Garage account and sends an introductory e-mail. After that, more than 90 percent of all driver communication takes place via The Garage.

Back in corporate headquarters, Sidecar employees use the JiveX public and private groups for product testing, driver training, general sharing, discussion, news, and events. National and local groups allow for easy targeting of communication, segmenting, and subsequent analysis. Ogneva notes that, compared to the old method, group administration is easier by orders of magnitude, as is moving content around.

JiveX also allowed Sidecar to collect driver feedback and usage data. The company used this information to improve subsequent iterations of The Garage. For example, Sidecar learned that separate groups for day and night drivers simply weren't necessary. They confused drivers more than they helped. The data proved that what appeared to be a good idea really wasn't so good at all.

Beyond that, The Garage lets Sidecar better understand driver sentiment and take necessary actions. A few examples illustrate this point. First, soon after its launch, drivers discovered a problem with the app's referral system. The team pushed a fix within a couple of days. Second, Ogneva discovered that drivers were posting their own promotional flyers for nearby cafés and events. A light bulb went on. The company rightly saw this as an opportunity to post an editable template equipped with each driver's referral code. By understanding what drivers really need, Sidecar is able to rapidly focus on the things that matter to its community.

Continuous Development

Much like their Klick Health brethren, Sidecar's developers don't posit and deploy features in a vacuum. To maximize the chance that features on The Garage actually took root, Sidecar launched a Captain's Program to solicit input from a select group of drivers. The company calls its most engaged community members *Driver Captains*. In effect, they act as peer mentors and trusted advisors to other drivers. They provided invaluable feedback on usability, group names, site navigation, and features. They welcome new drivers as they arrive.

Sidecar also suspected that its drivers would want to share tips, tricks, and information with each other, but what types? No one knew. Rather than trying to predict the future, Sidecar embraced an organic deployment method. Drivers would largely determine how The Garage evolved, not corporate staff. This stands in stark contrast to large organizations that dictate features from the top down, often unsuccessfully.

More than ever, the ability to quickly deploy, learn, and adapt is no longer a luxury; it's a necessity. "I didn't want our community to become a bunch of individual silos," says Ogneva. "Our vision is for The Garage to evolve, but we don't yet know exactly how or in which direction. JiveX offers a very flexible and robust platform that will support our growth and evolution." In Fraietta's words: "The company's drivers will ultimately shape The Garage. For its part, Sidecar can easily get critical information to and from its drivers."[*]

Lessons, Results, and Next Steps

The success of The Garage at Sidecar stems from many factors, not the least of which is its insistence on creating a truly collaborative, mobile-friendly experience. Sidecar built a better mousetrap, but it wasn't sure about how its drivers would use it. In other words, Sidecar didn't try to map everything out ahead of time. The company embraced uncertainty.

No one could have predicted some of the most popular and valuable content created and shared on The Garage. For instance, drivers don't work in proper offices during business hours. At some point, all drivers need to heed the call of nature. How could they easily find quality public restrooms, especially late at night?[†] This turned out to be a critical question that kept coming up. The drivers created their own city-specific methods and taxonomies to solve this problem. A screenshot is shown in Figure 8.7.

Useful and timely content like this has made Sidecar's drivers its biggest advocates. In turn, they effectively help spread the word and strengthen the company's brand. (Remember, to passengers, the drivers *are* Sidecar.) An arduous, ineffective, and kludgy communications tool would contravene that goal. It's not inconceivable for frustrated and disaffected drivers to go elsewhere to a competing service. A mass exodus isn't very likely, though. The Garage has kept Sidecar's drivers loyal, informed, engaged, and, most important, making money.

How often do employees say the same about e-mail?

The Internal Social Network

In my third book, *The New Small*, I examined a breed of emerging small businesses that is harnessing the power of new technologies. To briefly summarize the book, no longer are best-of-breed

---

[*] Conversation with Fraietta.

[†] I am reminded here of the scene in *Seinfeld* in which George can rattle off the best public Manhattan bathrooms by cross-streets. See http://tinyurl.com/ozjmetc.

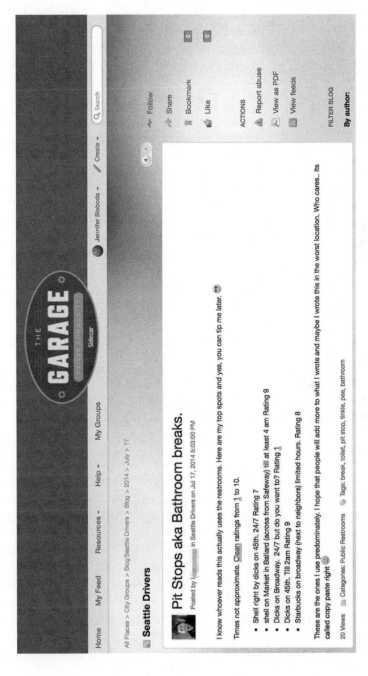

Figure 8.7 Pit Stops at The Garage

Source: Sidecar

applications and technologies the sole purview of large enterprises. Technology-wise, there's never been a better time to be small. The book covers 11 diverse and progressive small businesses that are symptomatic of a game-changing trend. Soon after the 2010 publication of the book, I came to know Paul Roetzer, the head of PR 20/20.

Company Background

Roetzer founded PR 20/20 in November 2005 with an ambitious vision: to transform the PR industry. Today the 13-person inbound marketing agency based in Cleveland, Ohio provides results-driven, integrated client campaigns. Its specialties include advanced analytics, content generation, public relations, social media, and search marketing.

"The fast-paced world of marketing demands that consultants stay on top of technology trends and changing consumer behaviors to remain competitive," Roetzer tells me. "At the individual level, navigating this endless sea of resources, updates, and technologies can be a daunting task. Simultaneously, top marketing talent—those individuals who can keep pace with all of these changes—is in high demand. As an agency, we needed the infrastructure in place to develop and retain these marketers."

Communication Issues and the Move to Yammer

Despite the company's relatively small employee population, it suffered from several internal communication problems. Employee inboxes were overflowing. A simple question via e-mail would often spark a chain of responses so deep that the discussion was nearly impossible to follow. As a direct consequence, employees throughout the day would sometimes lose track of valuable information. Examples included client developments, industry updates, and key events.

For these reasons, PR 20/20 sought a solution that would concurrently encourage collaboration, continuously transfer knowledge, and perpetuate its culture. In November 2010, the company conducted a one-month beta test with Yammer, a type of private social network. A small group of PR 20/20 employees kicked

Yammer's tires. (Microsoft purchased Yammer for \$1.2 billion in June 2012.)

The PR 20/20 test group instantly took to the intuitive application. Yammer isn't entirely dissimilar to Facebook, something that most of the company's employees already used on a daily basis. The staff began sharing information and resources with each other and connecting in ways that just felt unnatural via e-mail. Roetzer discovered that, although employees were e-mailing each other less frequently, they were actually communicating more. They had become more informed and engaged.

Soon after its successful pilot, the company rolled out Yammer in earnest. To date, PR 20/20 relies on the network as a valuable information outlet. Employees use it to post, edit, and find resources related to the industry, the agency, and its clients. What's more, Yammer provides PR 20/20 with the ability to quickly respond to demands and opportunities it confronts each day without over-whelming its employees.

Building on Early Successes

Roetzer immediately saw how well Yammer worked at spreading ideas, sparking innovation, and generating collective wisdom *within the agency*. As a result, he decided to build on its initial internal success. In October 2012, PR 20/20 created and launched an external Yammer learning community.

The launch coincided with a seven-part webinar series the company was hosting. Ideally, the series content would attract marketing agency professionals to the Yammer group. If outsiders found the content useful, they would engage, network, and share their knowledge and experiences with each other. PR 20/20 hoped that Yammer would serve as a central information repository and means of interaction, and it ultimately did. New and informative resources trickled in. Attendees asked each other questions, stimulated discussions, and posted key lessons within the network with nary an e-mail sent. Content easily flowed into Yammer for everyone to see.

The company then solicited attendee feedback and ideas. How should the curriculum be modified each week? This gave the webinar series a choose-your-own-adventure feel that strongly resonated with participants. Figure 8.8 displays a screen shot of the PR 20/20 Yammer group.

Paul Roetzer
To **All Company**

Q2/S1: In slide 44, we explored potential performance-based campaign recommendations. Knowing their goals, and priority key performance indicators (KPIs), are there any campaign concepts you would add or make the top recommendations?

Like · Reply · Share · More · 29 minutes ago

👍 Tracy Lewis and Mike Kaput like this.

Jessica Miller
I would prioritize top of the funnel activities for the first couple of months, because the company has limited brand awareness to date.

Like · Reply · Share · More · 21 minutes ago
👍 Tracy Lewis, Mike Kaput and Taylor Radey like this.

Tracy Lewis
cc: Jessica Miller

Agree with Jessica Miller. I'd focus on content strategy, production and promotion first. We may also want to consider a loyalty program to better engage existing customers.

Like · Reply · Share · More · 16 minutes ago
👍 Jessica Miller likes this.

Figure 8.8   PR 20/20 Yammer Marketing Webinar Group
Source: PR 20/20

Results and the Future

For PR 20/20, Yammer has been a rousing success. It has fundamentally improved the way in which its employees work and communicate with one another.

Since implementing Yammer, employees send considerably fewer e-mails while communicating better. Yammer's searchable and threaded discussions have allowed team members to access the information they need quicker and in a much more digestible manner. Employees are now more apt to share information, seek resources from each other, and ask questions.

As the company continues to grow, remote work will become more commonplace. (At present, one employee regularly works from Denver, Colorado, and another from her home.) Fortunately, this isn't a problem for Yammer. Like many of the tools covered in this chapter, it is location-agnostic. Yammer keeps everyone informed of what's happening in the office and vice versa. It has reduced the administrative burden at the company. Specifically, it has obviated the need for check-in calls and e-mails.

PR 20/20 regularly posts educational resources on Yammer. These include relevant news articles, upcoming events, and advancement opportunities. Employees also use Yammer to complete professional development exercises. For example, account managers may post prompts or hypothetical situations, such as "Client X saw a significant decrease in leads last month. How would you pinpoint the cause and position your findings to the client?" Employees then share how they would respond. These exercises represent a great way to encourage employees and groups to think critically, to see their peers' approaches, and to learn from them. Everybody wins.

Yammer is primarily a business tool, but it has become a vehicle for personal sharing at PR 20/20. The lines between work and home have been blurring for years, something that employees at Klick Health, Sidecar, and countless other companies have discovered. Employees gladly offer glimpses into their personal lives for all to see. Yammer helps employees get to know each other better. They can find wedding and baby photos, invitations to happy hours, amusing YouTube videos, sports polls, and more. Finally, Roetzer notes that Yammer has helped improve employee morale.

Lessons and Next Steps

Yammer has taught PR 20/20 several things. First, it's essential to determine an internal structure for organizing discussions. Communication about specific topics, projects, departments, clients, and teams is classified via different taxonomies. A structured system maximizes the chance that information is easily retrievable in the future. To this end, PR 20/20 uses Yammer's hashtag feature for this very purpose. Figure 8.9 shows an example.

Second, it was essential for employees to activate automatic notifications. As the company grew, the number of updates posted on Yammer did as well. By tagging the most relevant individuals in each conversation, employees ensure that the right people see pertinent updates. No one needs to send additional e-mails. Hashtags have

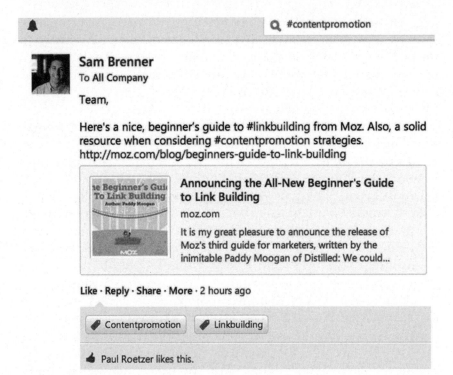

Figure 8.9   Yammer Conversation with Clickable Hashtag
Source: PR 20/20

minimized the chance that critical messages are not received and things fall through the cracks.

As PR 20/20 continues to grow, it will doubtless add more staff. The true value of its new collaboration tool will evolve and expand. "Yammer has proven to be an extremely effective communication tool at PR 20/20," says Roetzer. "We want to ensure our employees continue to share ideas and information. We want to identify, use, and grow our internal expertise in new directions. Finally, we want our team to feel connected. Yammer will drive these efforts to a significant degree."

New Tools: No Guarantees

The Klick, Sidecar, and PR 20/20 case studies have demonstrated that, by themselves, the introduction of new communications tools guarantees nothing. They are necessary but not sufficient for promoting effective business communications. Disinterested, over-whelmed, and otherwise disengaged employees won't flock to shiny new things just because management says so.

These case studies also illustrate the importance of timing. There is no such thing as a *perfect moment* for change. As the following story illustrates, though, some periods are far worse than others. Moreover, adding new tools and requirements to employees who are already swamped with work is almost always counterproductive.

Training Not Received: How to Circumvent HR

For nearly 20 years, I worked at AT&T. Whenever budgets got tight, all corporate travel would cease. To save money, Ma Bell would deliver training via the company intranet as streamed presentations. Unfortunately, my colleagues and I didn't have time to sit through half-day virtual courses every week. Yes, training was important. In the whole scheme of things, though, our team had much higher priorities. Ditching training wasn't even an afterthought.

After our team missed a few courses, someone high up in HR sent each of us a few threatening e-mails about our nonparticipation. We didn't know it at the time, but HR could easily determine when employees had logged in to the course, when they had logged out, and who had failed to log in altogether.

We soon realized that we could easily kill two birds with one stone. That is, we could still tend to our day jobs while ostensibly taking the courses online. We would just log in, minimize the screen, mute the audio, and go back to work. HR seemed pleased. We never heard from them again about training.

Colin Hickey spent nearly two decades at AT&T in different roles. He currently advises executives and entrepreneurs as an independent consultant.

Hickey's story nicely sums up perhaps the key point of this book: We frequently believe that our messages have been successfully delivered and received when nothing could be further from the truth. The fact that we've sent a message in no way guarantees that our fellow employees, customers, partners, and other third parties have received and understood it.

Next

This book concludes with a Coda.

Notes

1. David K. Williams, "Leading Like Jeff Bezos: Words Are More Important Than Numbers," September 4, 2013, www.forbes.com/sites/davidkwilliams/2013/09/04/leading-like-jeff-bezos-words-are-more-important-than-numbers/.
2. Jon Mitchell, "How to Train Your Internet Friends," December 10, 2012, http://readwrite.com/2012/12/10/how-to-train-your-internet-friends.
3. Personal conversation with Fraietta.

PART

IV

WHAT NOW?

This book closes with some final thoughts on business, technology, language, and communication. There's also a call to action and a brief look at personal responsibility. I challenge readers to look inward and examine some of their own motivations.

It includes the following:

- **Coda:** Was This Message Received?

Coda

Was This Message Received?

Someone's sitting in the shade today because someone planted a tree a long time ago.

—Warren Buffett

Now that you've reached the end of this book, it's fair to ask a simple, five-word question: Has *my* message been received?

This book has showed how people routinely use—and often *misuse*—language and technology at work. It has demonstrated how intelligent professionals and organizations are adopting simpler language, new technologies, and plain old common sense in an effort to do something that is more important than ever: communicate effectively.

I hope that *Message Not Received* has taught you a thing or two about why so much contemporary business communication ultimately fails—and the consequences of those failures. If I have done my job, you are now thinking about business communications at least a little bit differently. You might now even be a little self-conscious or uncomfortable about your own messages. This isn't a bad thing. Armed with this valuable new knowledge, the ball is now in your court.

You may be able to change your own communication style, but what about the styles of those around you? In many organizations, communication leaves more than a bit to be desired. If that statement applies to your current station at work, you have three choices:

Option A: Do nothing

You can ignore this book and its central premise. You can dismiss or discount its accompanying data, advice, examples, and case studies. You can revert to business as usual and accept your organization's status quo. Nobody's stopping you. Perhaps bad business communication simply doesn't bother you, or you just don't want to rock the boat.

Option B: Flight

If bad communication has driven you to the point of exasperation, you can choose to seek employment elsewhere. After all, you are the CEO of your own career. You wouldn't be the first person to quit in frustration over *Dilbert*-esque management and bureaucracy. Some companies and cultures just can't be fixed. A fresh start might be just the ticket for you.

Option C: Persuade and Lead

Perhaps you're not ready to call it quits just yet. You are prepared to fight the good fight. You're ready to change how you and others communicate—or at least try. If so, then you can start by doing the following:

- Ask yourself if you routinely say something as clearly as possible.
- Think about your audience before peppering your messages with arcane terms and acronyms.
- Pause and take a deep breath before immediately responding to everyone copied on a pointless e-mail.
- Realize the utter insanity of relying on e-mail as the default communications tool within your organization. Experiment with new technologies that encourage true collaboration.
- Refuse to engage in interminable e-mail dialogues, especially when you've expressed your desire to actually *speak* to someone.
- Politely point out to others that you don't remotely understand what "leveraging our current value-add use cases going forward to promote strategic alignments and synergies" means.

Your new tactics and language may not immediately bear fruit, and you may ruffle a few feathers. People may question what you're doing. You may not be able to abstain altogether from the occasional pointless e-mail chain and some level of jargon. As with all types of progress, sometimes you have to take a few steps back before taking a giant leap forward. As I know all too well, many people simply hate change.

I encourage you to persevere, though. You just might find that you actually like simpler language. You may enjoy communicating and collaborating through applications other than e-mail. I'll also wager that you and others around you will eventually start to see results. Once that happens, you'll enter a virtuous cycle. Others may start to ape your new, streamlined communications style and techniques.

Remember Warren Buffett's quote at the beginning of the Coda. I hope that you're sitting in the metaphorical shade soon—and *not* responding to e-mails.

Acknowledgments

Kudos to Team Wiley: Sheck Cho, Stacey Rivera, Susan Cerra, Todd Tedesco, and Andy Wheeler. Additional thanks to Johnna VanHoose Dinse, and Luke Fletcher.

Hat tips to Jay Goldman, Maria Ogneva, Mike Fraietta, Paul Roetzer, Bob Charette, Najeeb Ahmad, Tess Woods, Terri Griffith, Nick Morgan, Brad Feld, Sarah Gooding, and Marisa Smith for their invaluable stories and sidebars. Also, thanks to David Sandberg, Michael Viola, Joe Mirza, Chris McGee, Scott Berkun, Babs Hobbs, Todd Hamilton, Dorie Clark, Ellen French, Dick and Bonny Denby, Kristen Eckstein, Jimmy Jacobson, Aaron Goldfarb, Andrew Botwin, Mark Frank, Rob Metting, Melinda Thielbar, Jay and Heather Etchings, Chad and Sarah Roberts, Karen Davis, Alan Berkson, Mike Schrenk, Mark Cenicola, Barbara Green, Colin Hickey, Brian and Heather Morgan, Michael West, Jennifer Zito, John Spatola, Michael DeAngelo, and Marc Paolella.

For thousands of hours, the guys from Rush (Geddy, Alex, and Neil), Marillion (h, Steve, Ian, Mark, and Pete), and Dream Theater (Jordan, John, John, Mike, and James) have inspired me with their music. Keep on keepin' on!

A very special thank you to the mad genius Vince Gilligan, Bryan Cranston, Aaron Paul, Dean Norris, Anna Gunn, Bob Odenkirk, Betsy Brandt, Jonathan Banks, Giancarlo Esposito, Steven Michael Quezada, RJ Mitte, and the rest of the *Breaking Bad* team. Each of you has made me want to do great work.

Finally, my parents. I'm not here without you.

Thank You

Thank you for buying *Message Not Received*. I hope that the preceding pages will make you think differently about technology and how we communicate at work. Beyond achieving some level of enjoyment and education (always admirable goals in reading a nonfiction book), I also hope that you can apply your newfound knowledge at work.

And perhaps you are willing to help me. I am a self-employed author, writer, speaker, and consultant. I'm not independently wealthy. I don't have a big public relations machine working to get my name out there. My professional livelihood depends in large part on my reputation, coupled with referrals and recommendations from people like you. Collectively, these factors enable me to make a living.

Each of these actions is very helpful:

- Write a review of the book on amazon.com, bn.com, and/or goodreads.com. The more honest you are, the better.
- Mention the book on your blog, Facebook, Reddit, Google+, Twitter, LinkedIn, Pinterest, and other sites you frequent.
- Recommend the book to anyone who might find it interesting.
- Give it as a gift.
- If you know people who still work in newspapers, magazines, television, or industry groups, I'd love a referral or reference. Social media hasn't entirely replaced traditional media.
- Visit www.philsimon.com and read, watch, and listen to your heart's content. I frequently blog, post videos, record podcasts, and create other interesting forms of content on a wide variety of subjects.
- Check out my other books.

I don't expect *Message Not Received* to become a best seller, but stranger things have happened. Case in point: *Capital in the Twenty-First Century* by Thomas Piketty, an obscure French economist. In 2014, the 700-page tome on income inequality became the very definition of a surprise hit. It proved what the physicist Niels Bohr once said: "Predictions are difficult, especially about the future."

I'd love to be on *Charlie Rose*, but that is exceedingly unlikely. I write books for several reasons. First, that's just what a writer does. Second, I believe that I have something meaningful to say. I like writing, editing, crafting a cover, and everything else that goes into creating books. To paraphrase the title of an album by Geddy Lee, it's my favorite headache. Third, although Kindles, Nooks, and iPads are cool, I enjoy holding a physical copy of one of my books in my hands. In our digital world, creating something tangible from scratch just feels good to me. Fourth, I find writing to be incredibly cathartic. Finally, I believe that writing books will open new doors for me.

At the same time, producing a quality text takes an enormous amount of time, effort, and money. Every additional copy sold helps make the next one possible.

Thanks again.

Selected Bibliography

I read quite a bit. The following books weighed heavily on my mind as I penned *Message Not Received*. To the best of my recollection, here's the list of books that influenced the one that you just read:

Anderson, Chris. *The Long Tail: Why the Future of Business Is Selling Less of More.* New York: Hyperion, 2008.

Ariely, Dan. *Predictably Irrational, Revised and Expanded Edition: The Hidden Forces That Shape Our Decisions.* New York: HarperCollins, 2009.

Baron, Dennis. *A Better Pencil: Readers, Writers, and the Digital Revolution.* New York: Oxford University Press, 2009.

Battelle, John. *The Search: How Google and Its Rivals Rewrote the Rules of Business and Transformed Our Culture.* New York: Penguin Group/Portfolio Trade, 2006.

Berger, Warren. *A More Beautiful Question: The Power of Inquiry to Spark Breakthrough Ideas.* New York: Bloomsbury, 2014.

Berkun, Scott. *Confessions of a Public Speaker.* Sebastopol, CA: O'Reilly Media, 2011.

Berkun, Scott. *The Year Without Pants: WordPress.com and the Future of Work.* San Francisco, CA: Jossey-Bass, 2013.

Bierce, Ambrose, and Freeman, Jan. *Write It Right: The Celebrated Cynic's Language Peeves Deciphered, Appraised, and Annotated for 21st-Century Readers.* New York: Walker & Company/Bloomsbury, 2009.

Brynjolfsson, Erik, and McAfee, Andrew. *Race Against the Machine: How the Digital Revolution is Accelerating Innovation, Driving Productivity, and Irreversibly Transforming Employment and the Economy.* Lexington, MA: Digital Frontier Press/Amazon, 2012.

Cain, Susan. *Quiet: The Power of Introverts in a World That Can't Stop Talking.* New York: Broadway Books/Random House, 2013.

Carr, Nicholas. *The Big Switch: Rewiring the World, from Edison to Google*. New York: W. W. Norton & Company, 2009.

Carr, Nicholas. *The Shallows: What the Internet Is Doing to Our Brains*. New York: W. W. Norton & Company, 2011.

Christensen, Clayton M. *The Innovator's Dilemma: The Revolutionary Book That Will Change the Way You Do Business*. New York: Harper-Business, 1997.

Chui, Michael, Manyika, James, Bughin, Jacques, Dobbs, Richard Roxburgh, Charles, Sarrazin, Hugo, Sands, Geoffrey, and Westergren, Magdalena. "The Social Economy: Unlocking Value and Productivity Through Social Technologies," McKinsey Global Institute, www.mckinsey.com/mgi, July 2012.

Cialdini, Robert B. *Influence: The Psychology of Persuasion, Revised Edition*. New York: Harper Business, 2006.

Csikszentmihalyi, Mihaly. *Flow: The Psychology of Optimal Experience*. New York: HarperCollins, 2008.

Dubner, Stephen J., and Levitt, Steven D. *Think Like a Freak: The Authors of Freakonomics Offer to Retrain Your Brain*. New York: William Morrow, 2014.

Elberse, Anita. *Blockbusters: Hit-making, Risk-taking, and the Big Business of Entertainment*. New York: Henry Holt and Company, 2013.

Elkind, Peter, and McLean, Bethany. *The Smartest Guys in the Room: The Amazing Rise and Scandalous Fall of Enron*. New York: Portfolio/Penguin, 2004.

Feierman, Joanne. *Action Grammar: Fast, No-Hassle Answers on Everyday Usage and Punctuation*. New York: Touchstone/Simon & Schuster, 1995.

Flower, Linda. *Problem-Solving Strategies for Writing*. Fort Worth, TX: Harcourt College, 1993.

Freeman, John. *The Tyranny of E-mail: The Four-Thousand-Year Journey to Your Inbox*. New York: Scribner, 2011.

Gleick, James. *Faster: The Acceleration of Just About Everything*. New York: Vintage/Random House, 2000.

Jackson, Maggie. *Distracted: The Erosion of Attention and the Coming Dark Age*. Amherst: Prometheus Books, 2009.

Kahneman, Daniel. *Thinking, Fast and Slow*. New York: Farrar, Straus and Giroux, 2011.

Keynes, John Maynard. "The Economic Possibilities for Our Grandchildren," *Essays in Persuasion*. London, England: Macmillan, 1933.

Kurzweil, Ray. *The Age of Intelligent Machines.* Cambridge, MA: MIT Press, 1990.

Kurzweil, Ray. *The Age of Spiritual Machines: When Computers Exceed Human Intelligence.* New York: Penguin, 2000.

Johnson, Steven B. *Future Perfect: The Case for Progress in a Networked Age.* New York: Riverhead Trade/Penguin, 2013.

Lewis, Michael. *Flash Boys: A Wall Street Revolt.* New York: W. W. Norton & Company, 2014.

Maslow, Abraham. "A Theory of Human Motivation," *Psychological Review,* 50 (1943): 370–396.

Mellahi, K., and Wilkinson, A. "Downsizing and Innovation Output: A Review of Literature and Research Propositions," BAM Paper. London, England: British Academy of Management, 2004.

Micklethwait, John, and Wooldridge, Adrian. *The Witch Doctors: Making Sense of the Management Gurus.* New York: Three Rivers Press/Random House, 1998.

Orwell, George. "Politics and the English Language," *The New Republic,* June 1946.

Partnoy, Frank. *Wait: The Art and Science of Delay.* New York: PublicAffairs/Perseus Books, 2013.

Pieper, Josef. *Leisure, The Basis of Culture.* Translated by Alexander Dru. London, England: Faber and Faber, 1952.

Powers, William. *Hamlet's BlackBerry: Building a Good Life in the Digital Age.* New York: HarperCollins, 2011.

Rosa, Hartmut, and Scheuerman, William E. *High-Speed Society: Social Acceleration, Power, and Modernity.* University Park, PA: Penn State University Press, 2009.

Rosenzweig, Phil. *The Halo Effect: . . . and the Eight Other Business Delusions That Deceive Managers.* New York: Free Press, 2007.

Schor, Juliet. *The Overworked American: The Unexpected Decline Of Leisure.* New York: Basic Books, 1993.

Shea, Ammon. *Bad English: A History of Linguistic Aggravation.* New York: Perigee Trade/Penguin, 2014.

Simon, H. A. "Designing Organizations for an Information-Rich World." In Martin Greenberger, *Computers, Communication, and the Public Interest* (pp. 40–41). Baltimore, MD: The Johns Hopkins Press, 1971.

Stewart, Matthew. *The Management Myth: Debunking Modern Business Philosophy.* New York: W. W. Norton & Company, 2009.

Stone, Brad. *The Everything Store: Jeff Bezos and the Age of Amazon.* New York: Little, Brown and Company, 2013.

Taleb, Nassim Nicholas. *The Black Swan: The Impact of the Highly Improbable*. New York: Random House, 2010.

Truss, Lynne. *Eats, Shoots & Leaves: The Zero Tolerance Approach to Punctuation*. New York: Gotham Books/Penguin, 2006.

Walsh, Bill. *Yes, I Could Care Less: How to Be a Language Snob Without Being a Jerk*. New York: St. Martin's Press, 2013.

Watts, Duncan J., *Everything Is Obvious: How Common Sense Fails Us*. New York: Crown Business/Random House, 2012.

Zinsser, William. *On Writing Well, 30th Anniversary Edition: The Classic Guide to Writing Nonfiction*. New York: HarperCollins, 2006.

About the Author

Phil Simon is a sought-after keynote speaker and recognized technology authority. He has written six other management books, including the award-winning *The Age of the Platform: How Amazon, Apple, Facebook, and Google Have Redefined Business*. When not speaking and writing, Simon advises organizations on matters related to Big Data, communications, strategy, technology, and emerging trends. His contributions have been featured in the *New York Times, Wired, Harvard Business Review, Inc.* magazine, and *BusinessWeek*, Fox News, as well as CNN, NBC, CNBC, *The Huffington Post*, and many other sites. He holds degrees from Carnegie Mellon University and Cornell University.

Web: www.philsimon.com
Twitter: @philsimon
#MessageNotReceived

Index